RESIL

Resilience in Childhood

Perspectives, Promise & Practice

Erica Joslyn

 macmillan education palgrave

First published 2016 by
PALGRAVE

Palgrave in the UK is an imprint of Macmillan Publishers Limited, registered in England, company number 785998, of 4 Crinan Street, London, N1 9XW.

Palgrave Macmillan in the US is a division of St Martin's Press LLC, 175 Fifth Avenue, New York, NY 10010.

Palgrave is a global imprint of the above companies and is represented throughout the world.

Palgrave® and Macmillan® are registered trademarks in the United States, the United Kingdom, Europe and other countries.

ISBN 978–1–137–48614–1

This book is printed on paper suitable for recycling and made from fully managed and sustained forest sources. Logging, pulping and manufacturing processes are expected to conform to the environmental regulations of the country of origin.

A catalogue record for this book is available from the British Library.

A catalog record for this book is available from the Library of Congress.

Printed in China

Contents

Acknowledgements

The author and publisher would like to thank SAGE Publications Inc for their permission to reproduce Table 1.1 'Domains for resilience' from R. Gilligan 'Beyond Permanence? The Importance of Resilience in Child Placement Practice and Planning' in *Adoption and Fostering* 21/1

List of illustrations

Tables

Figures

Boxes

Introduction

The concept of resilience has been a topic of scholarly discussion for several decades. In recent years, interest in this matter has grown considerably, alongside a growing awareness of its importance in terms of developing useful, effective social policies and the promotion of behaviours and actions on the part of parents, teachers, social workers and others, that can all facilitate the development of qualities of resilience in the growing child and adolescent and, by extension, in communities and society at large.

Because resilience is a broad issue, with effects and impacts at every level of society, it is interdisciplinary by its very nature; as a result of this and of the innate complexity of the subject, arriving at a generally held understanding of precisely *what* resilience is can be a challenge. The water is further muddied by the use, in general discourse, of terms that can overlap in meaning with resilience while not conveying precisely the same implications – terms such as 'well-being', 'successful', and 'adaptability'. Although all these can be useful terms to discuss an individual's personal situation, none carries exactly the same meaning or weight as 'resilience'.

Yet the meaning of the term 'resilience' is not straightforward; it is commonly used to describe a variety of positive attributes and successes, and it may be used slightly differently in 'ordinary' conversation as opposed to academic discourse. Resilience in this text draws on a number of interpretations of the concept, for example, 'resilience' is accepted as a description of a collection of characteristics that young people or adults may exhibit despite having experienced significant disadvantage in their earlier years. In this sense, resilience refers to better than expected emotional and developmental outcomes, such as the child who grows up to have a successful life despite experiencing deprivation and violence in his or her early years.

Resilience is also used to refer to children and young people having high levels of competence even when they have been exposed to high levels of stress when dealing with threats to their well-being, such as the young person who emerges from a war-torn society, doing relatively well. In addition, resilience is accepted as positive functioning indicating recovery from trauma, such as in the case of the person who recovers well from an event such as assault, abuse or serious illness.

In contrast, when children and adolescents do not display the skills and attributes of resilience during their childhood, there is an expectation that, should they encounter difficult life circumstances, they could develop psychosocial problems ranging from academic difficulties to self-destructive behaviour.

Children and young people with low levels of resilience who are living in difficult circumstances are judged to be at risk of developing destructive or otherwise maladaptive behaviours leading to more negative lifestyles.

Whether one understands resilience as positive developmental outcomes, a set of competencies or coping strategies, the presence of resilience is associated with positive functioning and positive lifestyles for children, young people and their families. Despite these similarities, the detail of how resilience is manifested and how it can be fostered is often a matter for debate.

This text is designed to dissect, disassemble and examine the components and elements that underpin the contemporary understanding of resilience as a priority human asset. This text explores its foundations, meanings and conditions as well as practical approaches. It arises from a real consideration of resilience as an essential human asset and deconstructs the origins and foundations of our views on resilience, including its characterisation and theoretical perspectives as well as its significance in practice and policy. We explore the input of some of the earliest scholars and researchers working in this area and look at how their work has led to our current understanding and situation.

Today, understanding and knowing how to apply a working knowledge of resilience is essential in a wide range of arenas. Professionals as diverse as doctors, nurses, teachers, social workers, child care workers, psychologists, psychiatrists, economists, city planners, politicians, sports coaches and more can best serve their public when they understand what resilience is, why it is important and how they can contribute to fostering it. However, acquiring this knowledge and understanding is far from straightforward.

The complexity of resilience as a modern construct can be demonstrated by the range of disciplines and perspectives currently involved in the study of resilience – psychopathology, positive psychology, sociology and its branches such as socioecology, neuroscience and physiology. One of the commonly shared perceptions from across these many disciplines is the importance of building resilience in children and young people.

One of the key findings emerging from a range of multidisciplinary research is the importance of childhood, including the 'extremes' of very early infancy and late adolescence, for laying foundations for the characteristics and attributes of resilience to be able to flourish. The formative years of childhood and adolescence are seen as the seedbed for building skills, attributes and attitudes that will echo into resilience in later life. In effect, for childhood and adolescence, resilience is as much a promise as it can be a reality.

In childhood, the acquisition of resilience is a promise that a successful future is eminently possible. The promise is that resilient individuals will be able to contribute effectively and constructively within their communities and to become adults with every chance of living happy, fulfilled and productive lives, and of raising their own resilient children in due course.

In effect, resilience conveys the promise that children and young people can, despite inauspicious childhoods or traumatic experiences, become the agents of their own fate rather than being victims suffering the long-term effects of adverse life circumstances. Even in lives that are objectively very difficult, the promise of resilience can be envisioned as a beacon of hope, lighting the way to a better future. Moreover, fostering qualities of resilience in children from birth and throughout childhood has the potential to benefit not only individuals and their families but also entire communities and society at large. Resilient individuals are happier, have better physical and mental health, and are less likely to engage in antisocial behaviour, for example.

The premise that building the skills of resilience in childhood is primarily a promise of a successful future is a central tenet of this book. This text starts from the assumption that resilience is primarily a social construction based on an infrastructure of concepts, models and schemas, supported by a backdrop of shared understanding and practices, leading to a promise. It is principally concerned with understanding how this everyday intersubjective construct is constituted and how the promise and development of resilience are operationalised through childhood. It goes on to explore a range of perspectives, models and explanations of resilience. Its primary focus is a critical analysis of their contributions, both in the construction of the theory and in the building of skills and competence during childhood. It adopts a multidisciplinary approach to deconstruct the modern construct of 'resilience' and interrogates social knowledge, researched opinion and interpretative analysis to explore the active and conscious construction of our current understanding of resilience and its components.

Book outline

Part I is designed to both introduce the concept (Chapter 1) and explore the origins of resilience as a discrete field of study and research (Chapter 2). Part I explores definitions, characteristics and the research trail leading to our contemporary understanding of resilience. The first two chapters explore findings, perspectives and research from scholars working in various fields since the very early days of the study of resilience (including a glance at some earlier scholars whose work laid the foundations for this area). These two early chapters are designed to explore the complexities of the meaning, approaches and strategies commonly associated with resilience, to be revealed and understood using a deconstructionist format. These two chapters draw a plethora of published work together to demonstrate the modern understanding and field of resilience.

Part II explores theoretical and research underpinnings of the study of resilience. Knowledge and understanding of resilience can be considered to embrace three distinct discipline components: psychological, sociological and, more recently, neuroscience (Radke-Yarrow and Sherman, 1990, 100). In Chapters 3–5, Part II explores the contribution of these three disciplines. From a disciplinary perspective, each chapter explores various components, perspectives and research that contribute to our current understanding of resilience, and provides an understanding of the challenges inherent in building resilience in children and young people.

Chapter 3 explores the psychological inputs to resilience, starting with the early social and emotional development of children and young people. It also explores potential psychological hazards to the development of resilience. Chapter 4 looks at neurological inputs to resilience and at emerging research that shows that particular areas of the brain can be crucial in the development of resilience at a biological level. Chapter 5 explores important sociological factors and key sociological frameworks for the exploration of resilience. The current construct of resilience continues to evolve, drawing upon research from these disciplines, and cumulatively these areas contribute to our understanding of the phenomenon, its benefits, its potential and its promise.

In Part III, the text moves from the theoretical to the practical, considering a range of strategies that support and underpin current practice in relation to children, young people and families. These final chapters explore practices and strategies that can foster resilience and that may have the potential to make real the promise of resilience.

In Chapter 6, we explore ways in which the qualities of resilience can be fostered, developed and encouraged in children and young people through social care practice. Chapters 7 and 8 explore educational resilience in relation to children in the early years (Chapter 7) and during the school years (Chapter 8). Chapter 7 looks at the use of formal and less formal interventions with children during very early childhood, incorporating early childhood education, and can set the scene for better progress through education and the early years. Chapter 8 examines the utility of educational resilience in improving life chances and explores the enhanced role of schools as enablers of qualities of resilience in the developing child or adolescent.

Educational resilience has become a key driver to enable the development of a much more resilient cohort of young people into the twenty-first century, leading to a more resilient generation and ultimately to a more stable, functional and economically viable society as a whole. Chapter 9 explores the ultimate gift of 'resilient children in young people' to wider society and the promising aspects of resilience to individuals, communities and national and global society. This chapter also looks at the nature of citizenship and the interplay between resilience and the individual's capacity to perform his or her role as a successful citizen.

PART I

RESILIENCE:
THE CONSTRUCT

CHAPTER 1

Resilience – An Introduction

Introduction

'Resilience' is a word that one hears often but which often seems to defy a precise definition. In the context of this text, 'resilience' encompasses psychology, sociology and child and adolescent development to describe children and young people who flourish despite what can objectively be described as very difficult circumstances.

It is common to assume that children and young people are more likely to show strong negative reactions if they have been subjected to neglect or abuse during early childhood. It is also assumed that they are more likely to develop problems in subsequent life. However, research shows that not all do (Garmezy et al., 1984; Masten et al., 1990). Some children do not appear to be significantly damaged by their challenging backgrounds, and some even thrive; these children are considered to be resilient.

Although many studies have focused on children and young people growing up with varying degrees of dysfunction and/or deprivation, children in affluent and apparently ideal circumstances can also face challenges to resilience. Indeed, the concept of resilience can also be applied to those who do well despite not being exposed to significant personal difficulties.

The rationale for building resilience in children and young people is that, irrespective of background and or early experience, those who develop appropriate skills and competence will be able to cope constructively with challenges and difficulties that they encounter daily and will develop levels of resilience that could help them as adults. The modern social construction of resilience gives authority to the promise that, with the appropriate skills and capabilities, children and young people will develop into successful adults who will be able to steer a positive life course for themselves, their families, their communities and to the benefit of the state (Rutter, 1984). This is a promise that children and young people can emerge from a stressful childhood or traumatic period with strong personal strength – even made stronger in some cases – by the very difficult circumstances that they have lived through.

The acquisition of resilience in childhood is a promise of a successful future. Fostering qualities of resilience in children throughout childhood has the potential to benefit not only individuals and their families but also entire communities and society at large. In effect, resilience conveys the promise that children and young people can, despite inauspicious beginnings, become positively engaging adult citizens rather than suffering the long-term negative effects of adverse life circumstances. Even in lives that are objectively very difficult, the promise of resilience can often be envisioned as a beacon of hope.

Over the last 50 years, there has been extensive research and commentary on the components, characteristics and practice of building resilience. There is now no longer any doubt that the skills of resilience are important to children and adults. However, differences in the trajectories of diverse individuals in response to adversity provide a varied canvas for the study of both the construction and the determinants of resilience.

The literature on resilience spans a wide range of definitions, approaches and determinants. This chapter explores these definitions of, approaches to and determinants of resilience, and examines how these contribute to our understanding of the skills and competencies commonly associated with the building of resilience during childhood and adolescence.

The construction of resilience

The meaning of the term 'resilience' is not straightforward. It is commonly used to describe a variety of positive attributes and successes. Firstly, it may be a description of a collection of characteristics that children or young people may exhibit despite having experienced significant disadvantage in their earlier years. Thus, in this sense, resilience refers to better than expected emotional and developmental outcomes. Secondly, resilience may refer to young people having high levels of competence even when they have been exposed to high levels of stress when dealing with threats to their well-being. And thirdly, resilience may refer to positive functioning that indicates recovery from trauma.

A number of influential definitions (Box 1.1) have emerged from various disciplines and from research carried out in a variety of settings and life circumstances.

Box 1.1 Definitions of resilience

1. Resilience is a dynamic process when there is a threat to the child's well-being and the child demonstrates positive adaptation. Children deal with stress at a time and in a manner that allows them to develop their qualities of self-confidence and social competence (Rutter, 1971).

2. Resilience is a process and not a fixed quality. It is seen in the successive positive adaptations of those who are exposed to adversity (Masten et al., 1990).

3. Resilience comprises a set of qualities that help one to deal with or overcome a lot of the negative impacts of adversity in life (Gilligan, 2000).

4. Resilience is the compound of personal, cultural and environmental factors that combine to make it easier for the individual to navigate difficult periods in life and do well (Ungar, 2008).

5. Resilience evokes relatively good outcomes in the face of adversity, facilitated by personal qualities such as self-efficacy, secure attachments and good relationships, and resources within the family and in the broader community (Daniel, 2010).

Whether one understands resilience as positive developmental outcomes, a set of competencies, or as coping strategies, the presence of resilience is associated with positive functioning and positive lifestyles for children, young people and their families. These conceptualisations of resilience share the notion that resilience is influenced by a child's environment and that the interaction between individuals and their social ecologies will determine the degree of positive outcomes experienced.

Recent trends in research have moved the debate from the 'what' to the 'how' – *how* do resilience factors lead to positive outcomes, and what mechanisms are involved? These definitions also emphasise an understanding of resilience as a *process* rather than as a set of individual character traits. However, processes for developing resilience are complicated. Every successful young person may take a different path or trajectory.

Rutter (1999, 120) suggests that for resilience to have any meaning, it must also apply to differences in responses to a given dose of the risk factor and that it must be acknowledged that individuals will have different trajectories in response to adversity. For Rutter, these differences are important and, in effect, provide the infrastructure for the study of resilience. This view of resilience as a dynamic process has itself generated a number of perspectives on the methods and processes of adaptations that may or may not result in promoting features of resilience within the child, family and community contexts.

The concept of resilience has emerged most strongly over the last 50 years. On one hand, resilience has developed as an academic construct through sustained research and scholarly activity. On the other hand, resilience as a concept has caught the imaginations of the political and professional classes. The result has been the emergence of perspectives, approaches, interpretations and expectations. For many, resilience is perceived less as discovered knowledge and more as individual constructions of models and schemas.

This conceptual framework of resilience is based on two interacting features – the conceptual foundations of resilience (the left side of the framework) and the personal resources and assets (the right side of the framework) – with the ability to cycle back and forth from right to left and vice versa. In this model, resilience has been constructed against a backdrop of academic research and presents a flexible framework that can be applied to different contexts and can facilitate different trajectories towards resilience (Figure 1.1). Figure 1.1 presents a portrait construction wherein either side may vary according to factors that underpin and/or drive an individual's pace and trajectories.

The construction of resilience is presented here as one that can fluctuate and can be strengthened or weakened by different actions and interactions as well as experiences and practices. Resilience as an asset depends on its particular context, interactions and resources for change. The promise of resilience is its potential as a mechanism for positive citizenship into the twenty-first century – a citizenship permeated with sustainable, personal, cultural and social values (see Chapter 9). Cultural factors play a significant role in determining the legitimacy of the construct while individual factors govern the form and characteristics of resilience (Ungar, 2008). Figure 1.1 provides a framework wherein political, cultural, social and economic policies and factors can shape complex understanding of resilience at an individual level.

Figure 1.1 The construction of resilience

Monica is a young woman who lives in a farming community in the US. She is very close to her paternal grandmother, who lives close by. Her father was an alcoholic, and when he was drunk – which was most days – was abusive to her mother, Monica and her two younger brothers. Monica was 11 years old when her father left home and never came back. Monica helped her grandmother come to terms with this loss. Home life became better for a short time, and Monica was able to begin to enjoy sports – she joined a basketball team and became an athlete in track and field. However, her mother's partner, Tom, moved into the family home six months ago. Monica does not like her mother's partner, and there are constant rows between Monica and her mother and Tom. Monica became angry that her life had changed again and started drinking in high school. However, she continued with her sports to spite Tom, who kept telling her that she should be at home looking after her two brothers. She continued to live at home but had very little interaction with her mother and drifted away from family activities. In her third year of college, her drinking became out of control, and she was expelled. Her drinking continued and she moved in and out of low-paid work. She recently got a job at a local gym (as an assistant) and is desperate to keep this job and to go back to college – but she continues to drink.

Jenny lived in South London in a block of flats with her family. Jenny was always closer to her father than to her mother, but her father died suddenly when she was 11 years old. She felt the loss of her dad very deeply and felt lonely and left out because she believed that her mother preferred her younger sister. Her mother married again, but Jenny hated being around her mother and her new husband, as they would make explicit sexual references about her, such as 'Hey, Jenny, you look very sexy tonight'. As an adolescent she began to do very badly in school and to lose interest in her studies. When she was 14, she ran away from home and lived on the streets for two years, with no contact with her family. During that time, she worked as a sex worker and regularly presented for emergency contraception. Recently Jenny has got a couple of low-paid cleaning jobs. She is now 16 and hates her life but continues to have no contact with her family and has no friends her own age. She has now approached the Salvation Army to ask for help to find somewhere to live near her cleaning jobs.

Discussion

With reference to Figure 1.1, consider the two case studies in the vignette and answer the following questions.

1. Compare the different personal resources and assets available to the adolescent in each case.
2. Explore the different external factors that may help or hinder recovery in each case.

Approaches to resilience

Recognising the building of resilience as an interpretative and constructed process leads to recognising childhood as (i) having the rudimentary beginnings of resilience and (ii) having the potential to develop these fledgling beginnings into adept realisations. In essence, this forms the basis for understanding how resilience can be developed and fostered during childhood and into adulthood. An analysis of approaches to and perspectives of resilience provides an opportunity to critically explore the matrix of factors that constitutes the shaping of resilience through childhood.

Behavioural and adaptation perspectives

Olsson et al. (2003) identify two different approaches to resilience, the differences between which are not always clear, and considerable confusion can arise as they are often used interchangeably:

1. a behavioural approach – defined as an outcome characterised by particular patterns of functional behaviour despite risk;
2. an adaptation approach – defined as a dynamic process of adaptation to a risk and involving interaction between a range of risk and protective factors from the individual to the social context.

The behavioural approach focuses on individual behavioural deficits and shortcomings (Olsson, 2003) and utilises, for example, poor academic skills, chaotic anger management responses and unwanted behavioural characteristics as markers of resilience function. It adopts a psychopathology view of negative developmental outcomes (Box 1.2) to assess resilience function and focuses on a lack of coping strategies in the face of adversity.

The behavioural approach, therefore, appears to be limited insofar as it relies on a rather narrow response view of resilience. It is limiting to view resilience as purely applying coping strategies adequately to the daily challenges of life – particularly for children and young people who may be disadvantaged in a range of objectively considered ways such as poverty, abuse in childhood or poor physical health.

Box 1.2 Examples of negative behavioural outcomes

- Failing to reach social or behavioural milestones at an appropriate age
- Not acquiring the skills essential to functioning in adult life
- Engaging in excessive risk-taking behaviour
- Poor regulation of emotions
- Inability to develop positive relationships of attachment (disordered attachment) with the important people in his or her life
- Poor self-care, including problems with diet, alcohol and drug consumption
- Lower cognitive function, resulting in more difficulties communicating thoughts and feelings, and engaging in complex behaviours (i.e. at school or at work)
- Poor problem-solving skills

(See, for example, Gilbert et al., 1991.)

Rutter (2005) warns of the risk of drawing inappropriate correlations and conclusions from observable competing facts and explores the consequences of judging behaviour purely from one set of facts. In making the point, he argues, that we are ill-advised to assume a direct link between observed outcomes and observed social factors. As an example, Rutter (2005, 8) draws on a case study of a Native Indian community. The study found that poverty had been considerably alleviated when a casino was opened. It was also found that subsequently there had been a major reduction in disruptive behaviour on the part of the community's children. Rutter warned that this change in the children's behaviour and attitudes did not necessarily relate directly to the reduction of poverty associated with the opening of the casino, but to a tangential issue: parents started to engage more with their children.

In his 2000 paper, Rutter (2000, 654) writes that 'many studies of resilience have been based on a rather restricted range of outcome measures' and asserts that these can lead to misleading conclusions. Within this approach, he also identifies the notion that one pays a 'price' for resilience; that children and adults who demonstrate resilient behaviour may do so at the expense of some social function. Thus, although it is tempting to define resilience solely in terms of behavioural skills in the face of adversity, this may not reflect the complete context and/or circumstance that would explain these behaviours. Ong et al. (2009) also suggest that one runs the risk of inferring a strong deterministic perspective on how children and young people develop and respond to their environment. In addition, they suggest that children and young people may find themselves in situations that may, on the one hand, pose a hazard to their well-being but, on the other, may not present a setback in every instance.

Ong et al. argue that, 'within the developmental and academic literature, most researchers agree that it is important to consider adaptive functioning more broadly beyond just the skills of avoidance of negative developmental outcomes' (Ong et al., 2009). The adaptation perspective is based on a process design which emphasises the mechanisms or processes that act to modify the impact of risk factors and safeguard the developmental process to enable young people to develop resilience. According to Lee et al. (2013, 275), 'building resilience can be thought of as a dynamic cognitive process that both protects an individual in adverse situations and enhances his or her social and emotional development'. In effect, the adaptation approach presumes development over a period of time, characterised by effective responses despite the presence of developmental risk and acute stressors. It may refer to resilience not as a fixed quality but, instead, as a 'whole interaction between individuals and the environment around them, such as family, community or the social system' (Lee et al., 2013, 269). Importantly, the adaptation approach also recognises that, as environmental conditions change, the vulnerability or resilience of an individual can also change.

Developmental and emotional perspectives

Both developmental and emotional perspectives have strong support among politicians and professionals and are based on a strong belief in a cause-and-effect model of resilience. These approaches are seen in the work of Goldstein and Brooks, who define resilience as 'a child's achievement of positive developmental outcomes and avoidance of maladaptive outcomes under adverse conditions' (Goldstein and Brooks, 2006). They advocate that the achievement of positive development outcomes demonstrated through, for example, an ability to perform well at school and to interact with peers and adults in an appropriate manner, could culminate in resilience capability.

Goldstein and Brooks refer to resilience as a 'mindset' and describe a resilient mindset as 'the product of providing children with opportunities to develop the skills necessary to fare well in the face of adversity that might lie in the path to adulthood for that individual' (Goldstein and Brooks, 2006, 6). Their definition of the resilient 'mindset' as a 'product' promotes the view of inputs (actions and interventions) designed to craft and create certain qualities and characteristics leading to required outputs (competency and mindset). For children and young people, this 'mindset' can comprise, for example: a preference to focus and concentrate on schoolwork; the development of negotiating skills to help to avert conflict in social relationships; the ability to self-comfort when difficulties arise; an understanding of how to adapt behaviour to local social norms; and a rejection of antisocial behaviours.

This approach, which focuses on the social and emotional aspects of child development (see Chapter 3), suggests that children and young people who are exposed to appropriate social and emotional conditions during their developmental years are likely to exhibit better levels of physical and mental health

(Dowling, 2010, 77). Here, the craft of resilience lies in child development opportunities. The emphasis is on providing appropriate antecedent conditions to enable children and young people to become emotionally well balanced and adjusted to social and behavioural norms and values.

According to Schoon, individuals who have achieved positive outcomes in their lives despite experiencing difficult circumstances are considered to display positive social and emotional adjustment which, he argues, 'has been defined not only in terms of a lack of pathology, the attainment of psychosocial developmental milestones, the statistical average, the utopia of self-actualisation, but also as the ability to negotiate life's developmental and emotional crises' (Schoon, 2006, 11).

The importance of the cultural context

Michael Ungar (2008), in his work following the International Resilience Project, emphasises the importance of the cross-cultural perspective in resilience:

> In the context of exposure to significant adversity, resilience is both the capacity of individuals to *navigate* their way to the psychological, social, cultural and physical resources that sustain well-being, and their capacity individually and collectively to *negotiate* for those resources to be provided in culturally meaningful ways. (Ungar, 2008, 225)

This definition shifts the debate on resilience from an individual concept to one that is culturally sensitive. The individualised concept is, however, most popular in Western countries and is utilised extensively by Western-trained researchers and service providers. Ungar suggests that resilience should be understood as a social construct that leads the debate towards cultural norms, values, procedures and goals. Specifically, a cultural explanation (explored more fully in Chapter 9) makes explicit the notion of resilience as an outcome that may evolve if services, supports and health resources are provided in such a manner that makes it more likely for children and young people to do well in ways that are meaningful to them, their families and their communities. In this perspective, resilience emerges from successful navigation to resources and negotiation for resources, and builds confidence and identity based on culturally informed success.

The International Resilience Project highlights the importance of a sense of power and control and an understanding of place in family and community. This project recognises the value of spirituality to meaning and identity in many parts of the world, and the subsequent influence on children and young people building self-efficacy and competence within a cultural environment.

Ungar (2008) explored resilience among over 1500 young people from different locations around the world, finding that there are certain propositions that contribute to an understanding of resilience that is 'more culturally and contextually embedded'. Ungar argued that the focus on social and behavioural outcomes that are considered desirable in highly developed nations in Western culture is unlikely to be applicable to populations within other cultures. He warns that little attention has been paid to these many cultural factors and suggests that other factors that impact on how resilience is experienced and perceived in different cultural and community contexts are too important to be ignored.

In their investigation of resilience with 1500 young people in 14 different communities on five continents, exploring both global and cultural/contextual aspects of resilience, Ungar and his colleagues carried out an investigation of 'paying special attention to the influence of culture and context on definitions of risk, the mediating factors associated with resilience, and localized definitions of positive outcomes' (Ungar, 2008). Their work revealed major variations in how young people cope with different periods in their lives, depending to a great extent on their culture and context.

Based on this research, Ungar puts forward four propositions that he suggests will be useful in both researching and designing culturally relevant interventions:

1. There are global as well as culturally and contextually specific aspects to young people's lives that contribute to their resilience.
2. Aspects of resilience exert differing amounts of influence on a child's life, depending on the specific culture and context in which resilience is realised.
3. Aspects of children's lives that contribute to resilience are related to one another in patterns that reflect a child's culture and context.
4. Tensions between individuals and their cultures and contexts are resolved in ways that reflect specific relationships between aspects of resilience.

These propositions suggest that resilience can be seen as a component and consequence of environmental factors as well as a component and consequence of individual factors. In an effort to move away from heavily Western interpretations and understandings of resilience, Ungar (2008) suggests that in the context of exposure to significant adversity, whether psychological, environmental, or both, resilience is both the capacity of an individual to navigate his or her way to health-sustaining resources and a condition of the individual's family, community and culture to provide these health resources in culturally meaningful ways.

Vignette 1.2

Hamid is a 15-year-old Muslim boy who was born, educated and raised in Pakistan. Hamid was a good student who had previously done very well in school. However, recently Hamid began to draw away from school, not attending regularly, not handing in homework and presenting unusually poor-quality work. His teacher spoke to Hamid, who said that everything was fine. The teacher also contacted Hamid's parents, who said they would take him to the doctor. Hamid had recently been diagnosed with epilepsy. Following the teacher's enquiries, Hamid refused to go back to school because he was afraid that his friends at school might find out. He was given medication by his GP, and after two weeks began to feel better but hated taking these tablets. Neither Hamid nor his parents wanted the school or his teacher to know about Hamid's condition and instead told his teacher that Hamid had gastroenteritis. Three months later, his teacher continues to be concerned about Hamid and has had a meeting with Hamid and his parents. However, Hamid and his parents continue to say that Hamid is just tired and will be better soon. The teacher feels that Hamid should be over his gastroenteritis by now, and so feels that there may be more to this story but is unable to get to the bottom of the problem. Hamid has returned to school but continues to be withdrawn and underperforming, and tells his parents that he will do better next year when he gets used to the tablets, but not to tell his teacher.

Discussion

Explore the cultural factors that may be at work in the vignette.
Examine the positive resources and assets that may be helpful to Hamid on the path that he has chosen.

Domains for resilience

Much of the work on resilience (for example, Goldstein and Brooks, 2006; Schoon, 2006; Dowling, 2010) has highlighted the importance of positive characteristics as cornerstones to any display of resilience. Gilligan (1997) has identified six positive domains (Table 1.1) that he suggests can be used to frame our understanding of factors that can impact on childhood resilience.

The presence of these domains can often be perceived as providing a strong underpinning for good social and emotional adjustment. As a consequence, certain

Table 1.1 Domains for resilience

Domains for resilience	Descriptors
Secure base	When the child is physically healthy and robust and has a positive and functional home environment, he or she is said to have a secure base – a foundation upon which resilience can be built. Children with a secure base feel that they belong; they are secure in their identity; and they feel safe. The positive effects of a secure base can be seen in terms of physical, psychological and neurological well-being.
Social competencies	Socially competent children can engage easily with the world and the other people around them. They are able to regulate their emotions and behaviour, such as having the ability to engage in conversation and behave in a positive way with others and form rewarding friendships. They are also adept at assessing situations, understanding various perspectives and learning from social situations such that their competence continues to grow.
Positive values	Optimism, hope and a sense of empathy for other people are some of the positive values that contribute to resilience. Young people who have a sense of the importance of qualities such as integrity, social justice and equality, responsibility and honesty often experience that these values can be channelled into positive behaviour, including the ability to think critically and have better skills in the areas of conflict resolution and problem solving.

Talent and interests	A sense of 'being good at' something and caring about it – whether it is sports, the arts, music or any other interest. Feeling 'good at something' is an important contributor to healthy self-esteem. Talents and interests also provide many opportunities for the young person to engage with others and form positive relationships with them.
Friendships	Healthy, affirming relationships, especially with peers, are an important factor in securing positive relationships. These can potentially moderate the effects of negative aspects of the child's life that run counter to building resilience.
Education	Access to education and the ability to engage with an education system can provide the child with the academic and other skills necessary for a successful life in his or her cultural milieu. In many societies, education is also an important forum in which to create positive friendships, to grow social competence and to develop a sense of positive attachment to adults other than parents.

Source: Gilligan (1997).

domains are perceived as evidence that some of the attributes of resilience may be present or possible. According to Gilligan (1997), a combination of domains and behaviours are key components necessary for a child or young person to achieve greater competence and capability and should form the cornerstones for social care practice.

The texture of resilience

Resilience research has consistently emphasised what Barnett et al. (1996) referred to as 'keystone behaviours' (Table 1.2). These are drawn from a range of perspectives and are identifiable behaviours that are generally applied to all children and young people. In the context of resilience, key behaviours and attributes have been commonly applied. However, it is important to note that every child is wholly distinct from any other, with a different social and family background, a different genetic heritage and a different range of behaviours.

Table 1.2 Characteristics that support resilience

• Confident	• Optimistic	• Future-focused
• High in self-esteem	• Creative	• Rational
• Adaptable	• Flexible	• Persistent
• Autonomous	• Reflective	• Realistic
• Socially aware	• Solution-focused	• Articulate
• Responsive	• Help-seeking	• Courageous
• Empathetic	• Positive	• Self-aware

These descriptors highlight qualities that children and young people may display at various times and are also behaviours and qualities in which they can become more accomplished over time. Contrasting those who have developed resilience with those who have not can also be revealing:

- Individuals who are resilient tend to see themselves in terms of what they have accomplished and achieved, whereas those who are non-resilient believe themselves to be non-achievers (even in the face of objective evidence to the contrary).
- Resilient people can constructively recognise and build on their strengths and weaknesses and promote those areas in which they are skilled and competent. In contrast, those who are not resilient are more likely not to believe themselves to have valuable skills or be able to recognise and build effectively on their strengths.
- Resilient people typically have a strong sense of 'belonging' and connection to others, whereas non-resilient individuals generally feel detached from their family, community and those around them; they often describe themselves as feeling 'disconnected' from others.
- Resilient people generally feel a distinct sense of autonomy, expect positive things from their future and have good levels of self-esteem, whereas those who are not resilient feel powerless and as though they have little control over their future, do not see many good things in their future and tend to have markedly low levels of self-esteem.

According to Barnett et al. (1996, 95) key behaviours can be framed within three integrant parts:

1. pivotal behaviours associated with response to maladaptive behaviours that can positively influence other child behaviours;
2. behaviours that result in other beneficial child, peer and/or adult outcomes; and
3. foundation skills necessary for adaptation to present and future environments.

The varied texture of resilience is not only identified by key behaviours but also by behaviour traits that can act to buffer a child from risk or enable the child to navigate an alternate path (for example Werner and Smith, 1987; Morrison et al., 2006; Ward and Thurston, 2006).

Risk and protective factors

Considerable work has been carried out by a range of researchers towards determining the factors that confer risk or a protective effect on children and young people in terms of resilience. It is worth noting that these factors, when present, are not necessarily predictors of what will happen in their life – not least because everyone has his or her own individual story of risk and protection.

As Zolkoski and Bullock (2012, 2295) state, individual stories 'may be probability statements; the likelihood of a gamble where levels of risk change depending on the time and place'. It is important to reflect on the gamble between protective and risk factors, and to explore a fuller understanding of the contributions that these can make to different interventions (more fully explored in Chapter 6).

Risk factors

The risk factors associated with a lack of resilience are complex and nuanced. West and Farrington (1973) identified a number as relatively common in a cross-cultural context. In their study of juvenile delinquent boys, they determined that the most potent risk factors for delinquency were low family income, large family size, parental criminality, low levels of education and poor parenting. Brackenreed (2010) suggests that 'it is disheartening to note that these same risk factors are on the rise causing children to be vulnerable to failure in school and in life, despite widespread efforts on the part of the educational system to address risks and provide interventions'.

Recent studies have determined that, for example, similar categories may be considered as at-risk properties (Lee et al., 2013, 270), and according to Lee et al. (2013) these could include, for example, poor mental health, family and community dysfunction, high levels of individual stress and belonging to certain demographics. Lee et al.'s meta-analysis argues that depression is one of the 'strongest negatively related variables to resilience' (Lee et al., 2013, 274). In his 1990 paper *Resilience Reconsidered* (Rutter, 2000, 651), Rutter states that 'there is abundant evidence that disturbed parent-child relationships do indeed constitute an important risk factor for psychopathology'. Schultz et al. (2013, 697) demonstrate the effects of violence on children, and in their US study they reported that 61 per cent of all children had seen at least one type of 'violence, trauma and abuse' in the course of a year, and that 66 per cent of those children had seen violence more than once, with 30 per cent witnessing five or more types, and 10 per cent experiencing exposure to 11 or more types of violence in the course of their lives. Exposure to violence is associated with various negative outcomes, including behavioural problems and the onset of post-traumatic stress disorder (Schultz et al., 2013, 698). It is important to note that the cumulative effects of multiple risks as described above are perceived to be a major inhibitor to the building of resilience (Yates et al., 2003, 245).

Rutter cautions that, 'there have been many examples of risks that have been assumed to be due to one factor but that subsequently were found to be due to some other feature with which it happened to be associated' (Rutter, 2005, 5). He cites the fact that, previously, many focused on the risks thought to be associated with 'broken homes' (divorced or separated parents) where one parent was now absent from the child's life. However, with subsequent research it became apparent that the principal risk had more to do with parental conflict than the break up per se.

Rutter (2005, 5) suggests that whereas, statistically, children do better when there is a father in the home, this is contingent on the qualities that the father brings into the home environment. He argues that if the father displays anti-social behaviour, the child is at *greater* risk of doing the same with the father present than absent. Luthar and Zigler (1991) also stress the fact that the relationship between risk and a lack of resilience is often far from linear. Significant differences also exist between genders. A study carried out by Werner and Smith (1982) demonstrated that, 'whereas permanent absence of the father and maternal employment were related to resilience among high-risk girls, the same conditions were destructive for boys'. This study suggests that, in some circumstances, a child's gender can put him or her at elevated risk. Rutter (1990, 189) also recognised the depth of gender differences in relation to resilience and has argued that boys are 'more likely than girls to develop emotional/behavioural disturbances when exposed to marked family discord'. Various reasons for this have been posited, including the fact that boys are more likely to display disruptive oppositional behaviour than girls, which in turn makes it more likely that they will elicit a punitive response and/or be placed in institutional care (Rutter, 1990, 190–1).

A 2006 study of children at risk in Crewe in Cheshire, Britain, also found quite significant differences in terms of both risk and protective factors for girls and boys: 'There was a greater prevalence amongst the boys for aggressive and angry behaviour, difficult behaviour at school, difficult behaviour at home and their achievement at school being well below potential. The girls were more likely to have the risk factors of a low level of exercise, poor health and an increased likelihood of being bullied' (Ward and Thurston, 2006, 48).

However, the major concern with the classifications of risk factors is that the relationship between the degree of risk and the extent of adaptation and/or maladaptation is far from straightforward. In her research for the Scottish Government, Fox (2012) identified seven tensions (Table 1.3) that may exacerbate personal risk factors.

These tensions indicate that it is very important to recognise the complexity of risks in children's lives and the circumstances within which young people find themselves. The picture of risks and tensions can be much more complex than it may first appear. Tensions may be subtler, not least because they often impose similar constraints to known risks and are therefore easy to miss. They can also be easily overlooked, resulting in classic misdirection and misleading correlations.

Protective factors

Personal qualities identified by a range of researchers have included life satisfaction, optimism, positive affect, self-efficacy, self-esteem and identity (Lee et al., 2013, 270). According to Lee et al., 'the strength and predictive power of demographic and psychological factors can directly impact on resilience levels'. They determined that the greatest effect on resilience came from protective factors, with risk factors having a smaller effect, and demographic factors a smaller effect again (Lee et al., 2013, 273):

> Self-efficacy was the strongest positively related variable to resilience compared with the other variables (e.g. life satisfaction, optimism). That is, a greater level of self-efficacy was closely related to an increase in an individual's resilience, for example, having the ability to cope with change and to use a repertoire of problem-solving skills . . . positive affect was strongly correlated with resilience, which indicated that resilient individuals are able to use positive affect to protect themselves against the effect of traumatic life events. (Lee et al., 2013, 274)

Table 1.3 Tensions that exacerbate risk factors

	Tension	Factors
1	Access to material resources	Lack of availability of financial, educational, medical and employment assistance and/or opportunities to access food, clothing, shelter and safety
2	Relationships	Lack of relationships/models with significant others, peers and adults within one's family and community
3	Identity	Failure to develop a personal and or collective sense of purpose, self-appraisal of strengths and weaknesses, aspirations, beliefs and values, including spiritual and religious identification
4	Power and control	Experiences and feelings of lack of control factors that inhibit the ability to effect change in one's social and physical environment in order to access health resources
5	Cultural adherence	Non-critical adherence to one's local and or global cultural practices, values and beliefs
6	Social justice	Lack of opportunity to experience or communicate a meaningful role in community and social equality
7	Cohesion	Inability or lack of opportunity to balance one's personal interests with a sense of responsibility to the greater good; unable to feel a part of something larger than oneself socially and spiritually

Source: Fox (2012).

Individual, personal characteristics, such as the individual's academic performance, temperament or character, degree of motivation and, depending on the given situation, gender, can all provide a protective effect (Zolkoski and Bullock, 2012, 2298). Additionally, Yates et al. (2003) focus on the use of and access to social support as protective factors. According to Yates et al. (2003, 247), there are three 'fields of resources' that can help to protect children who find themselves in adverse conditions:

1. child characteristics (personal qualities of the child in question);
2. family characteristics; and
3. community characteristics.

In contrast, Rutter (1990) advocates that the focus should be on whether or not a child is able to navigate his or her way through risk factors. He therefore describes four types of protective processes that he argues are likely to moderate risk factors:

1. those that reduce a child's exposure to risk;
2. those that reduce negative reactions to bad experiences;
3. those that promote self-esteem through achievement; and
4. positive relationships that provide opportunities for success.

Following this theme, Ong et al. (2009) suggest 'ego resilience' as a 'stable personality trait that has emerged as an important psychological asset'. Longitudinal personality studies have shown the benefits of ego resilience in children and adults alike:

> For example, in a series of coordinated experimental and individual difference studies . . . ego-resilient individuals exhibited faster physiological and emotional recovery from stress. In one study, higher ego resiliency was linked to quicker cardiovascular recovery following a laboratory stressor. (Ong et al., 2009)

According to Ong et al. (2009) ego resilience, refers to a person's ability to respond adaptively and resourcefully to new situations. This, they argue, can be characterised as having the capacity to 'overcome, steer through, and bounce back from adversity'. Although ego resilience can be an important protective factor, they argue that it is not necessarily the same thing as resilience per se.

Luthar et al. (2000, 546) argued that 'the terms 'ego resiliency' and 'resilience' differ on two major dimensions. Firstly, ego resiliency is a personality characteristic of the individual, whereas resilience is a dynamic developmental process. Secondly, ego resiliency does not presuppose exposure to substantial adversity, whereas resilience, by most definitions, does' (546).

In exploring the underlying mechanisms involved in the acquisition and deployment of protective factors, Ong et al. (2009) focus on the role of positive emotions and the degree to which they can 'serve as a bulwark against the normative disruptions and setbacks in later adulthood'. They point out that multiple studies, especially since the 1980s, have indicated the useful protective qualities of positive emotions, which can 'sustain continued coping efforts and restore vital resources that had been depleted by stress' as well as promote flexibility in thinking and solving problems. They argue that positive emotions can counteract the physiological effects that can be caused by negative emotions, facilitating coping and building social resources that will serve to help the individual in the longer term. These, they suggest, generally contribute to greater well-being, creating what Ong et al. (2009) refer to as a 'resilience cascade'. Ego resilience, which contributes to the greater expression of positive emotion, can be an important contributor to the more positive ways in which some people appear to be able to respond and adapt to stress. Similarly, children whom Ong et al. designate as 'ego brittle' tend to display 'behavioural problems, depressive symptoms and higher levels of drug use in adolescence'.

Resilience commonly refers to protective factors that are internal and external to the individual, and like risk factors, protective factors are perceived to have a cumulative effect. Figure 1.2 draws together a picture of cumulative protective factors that are attributable to children and young people.

We know that splendid isolation (represented by the castle in Figure 1.2) is not effective in enabling children or young people to develop the skills of resilience. The building of resilience is entirely dependent on social interaction and is only important in a social context. Figure 1.2 outlines a cycle of protective factors needed to shape and craft resilience as a process of social and emotional development.

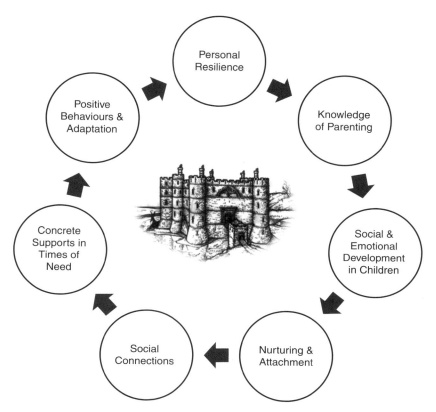

Figure 1.2 Cumulative protective factors

Goldstein and Brooks (2002) suggest that the more protective factors there are, the more likely children are to be resilient. However, Rutter (1990) argues against this optimistic spin. Instead, Rutter (1987) promotes social competence as a child's ability to think of several solutions to social problems, drawing on levels of autonomy, problem-solving skills, empathy, task orientation, curiosity, peer relations and a sense of purpose and future. Rutter continues to promote social and emotional competence as a primary protective factor.

Conclusion

Definitions of resilience vary, and diverse approaches have been taken to understanding the different facets of resilience and determining how it is formed. Researchers have identified approaches, domains, textures, behaviours and a variety of risk and protective factors which all demonstrate the complexities and multiplicities inherent in the construct. Although the breadth of interest in the subject hints at its complexity, it also provides us with a range of pathways and routes to understanding and building resilience. Resilience offers a very wide lens through which parents and practitioners can champion and nurture routes to its attainment.

Vignette 1.3

Robert and Albert are growing up in a depressed former mining town. The area is grim: most of the shops on the town's high street are boarded up; unemployment is high; and social problems such as vandalism and antisocial behaviour are common. Alcoholism, gambling and drug abuse are all significant issues here, as are occasional outbursts of racist violence against the town's few ethnic minority families. The local schools struggle with a school population that often seems to be characterised by apathy, at best. Robert and Albert's family shares many of the problems that are so common in the area. Their parents left school early, are only sporadically employed, and making ends meet is often hard.

Despite these difficulties, both Robert and Albert are doing well. They have a good relationship with their parents and with their grandparents, who live nearby. The family takes part in a local faith group that provides not just spiritual guidance but also a ready-made community of supportive friends and acquaintances. The boys' parents are determined that their children get the most they can from their education, and are keen to engage with teachers and ensure that homework is done properly and on time. Despite everything, the outlook for these brothers is quite good.

Questions and points for discussion

1. What are the risk factors facing Robert and Albert? How have these cumulatively impacted on their development?

2. What are the protective factors in Robert and Albert's lives? How have these cumulatively impacted on their development?

Thus, the level of complexity inherent in the construction and characterisation of resilience can also be seen as one of its strengths. There are many possibilities, framed in a multitude of ways, along the journey of childhood into adulthood. There is no one route to building resilience, and a route to resilience can potentially be shaped and crafted to accommodate the many configurations of life circumstances in childhood.

Even in lives that appear to be compromised by many difficulties, so long as there is capacity and capability, there is the potential to adopt an approach and structure domains that could effectively foster the development of resilience during childhood and adolescence. Resilience is a construct that is interpreted in a range of ways, which is one of the reasons why it draws from academic, political and social debates. Applying what we have learned in these diverse areas holds promise for many, in a variety of ways and at different times and in different places.

The promise of resilience, and its success in enabling people to live productive, happy lives despite difficulties and challenges, lies in the pliability of childhood and adolescence which facilitates the ebb and flow of social, emotional and behavioural competence over a sustained period of time.

CHAPTER 2

Resilience: Research & Development

Introduction

Decades of research and thinking in this field have contributed to our under-standing of the nature and development of resilience. Although the formal study of resilience as a discrete subject of research is relatively new, it has its origins in earlier multidisciplinary investigations.

In this chapter, we explore some of the writers and researchers, their schools of thought and their investigations, all of which have had a direct influence on the development of our understanding of resilience in childhood. Although each study is important in its own right, it is most useful to see the process as an incremental one; those working in the field have built upon the foundations created by previous generations of researchers and thinkers.

From the very early days of studies into resilience (in some cases, not even using the term) to more modern times, we have seen a gradual unwinding of a concept that continues to evolve to the present. It is strange to think that there was once a time when there was little understanding that an individual's experiences in childhood have a great impact on his or her future life – and yet this realisation was not widely accepted even in the early twentieth century and was still under consideration in the 1950s, when John Bowlby was carrying out work that is recognised as a cornerstone of resilience studies to this day. The interplay between the individual's physical and psychological well-being has become increasingly understood, and the appreciation of protective as well as risk factors, and the interaction between these, has grown. The understand-ing that one could identify the risks and opportunities in an individual's life gave rise to the idea that timely interventions could improve the outcomes for children and young people at risk, with profound implications for social and educational policy.

Early underpinnings

Whereas most modern theories of resilience as we recognise them today date to the 1950s, it is worth noting the endeavours of a number of earlier scholars in the emerging fields of psychology and psychopathology. Early research has provided an essential backdrop to the emergence of resilience as a concept for academic study as well as a key factor in positive growth and development (Bowlby, 1959, 1969).

Sigmund Freud (1856–1939) is well known as the father of psycho-therapy, to the extent that many of his claims – considered controversial at the time and for many years afterwards – are now well known. Many of his breakthrough understandings of the early psychological development of the human child are reflected in the scholarship of resilience today. We can point specifically to the notion that a person's experiences in early child-hood have the capacity to greatly influence the rest of the course of his or her life.

Early work on attachment, developed from research carried out largely with animals, has developed into attachment theory as we know it today (see also Chapter 3). Building on his work with women and children, Bowlby expounded his views on attachment in a number of papers including 'The Nature of the Child's Tie to His Mother', published in 1958 (Bowlby, 1958, 350–73), and 'Separation Anxiety' (Bowlby, 1959, 1–25). Also during this period, Mary Ainsworth carried out a detailed study on infants in Uganda, testing Bowlby's theories on attachment. Ainsworth's findings were instru-mental to Bowlby's further thoughts on attachment as elucidated in his pres-entation of attachment theory, published with the title 'Attachment' in 1969 (Bowlby, 1969).

Writing in 1989, John Bowlby stated:

> Evidence is accumulating that human beings of all ages are happiest and able to deploy their talents to best advantage when they are confident that, standing behind them, there are one or more trusted persons who will come to their aid should diffi-culties arise. (1989, 125)

The recent journey

Today, scholars working in the field that embodies resilience build upon the crucial early work that was carried out decades before. It is possible to identify three distinct stages in the journey of research into resilience in children and adults. This journey (Figure 2.1) has provided the under-pinnings for our understanding of the value of developing resilience in childhood:

1. a first stage of research studies indicating the importance of resilience in positive adult outcomes, building upon some of the earliest breakthroughs in the fields of psychology and psychopathology, with considerable leaps forward in the decades between the 1950s and 1980s;
2. a second stage of research studies focused on the identification of the char-acteristics of resilience, with important work having been carried out since the 1980s; and
3. a third stage of research studies that explore intervention activities, particu-larly those devised in the period starting with the beginning of the new mil-lennium (since 2000), designed to help children and young people develop the skills, attitudes and characteristics of resilience.

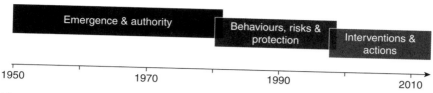

Figure 2.1 Journey of influence

Activity 2.1

With reference to each stage in Figure 2.1, explore the role of research and scholarship in shaping the value that we now place on resilience.

Stage 1: Emergence and authority

During the 1950s, the view of some children as inherently 'invulnerable' was a popular misconception. Michael Rutter (1987) notes that during the 1950s:

> the concept of invulnerable children became popular. Misleadingly, it came to be thought that there were some children so constitutionally tough that they could not give way under the pressures of stress and adversity. The notion proved to be mistaken in at least three respects: children's resistance to stress is relative, rather than absolute; the origins of stress resistance are both environmental and constitutional; and the degree of resilience is not a fixed individual characteristic. (Rutter, 1987)

Although the understanding that some children are more resilient than others emerged relatively early in the journey towards the modern study of resilience, an imperfect comprehension of the complex and multifaceted inputs to resilience led researchers to conclude that some people 'just are' more resilient than others. Thus the 1960s and 1970s represent very important decades for the study of resilience. The misconceptions of the 1950s began to lose ground.

The modern concept of childhood resilience began to coalesce into academic and popular constructs in the 1960s and 1970s as work being carried out by researchers such as John Bowlby, Mary Ainsworth and their colleagues and peers gained traction and acceptance.

In 1964, Michael Rutter carried out a series of studies with children on the Isle of Wight who had experienced risk factors including conflict between their parents, poverty, being part of a large family, criminal and antisocial behaviour on the part of the parents and growing up in care. Although it appeared that having to deal with one risk factor did not have a major impact on a child's progress, children were less likely to do well if they had to manage two or more challenges. The implication was that, by reducing or eliminating sources of stress for children, they could achieve much more positive outcomes (Zolkoski and Bullock, 2012, 197). Rutter's work on the Isle of Wight pointed to the idea that the individual's level of resilience was not an immutable factor, but could be influenced by changes in his or her environment, suggesting that specific interventions could have long-term implications for a person's resilience over the course of a lifetime.

In 1968, psychologists J. and J.H. Block of University of California, Berkeley, conducted a longitudinal study of cognitive and ego development. They defined as 'ego resilient' people who 'are resourceful in the face of new, un-mastered situations, maintain an integrated performance under stress, are better able to process two or more competing stimuli, and are better able to resist illusions' (Cook, 2012, 328). Ego resilience, they argue, reflects the ability to adapt to changes in the environment in a flexible way and includes the ability to see opportunities and to deal well with problems (Block and Kremen, 1996).

Building on Block and Block's earlier work, Block and Kremen (1996) go on to devise the characteristic 'trait resilience' in the context of their concept of a continuum. They describe this continuum as moving from people with high levels of ego resilience (and strong abilities in the area of self-regulation) to those with low levels of ego resilience (and poor abilities in the area of self-regulation, tending to over- or under-self-regulate).

Trait resilience – referred to as an integral personality trait – can be defined as an instinctive ability to adapt to the changes people experience in life, and to recover quickly from factors that are stressful, including the ability to allocate emotional, physical and intellectual resources efficiently and well (Block and Kremen, 1996). Block and Kerman argue that treating resilience as a personality trait may be one way to explain 'significant individual differences in the capacity to adapt in the face of trauma and stress given the same risks, as well as the fact that these individual differences may be present as early as birth'.

Block and Kremen's conception of resilience as a personality trait is at odds with what some other researchers believe; some feel that everyone is potentially resilient, and see resilience as resulting from 'normal adaptive functioning' (Waugh et al., 2008).

Norm Garmezy (1974, 1983, 1990, 1991) was one the most influential researchers from the early 1970s onwards. His work has been crucial and his contribution distinctive, emerging from the field of psychopathology and the connectivities between normality and mental disorder.

Garmezy has taken inspiration from the work of Bleuler (1978), which showed that even in high-risk groups, such as children of mothers with schizophrenia, there were numerous examples of children who showed adaptive patterns of social behaviour and positive employment experiences. Garmezy, recognising the importance of a range of influences on resilience, chose therefore to direct his research activity to the study of stress resistance in high-risk groups, with a focus on psychosocial disadvantage as opposed to character traits. His research emphasised the study of resilience as a process and not as a fixed attribute of an individual.

During the 1970s, the focus of research on childhood resilience shifted from psychopathology to emphasise the positive rather than the maladaptive – spurring an emergence of positive psychology and positive mental health. More specifically, studies in the field of childhood resilience in the 1980s began to focus more on acquiring relatively better social and emotional functioning rather than on the search for superior psychological traits or functions.

From the early 1980s, Emmy Werner and Ruth Smith published the results of their classic longitudinal study of a group of children growing up in the island of Kauai in Hawaii in difficult circumstances. The study, widely considered to be a 'foundational study' (Richardson, 2002, 309), followed the children from their birth in 1955 (before Hawaii joined the United States), with reports on the subjects being published periodically as they grew up. These children had experienced poverty, family dysfunction and other challenges. Unsurprisingly, many of them grew up to be adults with multiple problems of their own or to experience problems at various stages of their development. However, Werner and Smith wrote in their introduction:

> [W]e could not help but be deeply impressed by the resilience of most children and their potential for positive growth. Most young people in this cohort were completely coping with their problems, chose their parents as their models, found their family and friends to be supportive and expressed a strong sense of continuity in family-held values attached to education, occupational preferences and social expectations. (Werner and Smith, 1982, 2)

Werner and Smith were extremely struck by the fact that such a large proportion of these children managed to become resilient adults – including many who had had some serious behavioural or learning problems during their childhood or youth and who had seemed to be on course for a life full of problems and maladjustment. By the age of 10, a full third of the children in the study had required educational or mental health support or both. By the age of 18, only 10 per cent had mental health problems (Werner and Smith, 1982, 26).

According to Werner and Smith, their study demonstrated that the outcome of virtually every biological or psychological risk condition was dependent on the quality of supportive relationships and new opportunities as their lives unfolded (Werner and Smith, 1982). They demonstrated that the seeds of resilience were sown at a very early stage of child development. It became clear that resilient children were at an advantage from early childhood and throughout every period of their lives (Werner and Smith, 1982, 154–5). They were more resilient in terms of both mental strength and physical health, suffered fewer illnesses in their first two decades of life, and tended to recover more quickly when they did get sick. They had more advanced language development, problem-solving and communication skills. They coped better with the challenges of adolescence, with higher levels of self-esteem and the consciously expressed intention to work to make their lives better.

In exploring the difference between this group of resilient children and their peers, Werner and Smith were able to isolate a number of factors that combined to make them so different:

> [A] characteristically strong bond was forged between the infant and the primary caregiver during the first year of life. The physical robustness of the resilient children, their high activity level, and their social responsiveness were recognised by the caregivers and elicited a great deal of attention. There was little prolonged separation of the infants from their mothers and no prolonged bond disruption during the first year of life. The strong attachment that resulted appears to have been a secure base for the development of the advanced self-help skills and autonomy noted among these children in their second year of life. (Werner and Smith, 1982, 156)

Werner and Smith's research indicated that there were strong social bonds among the families of resilient children, whereas children who were more likely not to display qualities of resilience tended to have experienced a lack of dependable early years care and education in the absence of the mother and more frequent periods of ill health during childhood as well as higher levels of discord within the family. Werner and Smith were instrumental firstly in signalling the value of resilience from childhood; secondly, in demonstrating the importance of the role of social support; and thirdly, in promoting the recognition that resilience should be viewed across the human lifespan.

In 1984, Garmezy et al. also published an influential paper: 'The Study of Stress and Competence in Children: A Building Block for Developmental Psychopathology' (1984). They pointed out that formal studies of resilience tended to focus very much on children who were considered to be at greatly elevated risk of developing serious problems in later life. The authors studied three cohorts of children: a heterogeneous group selected from two urban environments; a group of children who had been born with a serious heart defect; and a group of children with physical disabilities who were about to enter mainstream schooling for the first time. Regardless of the group the children belonged to, it was determined that stress could be counteracted or compensated for by their personal qualities of strength:

> [W]hen certain positive personal attributes (or positive factors) are present, variations in stress will be less strongly reflected in variations of quality of adaptation than when these attributes are lacking, suggesting that the personal qualities in question impart a kind of 'immunity' against stress. The reverse is true for attributes of vulnerability; in their presence the impact of variations of stress on competence becomes more, rather than less, pronounced. (Garmezy et al., 1984, 102)

The search for definitions and descriptors had moved into the search for characteristics, risks and notions of immunity.

Stage 2: Search for behaviours, risks and protection

In 1971, Rutter, using divorce, bereavement, happy and unhappy separation as variables, found that the risks of antisocial behaviour in children were far greater in the case of divorce or unhappy separation compared to bereavement or happy separation. By the late 1980s and 1990s, groups of researchers (Rutter, 1971, 1999; Harris et al., 1986; Cherlin et al., 1991) had begun to concentrate research efforts on testing for environmental factors associated with risk, mediation and protection.

For example, Cherlin et al. (1991), considering specifically the effects of divorce, studied whether risk was a function of parental psychopathology. Findings related to children of 11 years of age demonstrated that the risk of pre-divorce conflict had a greater impact than the divorce itself.

Studies on other risk factors such as parental depression pursued a genetic as well as a psychosocial research trail. For example, early research that focused on the study of parental depression had a tendency to assume that the intergenerational risk effects on children were likely to be genetically determined.

However, more recently, further research has shown a more complicated picture of risk factors. Silberg and Eaves (2012) have shown, for example, that the effects of parental depression on child depression seem to emerge mainly from environmental factors.

In the 1990s and into the new millennium, the formal study of resilience increased, with particular interest in contributory factors. Perceptions that we live in more disjointed and stressful social societies have been driven by political and social factors, such as rising youth unemployment and persistent imbalances between the life chances of children and young people from disadvantaged communities compared to those of middle-class children. As a consequence, politicians, academics and practitioners have all sought to find ways to improve the quality of lives and environments for children, young people, their families and their communities. In relation to resilience, characterising children as 'at risk' has become a means of predicting vulnerability or risk for a wide range of negative outcomes such as school failure, delinquency and crime.

Activity 2.2

Summarising some of the major avenues of research explored during the course of the 1990s, Rutter (2000, 652) writes:

> Four general areas of interest may be identified. First, many investigators emphasize the value of focusing on positive outcomes, and not just on psychopathology. Thus, Masten et al. (2011) and Luthar (1991) investigated the factors associated with the development of social competence. Similarly, Bandura (1995, 1997) and others fostered numerous studies of the causes and consequences of self-efficacy. Second, there has been attention to the effects of positive experiences of various kinds. Thus, particularly in the field of depression, there has been much interest in the protective effect of social support . . . The third area of interest has concerned the study of the process of how individuals cope with stress and adversity . . . it has become clear that there is a substantial range of effective coping mechanisms (or psychological defences), that the coping style that works best for one sort of stress experience may not work equally well with a different kind of adversity, and that there are substantial individual differences in the coping styles with which people are most comfortable . . . Fourth, research has focused on the features or the processes that differentiate people's responses to serious stress or adversity.

Discussion

With reference to the four general areas of interest identified by Rutter, explore the impact of shifting research from psychopathology towards a more positive psychological approach.

Whereas earlier researchers in the field of resilience tended to focus on specific strengths displayed by resilient people, including children, the understanding of the characteristics of resilience has become progressively more nuanced:

> Resilience moved beyond the scope of just recognizing personal traits that contributed to the protective process[,] and included the interaction of environmental and contextual factors external to the individual – family, school, community and other external systems. (Benard, 2009, 208)

Work carried out in this period also revealed resilience to be 'neither linear nor permanent' (Benard, 2009, 208). According to Rutter, it is important to note that people who appear to be resilient on the basis of one measure of outcome may not be resilient according to other measures (Rutter, 2000, 663). The fact that resilience may not always manifest in socially desirable ways must also be recognised.

Benard (2009) supports this view and argues that:

> [w]hat may be considered a manifestation of resilience to one population may be undesirable to another. Take the example of the teen who chooses to be in a gang. By most normative social standards, this behavior would be labeled as being undesirable, if not blatantly deviant. Embracing a different perspective and using a 'resilience lens' yields an alternative explanation of why a youth may join a gang. What if the teen was to feel vulnerable and targeted for some unconscionable consequence because he was *not* in a gang. In this case, the teen may suggest that he or she became part of a gang in order to stay alive on the streets. (Benard, 2009, 209)

In general, the twentieth century saw the contributions of a wide and growing range of researchers into resilience and related fields, not all of which can be considered in full detail here. Table 2.1 provides examples of a range of risk factors that have emerged over time.

Table 2.1 Examples of risk factors

Researchers	Risk factors	Descriptors
Bowlby (1950s)	Lack of secure attachment	Separation from, or failure to develop attachment to the mother or primary caregiver is a risk factor to the developing child.
Rutter (1960s and 1970s)	Presence of two or more risks in a child's life	The presence of multiple risk factors, such as divorce, poverty, maltreatment, etc., have a negative impact on a child's qualities of resilience, when he or she might be able to deal with one risk factor.
Garmezy (1983)	Stress in childhood	Stress, including loss and separation, neglect, or the experience of extreme events such as war, all pose significant 'psychological threats' to the developing child.

Schoggen and Schoggen (1989)	Over-populated environments	Environments with few opportunities and roles and where individuals are likely to be exposed to less tolerance and more prejudice constitute a risk factor to a child's resilience.
Werner (1993, 2012)	Poor health in early childhood	Physical ill health and other risk factors experienced during early childhood are major predictors for problems with resilience throughout life.
Csikszentmihalyi (1993)	Depersonalisation	A shift from face-to-face interactions to an anonymous social context can mean increased vulnerability of youth and families, as can lack of community involvement.
Wolin and Wolin (1993) and Weist (1997)	Family limitations	Absence of a significant adult in a child's life and reduced opportunity to develop skill and competence in a safe environment are risk factors.
Wolin and Wolin (1995)	Lower socio-economic status	Children from lower socio-economic back-grounds experience a greater number of risk factors than children from more affluent back-grounds, and they are open to cumulative risk.
Brackenreed (2010)	Ethnicity and social labels	Ethnicity, racial, social class and gender groups, immigration and first and second language, per-sonal beliefs, traditions, practices and customs are all labels that pose risk factors.
Gilligan (2000, 2004, 2009)	Placement in care and the disruption to life trajectory	Young people in care face considerable chal-lenges: loss, separation from their families, friends and communities and, often, disruption to their education.
Daniel and Wassell (2002a) and Daniel et al. (2010, 2011)	The cumulative effect of multiple risk factors	This results from, e.g., chaotic family back-ground, lack of support at home and challenges at school. The absence of an environment suited to the development of resilience of the child, especially in relation to gender, is a risk factor to a child's resilience.
Silberg and Eaves (2000s)	Biology and environment can conspire to increase risk.	Behaviour problems in childhood pose a risk to resilience and can be attributed to both genetic and environmental factors. It is important to understand the complex nature of risk rather than assuming that one or the other factor is more important.

Thus, although we acknowledge the presence of risk factors, many scholars have contributed to our growing understanding of the role of protective factors as a counter measure to the severe consequences of risk factors.

Brigid Daniel and Robbie Gilligan have isolated characteristics of resilience that may be considered protective at various and varying stages of a child's development (Gilligan, 2000; Gilligan, 2004; Daniel, 2010; Daniel et al., 2010). As children grow up and more influences enter their lives, their development becomes more complex, requiring more complex patterns of protection. For example, resilient girls are notably more autonomous and independent than boys, being more expressive of their emotions, more socially perceptive and with well-developed nurturing skills (Daniel et al., 2010, 66–7). According to Daniel et al., everyone can experience protective and risk factors in the wider (extrinsic) environment (Daniel and Wassell, 2002a, 11).

Table 2.2 provides examples of a range of protective factors that have emerged over time.

Table 2.2 Examples of protective factors

Researchers	Protective factors	Descriptors
West and Farrington (1973)	Family competence	Importance of adequate and consistent parental role models: parents who spend time with children and pass on social achievements and parents who present as firm and consistent without the use of rejection.
Block and Kremen (1980s and 1990s)	Adaptability	Individuals with the ability to adapt responsively and flexibly to potential risks in their environment.
Morse, Rojahn and Smith (2014)	Structure and control factors	Families that celebrate birthdays, have a stabilising effect during times of crisis, believe in their ability to control life and have established routines, including meal times.
Rutter (1984)	Positive outlook Self-esteem and self-efficacy	A sense that one can withstand challenges. A feeling of self-worth and a feeling of control over what happens to you.
Garmezy (1983, 1991)	Developmental milestones	Resilience being not just a fixed trait, but a process, a dynamic pattern of adaptation to an environment that is always changing.
Rutter (1987), Masten et al. (1995) and Wolin and Wolin (1995)	Community and networks	A basis for healthy development, centrality of family and community – 'no family is an island', participation in family coping strategies, familiarity with relevant support systems.
Pence (1996)	Social services	Support and services afforded to children, young people and families.
Werner (1989), Benard (2001) and Marshal (2004)	Education and achievements	Opportunities to establish relationships with peers and adults, build social and academic competencies, meaningful engagement and responsibility within school and community.

Werner (1989)	Roles and responsibilities Rules and structure	Experiences that include responsibilities and tasks that involve working with and on behalf of others. Family size (fewer than four children being optimal), number of caregivers, structures and rules, and few chronic stressful life events during childhood and adolescence.
Benard (1993, 2001)	Significant adults	Teachers who provide and model care that enables positive development by fostering social relationships, listening to students, offering validation of feelings and showing respect and compassion.
Winfield (1991)	Education and aspiration	Having parents who are concerned about their children's education and are aware of their interests and aspirations.
Wolin and Wolin (1995)	Cluster of factors	Including resilience of insight, independence, relationships, initiatives, creativity, humour and morality.
Bandura (1995, 1997)	Self-efficacy	Developing qualities of self-efficacy that can assist with the development of resilience.
Gilligan (2000s) and Daniel (2000s)	Intrinsic and extrinsic factors	Understanding that although some individuals are born with a greater tendency towards resilience, resilience can be fostered in anyone, given a supportive environment at home, at school and in the community; and that protective factors tend not to be exactly the same for girls and boys.

As with risk factors, the protective factors in any child's life can be complex, multifaceted and not necessarily obvious at first glance. Research into resilience, including the identification of appropriate risk and protective factors, demonstrates some of the complexities inherent in the construction of resilience. Moreover, the dynamic of risk and protective processes that underlie resilience can be characterised as existing in two opposing directions. On the one hand, risk and or protective factors can operate before the experience of stress/adversity to increase resilience and, on the other, similar risk or protective factors can operate after an experience to foster resilience. In addition, research activity has sought to examine complex social contexts in order to consider which particular aspects of, for example, broken homes, poverty, school support and social capital networks actually contribute to risk or prevention. Masten et al. (1995), however, advocate caution in ascribing 'risk' and/ or 'resilient' factors to children and young people. They suggest that labelling children as 'resilient' can be as misleading and potentially harmful as labelling children as 'at risk'.

Stage 3: Interventions and actions

Various intervention techniques have been developed that are intended to help children to become more resilient. In the 1980s, for example, Fraiburg developed a 'set of intervention strategies based on psychodynamic principles' (Yates et al., 2003, 256) which focused on developing secure attachment between parents and children. In the 1990s, an approach that centred on helping parents to become more sensitive to their infants' needs was developed by van den Boom (Yates et al., 2003, 256). Daniel warns that any intervention intended to build resilience in children and families should take into consideration the specific protective and risk factors inherent in each child's situation (Daniel et al., 2011, 122).

However, it appears that such interventions tend not to be very successful when it comes to children growing up in high-risk environments. The most recent work in this area indicates the need for 'interventions that strive to ameliorate multiple risks while promoting successful adaptation in several settings' (Yates et al., 2003, 257).

By the mid-1990s, schools had been identified as key institutions providing mediation from risk and structured support to promote the development of resilience. In the following decade, there have been many changes in terms of how schools intervene to promote social and educational competence – important indicators of resilience – among students. For example, during this period, the US-based Carnegie Council on Adolescent Development (1995) notes that estimates suggest that 25 per cent of Americans between 10 and 17 years old are extremely vulnerable to the negative consequences of engaging in multiple high-risk social and health behaviours. At this time, the Council considered the current programmes then in use for promoting social competencies – which focused on problem solving, decision making, social approach and engagement, stress management and communication skills – as being of insufficient duration, and not adequately researched.

In 1965, Bronfenbrenner (1917–2005) spurred the US federal programme Head Start, designed to provide support to families on low incomes (see also Chapter 5). He influenced the political agenda at the time by establishing the notion that early intervention approaches, such as the Head Start programme in the US (Box 2.1) and Sure Start in the UK (Box 2.2), could lead to significant social and economic gains. The outcome of these programmes has typically been that children demonstrate 'initial IQ gains followed by subsequent declines' (Curtis and Cicchetti, 2003, 471); however, they do display enhanced competence academically and socially.

Box 2.1 Support in early years – the US model

The **Head Start** programme in the United States focuses on issues including early childhood education, health, and parenting. Growing from its beginnings as a summer school programme founded in 1965 under the government of Lyndon Johnson and intended to help very young children from deprived backgrounds (including homeless children, the children of migrant workers, and children from

Native American backgrounds) to acquire the skills they would need for primary school, it was expanded in 1981 and again in 2007. Head Start was also involved in the development of Sesame Street, a children's television programme.

The actual success rate of Head Start has sometimes been queried. However, research has shown that children who started the programme aged 3, and who remained in the programme for two years, had higher scores in various areas than children who entered when they were older and stayed in the programme for less time (MacWayne et al., 2012). Other research indicated that Head Start may make it more likely that young people eventually graduate from high school, and might contribute to higher earnings in adulthood. One particularly encouraging study suggested that young people who attended Head Start were given a long-term academic advantage over those who did not, and were less likely to be diagnosed as having a learning disability, as well as more likely to experience good health in adulthood and less likely to become involved in crime (Deming, 2009).

Critics of the Head Start programme suggest that apparent initial gains are not sustained over time. Although children appear to gain a higher IQ from their participation, when they are tested a few years later, studies seem to show that this advantage has either disappeared or has diminished. However, some researchers point out that this is most likely because the children likely to attend Head Start programmes are also the children most likely to attend low-performance state schools. The problem, therefore, is less with Head Start than with the fact that many children who have been through the programme are released to an educational system that does not provide them with sufficient supports to build upon their initial gains. (Lee et al., 1990)

Box 2.2 Support in early years – the UK model

Sure Start was founded in 1998 by the government then under Tony Blair, overseen by the Department for Children, Schools and Families, and the Department for Work and Pensions, with the stated aim of 'giving children the best possible start in life' by focusing on improving the quality of child care, education in early childhood and support in terms of health and family. The emphasis was on community developing and care within the community. Substantial state funding was provided to set up Sure Start programmes intended to target children living in deprived circumstances (Roberts, 2000) and to reduce levels of poverty in childhood.

At a local level, the views of parents and the organisations involved determined to a great extent how each chapter developed. As Sure Start evolved, the emphasis changed from local programmes to more formal 'Sure Start Children's Centres', which are controlled by local authorities.

Despite early reservations about how successful Sure Start actually was, various studies showed tangible benefits. One study, carried out in 2007, explored families in Wales in which parents in a deprived area had taken a course on parenting skills, leading to a lower incidence of problematic behaviour in their children. (Hutchings et al., 2007)

Vignette 2.1

Natasha is a single mother of three children living in a run-down part of a large industrial city. She is still young, in her mid-twenties, but her parents have already passed away. She has minimal contact with the two men who fathered her children. Because the family lives in poverty and has few social or familial supports, Natasha's children have been identified as at risk. When a 'Sure Start' programme was initiated in her area, Natasha was encouraged to enrol her children and to become involved. She was initially quite sceptical, but feeling that she might have the opportunity to meet other young mums in the same situation, she did as she was advised.

For Natasha, the biggest impact of Sure Start was her feeling that it 'took the pressure off'. The children were cared for in a crèche in the morning, enabling her to get a part-time job. She also attended classes on parenting and nutrition, and learned about how to discipline three active youngsters more effectively, as well as about how to provide nutritious meals on a tight budget. Work went well, and she has been promised more hours as soon as all three children are in school and she has more time. She did also meet other young mums, and has made a few friends – they have all agreed to help out each other as much as possible.

Discussion

With reference to the vignette, critically discuss the role of social policies designed to support families with multiple risk factors.

As well as the benefits outlined in the vignette, investigate what other benefits early interventions programmes – such as Head Start and Sure Start – might achieve that could support the development of resilience in children and families.

By the latter years of the twentieth century, interest among scholars of resilience had turned to positive psychology (which had first attracted attention from earlier researchers in the field) because, as Yates and Masten (2004, 522) say:

> [T]hese investigators studied, wrote and spoke about the human capacity for positive adaptation and achievement in the face of adversity. The resilience perspective stressed the importance of *promoting competence* through positive models of intervention and change, in addition to reducing or ameliorating the effects of adversity on children.

Schultz et al. (2013, 698–9) highlight interventions that have been created to help the promotion of resilience in children exposed to violence by focusing on developing or strengthening recognised protective factors that can lead to better outcomes 'by ameliorating existing harms or shielding children from further harm in the event of violence re-exposure'.

In Schultz et al.'s study of the effects of exposure to violence on children, they demonstrated that children with levels of self-control that increased over time were less likely than those with poor relationships with their parents to respond negatively as a result of this exposure (Schultz et al., 2013, 707). Although Fergus and Zimmerman stress that:

[a] resilience approach . . . emphasizes assets and resources as the focus for change. Internal assets that may be particularly critical to develop social skills for peers, self-efficacy for health-promoting behavior, academic skills and participation in extracurricular activities . . . skill building for life in general, such as the development of generic social and problem-solving skills, can be just as important as building skills for risk avoidance. External resources that may be developed include opportunities for adult mentorship, parenting skills, and provision of health-promoting settings for adolescents. (Fergus and Zimmerman, 2005, 411)

Examples of population-based interventions across the lifespan that are likely to support resilience include social policies and support for parents of infants, early childhood intervention programmes, school-based interventions, workplace and unemployment programmes, and activity programmes for older adults. Population-based programmes typically target everyone in a given population, with a view to improving levels of resilience across the board. The programme may target one or more issues, striving to eliminate or reduce risks or to enhance or create protective factors.

In the United States, the issue of child maltreatment has been identified as a matter that requires a population-based approach. Prinz et al. identified child maltreatment as being a problem not just for the child in question and his or her family, but society as a whole. They proposed the adoption of the 'Triple P' system, which was designed to give parents greater competence in caring for their children and to change or prevent parenting practices identified as dysfunctional. The Triple P system is predicated on five core principles of positive parenting: ensuring a safe, engaging environment; promoting a positive learning environment; using assertive discipline; maintaining reasonable expectations; and taking care of oneself as a parent (Prinz et al., 2009, 5).

The Triple P system has various 'layers' of intervention, each one focused on a progressively smaller element of the population, to enable the process to reach the widest number of people possible and to be tailored to meet the needs of the families and children most at risk.

Population-based approaches can be used to support population-wide behaviours and environments that exert a protective influence and enhance resilience. Community-based programmes have also been used to support, for example, early child development (Herrman et al., 2011, 264).

Vignette 2.2

Talvintol is a community with a large immigrant population, including a large influx of people who arrived only recently, fleeing war in their own country. Here there are multiple risks to resilience at both the individual and the community level. Many of the newer arrivals have post-traumatic stress disorder (PTSD). Poverty is endemic. Many do not speak English as a first language. A large number of children are being brought up in one-parent homes, and many struggle at school for a range of reasons. The community also suffers from a substantial degree of exclusion from the wider society in the area because of linguistic reasons, a degree of self-exclusion on the grounds of wishing to remain true to their roots, and a degree of racism and discrimination.

Rather than allowing this situation to continue unchecked, a community-based programme was set up to tackle a wide range of risk factors, including extra language support for children at school, language classes for adults (with special classes for women, who tend to be even more isolated than men) and 'meet and greet' events at which attempts are made to break down barriers between the newer arrivals and more established populations in the area. Psychological support in the relevant languages has been made available to those who need it. The community has also been encouraged to set up social events for women and children, and to enrol children in the local Sure Start programme.

Discussion

Explore how social exclusion can limit the social and emotional development of an adolescent.

Examine the consequences (barriers and opportunities) for developing resilience in the cultural context described in the vignette.

Yates and Masten (2004) write of the importance of intervening early, asserting that this can prevent children from 'derailing' from positive adaptation. They state:

> Interventions must focus on the initiation of positive developmental pathways, as well as on their maintenance over time. Early competence promotion efforts scaffold success that, in turn, provides a platform on which future developmental achievements are built. Yates and Masten (2004, 529)

In fact, numerous studies have highlighted the benefits of early intervention, not just to the children themselves in terms of enhanced quality of life, greater educational outcomes and so forth, but also for society at large. Karoly et al. (2005, 21) point out that the evidence suggests that learning in early childhood is cumulative in nature and therefore that the skills acquired in early childhood are necessary for learning in later childhood. Young people who are designated at risk, and who receive interventions as early as possible, are likely to experience benefits in areas including their performance at school and their outcome as adults.

Community-based interventions focus on specific communities, often within a larger group, that have been identified as being at particular risk. These communities might represent, for example, a particular ethnic minority or a specific socio-economic group. By engaging directly with community members, interventions benefit from local knowledge of needs and perspectives, and are more likely to result in a beneficial outcome to the community (Mooney-Somers and Maher, 2009, 3). Community-based interventions frequently focus on a specific issue that is posing a risk across the community. In community work, carrying out research tailored towards interventions is normally best done in the context of partnerships between researchers and the communities themselves (Mooney-Somers and Maher, 2009, 4), and peer researchers (members of the communities) are often also best placed to use their knowledge of the local culture to explore the issues around the risks at hand.

Conclusion

Our current understanding of resilience rests on the work of a wide range of researchers and scholars whose efforts combine to provide us with the nuanced, still-evolving knowledge that today is brought to bear on both social policy and direct intervention. From the basic understanding that one's early experiences impact on one's future well-being to Bowlby's breakthrough work in the area of attachment, we have come a long way. Understanding the journey that we have taken, from the first intimations that there might be a better explanation as to why some people do better than others in difficult circumstances than 'just because', is valuable also in helping us to appreciate how these insights are influenced and are applied in the context of politics and policy, and the role that timely and informed interventions can play in securing positive futures.

Research into the area of resilience continues to grow, and its journey of influence has led to a steadily more refined understanding of the edifice of resilience and its construction over time. This means that understanding what resilience is, how it is expressed and how it can be nurtured is itself a journey that continues to change and evolve, alongside the cultures, societies, families and individuals in which it is expressed.

The many lessons and key findings from earlier and current generations of researchers mean that resilience is now more fully understood from academic and political as well as practitioner perspectives. Of course, resilience does not occur outside a social context, and as we continue to explore its compounds in incrementally more detail while searching for relevant ways to intervene, we apply all that we have learned from earlier researchers and practitioners as well as from those working currently in the field. All of this takes place amid the ever-shifting sands of family structures, community coherence and employment across cultures.

KEY PERSPECTIVES

Building Blocks from Psychology

Introduction

In this chapter, we explore the importance of psychological health and wellness in early childhood and adolescence, as well as a range of psychological factors that influence how children and young people can and should develop the attributes and characteristics of resilience. We start with the very earliest days of individuals' lives and explore how their first forays into relationships with the important people in their lives can lay the foundations for well-being later on.

Even in the presence of poverty and other risks to resilience, establishing a positive relationship with a primary caregiver or caregivers can help to protect the growing child in numerous ways, including the development, throughout childhood and adolescence, of skills that will be essential to resilience later on. The ability to develop strong attachments to caregivers is innate in most children and can be facilitated. In early childhood, the individual's social and emotional experiences will impact on his or her neurological (see Chapter 4) as well as psychological development – and these two are inextricably intertwined.

It is known that resilience flourishes and exerts a protective influence in the context of sound mental health. Thus, in order to understand how resilience can be built up through childhood, we need to start by understanding the rudiments of inputs to mental health. As children grow, each will encounter potential hazards to his or her mental well-being; some more than others. For children and young people, there are many potential hazards, and life can offer a range of diverse negative and or positive opportunities.

Significantly, research has shown (Gilligan, 2000; Luthar, 2003; Mason, 2012) that even in people who have not experienced ideally close relationships in infancy, later childhood and adolescence can still provide opportunities for the development of the skills that help to build resilience. Some of these skills, such as positive thinking and emotional intelligence, can be taught, or at least deliberately developed, and have the potential to make a real and lasting difference.

Understanding how resilience can be developed begins with understanding the opportunities for the positive psychological development of children, and the factors that foster good mental health throughout their lives. This chapter explores the paramountcy of supportive relationships in shaping resilience and focuses on the relevant psychological factors as the building blocks of these relationships.

Early attachment

The first and most significant relationship in childhood is the attachment bond between the newborn and the primary caregiver, usually the mother. The importance of attachment in the early years is well established, and research has confirmed the formative months and years as crucial to the development of future individual qualities and attributes of resilience.

Despite their weakness and vulnerability at birth, newborn human infants are equipped with the first tools they need to start developing resilience. On a very basic level, they show their determination to stay alive by suckling. Many suckle for hours immediately after birth, stimulating their mothers' milk flow and providing themselves with colostrum, which is important for infant development. The suckling also serves to stimulate the mother's production of oxytocin, which is a 'feel good' hormone that helps her to bond with her newborn infant after the trauma of birth (Strathearn, 2007). As a close relationship with the caregiver is a positive indicator of the capacity to build resilience, these infant behaviours are important factors in enhancing the child's likelihood of developing relationships that can support resilience.

Newborn babies are also intensely interested in developing emotional relationships with their caregivers. This innate propensity towards attachment can be seen as an important protective factor. Babies' innate ability to initiate attachment with their caregivers was described in 1957 by John Bowlby, who wrote of the role of babies' smiles in eliciting loving attention from their mothers, describing it as

> a social releaser – a behaviour pattern, probably species-specific to Man, which in ordinary circumstances matures in the early weeks of life, one of the functions of which is to evoke maternal behaviour in the mother. (Bowlby, 2005, 48, orig. 1957)

According to Bowlby, these early smiles facilitated the babies' survival. Despite their constant cries to be fed, cleaned and cared for, babies offer a great reward to their caregiver in the form of their smile. In this respect smiling can be understood as an adaptive response: it is not hard to imagine smiling babies receiving more and better care from their mothers, ensuring that this behaviour persists into future generations. Thus, babies who are happy, and who are able to communicate this emotion to their caregivers, already display a powerful ability to initiate attachment and enhance their likelihood of fostering positive relationships.

Babies are born equipped with the ability to identify and, to some extent, empathise with those they interact with. They are sensitive to faces, and will stare at a face (or even a rudimentary drawing of a face) for longer than at other things in their environment. They also very quickly learn to differentiate the face, voice and smell of their mother from everybody else's, facilitating the development of a close and exclusive relationship between caregiver and child.

The time that very small babies spend staring at, smiling at and interacting with their caregiver is when they start to learn about communication, and to acquire (initially rudimentary) social skills. These are some of the fundamental building blocks of resilience. Children start to build these skills in the context of interactions with just one person (at any one time). When they have learned how to interact with one person or a few people – extending to social networks to more people, typically initially to others within the family circle and community.

The interactions that a child experiences in infancy are also crucial to language acquisition, which 'supports cognitive and social development, enhances memory and reasoning abilities, and underpins the development of executive function – the capacity to organise and manage one's own behaviour' (Waxman and Goswami, 2012, 89).

According to Flouri et al. (2015):

> Although most studies find that the relationship between exposure to environmental risk and child adjustment is linear, there is also some evidence for nonlinear (e.g. threshold) effects. A threshold pattern suggests that after a certain number of risk factors are experienced, behaviour changes. Researchers find that threshold effects usually fit quadratic trends showing that, as their number increases, risk factors potentiate each other such that their combined effect on child adjustment is far worse than a mere summation of their separate effects. (Flouri et al., 2015, 746)

The importance of attachment to a positive caregiver in the very young child's life lies in the role they play in managing anxiety and responding appropriately to the child's needs. Thus, they can help the child to form a secure emotional attachment that provides a base from which the world can safely be explored (Atwool, 2006, 316). According to Atwool, how babies' parents respond to their reactions to stress, and model behaviours in this context, can have a tremendous impact on the coping mechanisms that babies develop. Rutter, for example, has indicated the great importance of 'secure and harmonious love relationships' and 'success in accomplishing tasks' as key to establishing a 'positive self-concept' (Atwool, 2006, 321).

Understanding the role of attachment in the development of the child is crucial to understanding how resilience can be developed. Studies on attachment behaviour have identified a number of clear patterns. For the purposes of understanding resilience, two are particularly relevant (Figure 3.1).

Figure 3.1 Secure attachment v. insecure attachment

Secure attachment

Children who display secure attachment to a primary caregiver 'play happily when their caregiver is present, protest when they leave and go to them for comfort on their return' (Daniel and Wassell, 2011, 27). They find it easier to settle in at school, make friends and develop useful coping skills.

Children who experience secure attachment find it easier to develop empathy and to understand that other people have feelings that they might be able to influence (Bowbly 2005). Without empathy, it is difficult for people to form the close social networks and personal friendships – with both peers and adults from outside the family unit – that are an important contributing factor to building confidence in one's own ability, which is a foundation stone for resilience.

It has been argued that when an infant is exposed to the primary caregiver's regulatory capacities, their ability to adapt is facilitated. Without this, their brain would struggle to develop the ability to 'approach, tolerate and incorporate new experiences'. By developing a secure sense of attachment, and confidence in a co-relationship, children and adolescents become able to explore and manage new experiences that are potentially stressful (Atwool, 2006, 317). 'Attached' children have the ability to develop self-regulation. Together with attachment, this ability has been identified as a 'fundamental developmental task' of the early phases of life (Atwool, 2006, 321). Starting in infancy and continuing in childhood, attachment promotes the development of the growing brain, and the individual is facilitated in acquiring mastery over new situations (Atwool, 2006, 318).

After infancy and very early childhood, children need to accomplish certain developmental tasks such as acquiring the ability to get along well with friends, to behave in a way that is socially appropriate and to make progress in academic and other activities – all factors that have also been identified as essential to resilience. Secure attachment facilitates the acquisition of all of these skills (Atwool, 2006, 321).

Atwool (2006, 321) states that the 'quality of attachment is instrumental in the four central areas associated with resilience, individual characteristics, supportive family, positive connections with adults or agencies in the environment, and culture'. She points out (322) that research has demonstrated clear links between secure attachment and competence, and that competence and problem-solving abilities are clearly linked to self-esteem.

Insecure attachment

Since the early days of attachment theory, it has been recognised that:

> . . . when deprived of maternal care, a child's development is almost always retarded – physically, intellectually and socially – and that symptoms of physical and mental illness may appear. (Bowlby, 1953)

A child who has not developed a positive supportive relationship with his or her primary caregiver may display insecure attachment characterised by, for example, one of four behavioural patterns:

- Avoidant behaviour: If *avoidant*, the child tends to shun the caregiver after a separation and appears not to discriminate markedly between a stranger and a caregiver in his or her behaviour towards them. Avoidant children have to learn how to become self-reliant at a very early age; they learn not to engage in attachment behaviour so as to protect themselves from rejection. Although they continue to develop cognitively, attachment behaviour is not integrated and can even be repressed (Atwool, 2006, 319).
- Ambivalent behaviour: If *ambivalent*, the child appears to want comfort from the caregiver after a separation, but at the same time shows resistance to comfort, for example by squirming out of a hug (Daniel and Wassell, 2012, 28).
- Disorganised behaviour: If *disorganised*, the child can display a range of reactions, appearing to be confused and unable to accept the caregiver's attempts to provide comfort (Daniel and Wassell, 2012, 28).
- Anxious behaviour: If *anxious*, the child can be very preoccupied with the caregiver's availability to him or her (Daniel and Wassell, 2012, 28).

These behavioural patterns are easier to see in toddlers and become less evident as children grow older and more autonomous.

Vignette 3.1

Lisa was seven years old and had been referred for assessment because of her inappropriate behaviour in school. She veered wildly between wanting to be 'best friends' with everyone and engaging in rough, bullying behaviour when she didn't get her own way. Although she was bright, she found it difficult to concentrate in class and often seemed very reluctant to look her teacher in the eye.

When Lisa was assessed together with her family, a number of pertinent issues emerged. Lisa's mother suffered from postnatal depression for eight months after her daughter's birth and found it very difficult to bond with her. Then she found that she was pregnant again, and Lisa's younger brother was born before Lisa turned two. Lisa's parents freely admitted that she didn't get nearly enough one-on-one attention when she was small and that they still often found her hard to deal with. She was often very jealous of her younger brother but appeared to resist her parents' attempts to hold her or embrace her or draw her into games. She was not good at identifying her emotions and tended to lash out when she was frustrated about something.

It seemed quite clear that Lisa was demonstrating insecure attachment; because she had not been able to form close bonds with her caregivers in her early years, she found it hard to deal with her emotions. Sometimes it all became too much, and she got so frustrated that she misbehaved. Understanding this, it was easier for her parents to devise a strategy, together with Lisa's care worker, that would focus on the root cause of the child's problems rather than simply punishing her for their manifestations.

Discussion

Explore the factors in the relationship between Lisa and her parents that may have contributed to her behavioural difficulties, and examine how these difficulties may impact on Lisa's ability to develop resilience.

Explore how problems associated with insecure attachments may be addressed in adolescence, and suggest strategies that may help Lisa to develop more secure relationships.

Early co-regulation

The psychologist Alan Fogel coined the term 'co-regulation' to explain the notion that communication is not just an exchange of information, but a dynamic, continuous and complex process. As two or more people interact, they adjust their tone and words depending on the cues they receive from the listener in the form of body language, expression and so on (Fogel and Garvey, 2007). Because this process is central to the development of rewarding inter-personal relationships, engaging in co-regulation can be seen as an important element in developing the sort of socio-emotional relationships that facilitate the development of resilience in the growing child.

In the context of the relationship between a mother and her baby, Fogel and Garvey describe their interaction as follows:

> A mother … 'wants' her baby to smile at her so she initiates communicative actions that are likely to 'elicit' smiling, to which the baby may or may not smile 'in response', thus communicating some emotional information back to the mother. In this case, the total amount of information is the sum of the discrete states, the mother's intention, the mother's actions guided by her intention, and the infant's pleasure in response. (Fogel and Garvey, 2007, 252)

Co-regulation is not just a way to exchange information; it provides a means for the individual to learn how to interpret social cues and respond appropriately. Siegel (2001, 79) refers to the process of co-regulation as 'reflective dialogue'.

Activity 3.1

With reference to Figure 3.2, examine the role, value and benefits of co-regulation in facilitating social and emotional development.

Explore how theories on co-regulation and attachment interact with together in the context of resilience.

Figure 3.2 Co-regulation

Siegel (2014) considers co-regulation to be a fundamental quality of secure attachment relationships between children and their caregivers, and fundamental in terms of children developing the neurological/psychological abilities that will allow them to understand both others and themselves:

> Attachment figures recognize the signals sent by the child, attempt to make sense of them in their own minds, and then communicate to the child in such a manner that creates 'meaning' for the child in the shared dialogue about the mental states of the child and of the caregiver. Internal experience, or 'states of mind', can involve emotions, perceptions, thoughts, intentions, memories, ideas, beliefs, and attitudes. By directly focusing on these aspects of mental life, the adult can create a sense that subjective experience is both important and can be communicated and shared. In this manner, the 'mind' itself becomes a central focus of sharing in the discussions between two minds. Such a meaning-making process coupled with collaborative, reciprocal communication allows the child to develop 'mindsight': the capacity of the mind to create the representation of the mind of others, and of the self. (Siegel, 2014, 81)

Siegel (2001, 82) believes that the child's mind develops in such a way that the 'mental states' of the people he or she interacts with are represented as part of the brain's neural functioning, helping the child to formulate a sense of self, both in the present and autobiographically – a sense of self that extends into the past and the future. Siegel refers to this process as 'mindsight' and defines it as 'the capacity of one mind to 'perceive' or create representations of the mind of oneself or of another'. If the child experiences stress in early life, such as child abuse, this disrupts the development of mindsight and can even lead to a 'diminished development' of the brain as a whole and to 'marked impairments in both their capacity to understand basic social information and to behave in socially and morally meaningful ways' (Siegel, 2001, 83–4).

Research in the area of infant mental health indicates that when families 'begin to appreciate their infant's intentions and emotions, their communication systems will spontaneously come alive' (Fogel and Garvey, 2007, 256). Although more work needs to be done, this particular research suggests that even children who face considerable challenges to resilience can develop appropriate skills as long as their relationships with their primary caregivers enable them to rely on the signals and communications systems to understand and engage effectively and positively with their environment for their short- and long-term future.

Attachment and co-regulation in adolescence

Adolescence has long been thought of as a notoriously difficult life stage. Research indicates that even if adolescence isn't always as tumultuous as the popular imagination assumes, there is something to be said for the stereotype (Arnett, 1999, 319). Relatively frequently, individuals who have displayed resilience in early childhood become less resilient during this period, which Luecken and Gress (2010, 247) refer to as 'emerging adulthood'. Ebata et al. (1990, 312) argue that 'adolescents' increased needs for autonomy often require transformations in adolescent-parent relationships' and suggest that during adolescent years both parents and their children often have to make a considerable effort to reconfigure their relationship.

Writing on resilience in adolescence has, according to Fergus and Zimmerman, tended to focus on psychopathology, emphasising negative behaviours, and on a relatively small number of challenges that are well-established in the adolescent population, particularly substance abuse and violent and sexual behaviour (Fergus and Zimmerman, 2005, 407). However, 'epidemiological research, both in the United States and in Europe, suggests that no more than 20 per cent of youngsters in the adolescent age span manifest diagnosable disorders during these years' (Ebata et al., 1990, 309).

Nonetheless, adolescence is an important life stage when it comes to both expressing and developing resilience. The growing individual experiences rapid physical, hormonal, psychological and neurological changes (see Chapter 4), while also coping with more demands from family and the wider community (see Chapter 5). The degree to which adolescents have experienced attachment has considerable implications for the extent to which they display resilience. Those who have a history of secure attachment are typically 'confident, outgoing and able to access support when necessary' (Atwool, 2006, 318).

Conversely, adolescents who are avoidant typically appear 'sullen and withdrawn with intermittent outbursts of rage' and often have only superficial relationships with their peers. They can be aggressive in the context of their close relationships because they have learned not to trust others, and in particular to distrust those close to them (Atwool, 2006, 319). Similarly, ambivalent adolescents often have 'intense and explosive' relationships with the attachment figures in their lives. It is suggested that although they might want to have relationships with others, they often end up driving people away because they are afraid of rejection (Atwool, 2006, 319).

In a longitudinal study of adolescents who were 'seriously troubled' in their adolescent years and attended psychiatric hospitals for a period of time, Hauser et al. (2012, 232) found that some of them were leading healthy, productive lives ten years later. At the outset of the study, participants were categorised as belonging to one of three diagnostic groups: 'disruptive behaviour disorders, mood disorders and personality disorders'. Of an original group of 67, nine were determined to have achieved 'exceptional outcomes' (Hauser et al., 2012, 233). The researchers used a narrative approach to explore common themes and reported that:

> Four themes ultimately emerged that characterized the narratives of the exceptional adolescents: narrative coherence, self-reflection/self-complexity, sense of agency, and continual gravitational pull towards forming relationships, however problematic and challenging these might be at first. (Hauser et al., 2012, 235)

Hauser et al. determined that adolescents with average outcomes 'experienced greater helplessness, rage, and diminished self-esteem as adolescents than exceptional adolescents' (Hauser et al., 2012, 245). The exceptional adolescents had clearly developed qualities of resilience that had enabled them to move beyond a very difficult period in their lives to achieve a successful outcome later on. Lessons from this classic study show that early childhood experiences are hugely important and may well manifest positive outcomes as much as ten years later.

Whether adolescents have already developed qualities of resilience has much to do with their earlier experiences. However, regardless of the individual's experiences thus far, things could still 'go either way' for them; even in adolescence, qualities of resilience can be acquired that will help the individual throughout this period and in adulthood:

> [A]dolescence can exacerbate or buffer against early disadvantages or other childhood experiences in ways that affect adulthood. Experience in adolescence may also provide turning points that deflect earlier behavioral trajectories, and the unfolding of adolescence may allow for the accumulation of prior life advantages and risks that send young people on divergent paths into and through adulthood. (Johnson et al., 2011)

Despite the challenges of adolescence, it offers many opportunities to develop resilience. In many countries, this is also a time when important decisions are made. Young people decide whether to stay in school, whether to start a family soon or delay it until they are established in a career and whether to stay in the family home or to start living independently.

> **Vignette 3.2**
>
> Matt, who was 15 years old, was referred to social services when he ran away from home for the third time. He had been picked up on the streets of London, drunk and with just three pounds in his pocket. Although his parents wanted him back, he was placed temporarily in care until the social workers had a better understanding of his situation. It turned out that Matt, who self-identified as gay, had been living rough and had been exposed to extremely vulnerable situations on numerous occasions.
>
> Matt's parents expressed dismay at the revelation that their son was gay, but stated their desire to have him back anyway. They explained that Matt had been raised by an aunt and uncle in his earlier years, as his father was working on an oil rig and his mother had 'problems' at the time. Matt had found this experience very rejecting, and although his aunt and uncle had never been rejecting of him, he had always felt second best to their own children. Desperate for affection, he had become involved in a sexual relationship with a slightly older boy. Eventually, it all seemed too much and he ran away, thinking that maybe he could start a new life in the capital.
>
> **Discussion**
>
> Explore the psychological factors that have influenced Matt's relationships, and discuss how these have led to his particular circumstances.
>
> With reference to Matt and his extended family, discuss strategies that could help Matt to build a confident self-identity and construct a positive future.

Positive psychology

The role of positivity in healthy emotional development has enjoyed widespread appeal, and popular application of ideas about how to control personal narratives have been promoted, for example in the form of Norman Vincent Peale's *Power of Positive Thinking* (1952), which had considerable popular success and inspired many subsequent publications along similar lines.

The subject of positive thinking and positive psychology has also attracted attention from researchers working more strictly in the academic realm. Feder et al. (2010) state:

> An increasing number of studies have provided evidence for the key role of dispositional optimism and positive emotions in enhancing psychological resilience. Positive emotions frequently co-occur with negative emotions in the face of highly stressful personal situations. According to the broaden-and-build model, positive emotions provide a buffer against the adverse consequences of stress by decreasing the automatic arousal produced by negative emotions, and by increasing the flexibility of thinking and problem solving. In fact, studies have shown that positive emotions are associated with faster cardio-vascular recovery compared to negative emotional arousal and decreased stress activity. (Feder et al., 2010, 36)

Optimism appears to have a protective effect against stress and to be associated with better physical health. Schwartz (1986) suggests that positive thinking can be taught to children with, for example, problems of impulsivity. Citing a 1978 study by Kendal and Finch, he says:

> They found that impulsive children increased their on-task verbal behavior (positive self-statements) as a result of therapy when measured immediately at post-treatment. At follow-up, the total amount of on-task verbal behavior decreased, but the task performance remained significantly improved relative to the pre-therapy assessment. (Schwartz, 1986, 601–2)

In other words, when children are enabled to learn the skill of positive thinking, whether in the course of their upbringing or IN therapy, this can become embedded into their approach to life generally, with a positive impact on their level of resilience. Yates and Masten (2004, 529) assert that applied positive psychology is more likely to be useful when interventions in the child's life start early and are maintained. Positive adaptation in early developmental periods, they argue, 'provides the child with a foundation that enables successful encounters with subsequent stage-salient challenges'.

Synthesising the findings of various researchers, Fox (2008) reports:

> The overarching assumption is that positive emotions have been selected by evolutionary pressures to facilitate social interactions and cohesiveness, and there is growing evidence for this perspective . . . people who express positive emotions are better able to cope with chronic stress and less likely to suffer from a stroke in older age, and those who express the most positive emotions even seem to live longer. (Fox, 2008, 335–6)

According to this hypothesis, the more positive the person, the broader his or her mindset and this, in effect, makes it easier for the person to develop resources that will be of benefit to resilience in the future.

Internal dialogue and problem solving

The role of experimentation and reorganisation within resilient adaptation (see Chapter 1) often relies on the process of internal dialogue – the stories that people relate to and about themselves. The matter of internal dialogue has attracted a great deal of attention and over the years has been the subject of extensive psychological research. An understanding of the value of internal dialogue to emotional development is not new. Ryle (2009, orig. 1949, 29) observed that 'much of our ordinary thinking is conducted in internal dialogue or silent soliloquy, usually accompanied by an internal cinematograph-show of visual imagery'.

One of the major hazards to resilience in children who have experienced maltreatment is 'the belief . . . that they are at the mercy of fate and can do little to influence their lives' (Rutter, 1999b, 130–1). In other words, 'the narrative that they relate to themselves about their life's trajectory gives them no reason to develop an affirming 'silent soliloquy' or to envisage positive 'internal visual imagery' in relation to their futures. Conversely, young people who are able to 'exert positive planning and imagery in relation to key life decisions' tend to do much better in terms of their emotional functioning as adults' (Rutter, 1999b, 131).

Another interesting characteristic of the internal dialogue pertinent to resilience involves the asymmetrical relationship between positive and negative coping thoughts. Extensive research by Schwartz (1986) demonstrates that:

1. Appropriately functioning groups and individuals may be characterised by a 1.7 to 1 ratio of positive to negative self-statements (this ratio is deemed positive dialogue).
2. Mildly dysfunctional groups demonstrate a 1 to 1 ratio of positive to negative self-statements (this ratio is deemed internal dialogue of conflict).

However, that is not to assume that internal dialogue and coping thought processes follow a linear path of engaging with either positive thoughts or negative thoughts. Research shows that internal dialogue should most appropriately be recognised as an inner struggle between positive and negative coping thoughts and that this is characteristic of the *dialectical* nature of human thought (Figure 3.3).

It is important to recognise the nature of the dialogue that young people go through as they progress through the stages of actions and reasoning. This internal dialogue, with its inherent conflict and tension, and positive and negative coping thoughts, is thus an inevitable and important feature of helping young people to build sustainable resilience. According to Rychlak (1968, 628), the dialectical model of positive psychology holds that reasoning proceeds through the 'opposition of contradictories' – that the human capacity to conceive of opposing ideas provides the dynamic behind thinking itself.

Figure 3.3 Dialectical nature of human thought

Emotional intelligence

Psychologist Daniel Goleman popularised the concept of emotional intelligence (Goleman, 1996), building on the research and debate that had been mooted by other sources from as early as the 1980s. A widely accepted definition of emotional intelligence is the 'ability to recognize and manage one's own emotions and relationships, and acknowledge the emotions of others' (Windingstad et al., 2011, 109).

In 1998, Goleman (1998) isolated the key elements that he considers to be fundamental to emotional intelligence:

1. Self-awareness
2. Self-regulation
3. Social skills
4. Empathy
5. Motivation.

Goleman believes that although people are born with a general level of emotional intelligence that makes it more or less easy to acquire emotional competencies, these are not innate but can be acquired. In recent years, researchers working in the field of emotional intelligence tend to view it in terms of one of two theoretical perspectives on emotional competencies can be understood and addressed (Hansenne and Legrand, 2012).

Ability perspectives

Ability perspectives, such as the Mayer and Salovey model popularised by Goleman, see emotional intelligence as an ability that includes identifying, utilising, understanding and regulating emotions. From this perspective, emotional intelligence can be assessed by using tests with 'right' and 'wrong' answers (Hansenne and Legrand, 2012, 265).

Trait perspectives

Trait perspectives 'consider emotional intelligence as a multifaceted construct encompassing emotion-related behavioral dispositions thought to affect the ways an individual would cope with demands and pressures (e.g., self-control, well-being, emotional sensibility and sociability)' (Hansenne and Legrand, 2012, 265). Tests to measure trait emotional intelligence try to determine how the subject typically performs.

Many studies (e.g. Petrides et al., 2004) investigating the role of emotional intelligence on academic achievement are often carried out using the 'trait' perspective, and the strong correlation between emotional intelligence and educational achievement has been replicated across a number of studies from different Western countries.

An Italian study (Agnoli et al., 2012) explored whether emotional intelligence (trait) was a predictor of academic success in school. They studied a large cohort of children (447) aged between eight and 11. The results showed a clear correlation between higher levels of emotional intelligence and better performance in the areas of maths and language (Agnoli et al., 2012, 667). In a study of academically talented African-American students in the United States, Morales (2010, 172) identified high levels of emotional intelligence as intrinsic to a number of qualities that he isolated as crucial to academic resilience.

A similar study carried out in the United Kingdom (Vidal Rodeiro et al., 2012) reported on the role of emotional intelligence (trait) in the academic performance of a group of secondary school students aged 15 to 16. The study determined that there was indeed a strong association between levels of emotional intelligence and both high and moderately high levels of academic achievement (Vidal Rodeiro et al., 2012, 528). However, the researchers also found that factors that related to sociability did not appear to have an impact on academic achievement (Vidal Rodeiro et al., 2012, 529).

A recent Belgian study explored the impact of emotional intelligence and creativity on educational outcomes in a group of 73 children: a group of 44 with a mean age of 8.2 and a group of 33 with a mean age of 11.2 (Hansenne and Legrand, 2012, 265). The study found that, in this group, levels of emotional intelligence did not appear to have a significant impact on educational outcome for either gender, but that creativity did. Hansenne and Legrand argue that less quantifiable educational advantages are also associated with emotional intelligence, such as a reduced likelihood of suspension and better socialisation (Hansenne and Legrad, 2012, 265). Thus, irrespective of the ratio combination of emotional intelligence, education achievement, increased socialization and/or creativity, the presence of any or all of these contributes to the development of resilience over time.

Emotional capital

Zembylas worked with the notion of 'emotional capital', which refers to how emotions can serve a useful, productive purpose. In the context of classrooms and schools, he suggests that:

> emotional capital – expressed through the circulation of emotional resources among teachers and students – is systematically transformed into social and cultural capital – such as stronger relations in the classroom and empowered feelings in the school community. (Zembylas, 2007, 453)

An important element of emotional capital is the fact that it involves the management of 'emotional competencies', 'controlling undesirable emotions and acquiring desirable ones. In this way, emotional capital is used as a component of emotional intelligence and emotion management calls that are directed toward a particular kind of self-policing the affect' (Zembylas, 2007, 456). This ability to self-police emotions within a social context, especially those that are potentially damaging to self-esteem or more likely to prompt the individual to engage in violent behaviour, is an important indicator of resilience.

Gendron (2004, 6) believes that emotional capital is the factor that 'allows and boosts' the formation of human capital; in other words, that permits the individual to develop the skills, relationships and connections that will allow him or her to create a successful life. Emotional capital is the sum of emotional intelligence, emotional competence and social competencies (Gendron, 2004, 7–8).

According to Gendron (2004, 9), emotional capital is a catalyst; in other words, it permits the development of human capital generally. Without emotional capital, a person has very few resources. Emotional capital, Gendron believes, is primarily a learned skill. That is, it is not learned necessarily through formal channels such as school, but in all the social contexts, including the family, school, sports groups, with peers and so forth (Gendron, 2004, 10). Nor is it a fixed quality, but one that continues to develop and adapt throughout the life of the individual. However, it is important to note that the emotional competencies that are useful in one culture or at a particular period in time may not be the same in another.

McGrath and van Buskirk (1999, 15) discuss the issue of emotional capital with respect to students at community colleges in the US. The educational environment has become one of increasing diversity, and yet often the students who are most at risk are also the ones least likely to become involved in 'the social and academic infrastructures of institutions'. They refer to emotional capital as the 'social and psychological dimension of social capital' and describe it as consisting of 'the translation of the social bonds and shared norms created by social capital into emotions that shape the actions and perceptions'. In other words, their view is that emotional capital enables people to have a full and rewarding experience of their social context – in this case, a community college. For McGarth and van Buskirk, the likelihood of a good educational outcome for these students is considerably enhanced by building their access to emotional capital in the form of tangible emotional engagement within the educational structure (McGrath and van Buskirk, 1999, 34).

In a similar study in Australia, Reid and Reynolds (2013) explored ways in which the concept of emotional capital could help school leaders to engage students who were considered to be at risk of involvement in criminal activity, drawing on themes including safety, hope, engagement, justice and fairness. According to Reid, these students often did not have the same degree of emotional capital as more fortunate students, which, he argues, may have a great deal to do with the choices they made with respect to their behaviours and future aspirations.

Hazards to good mental health

Long-term psychological consequences research shows that most children experience hazards to good mental health as they are growing up. For example, one US survey of over 8000 households found that 74.4 per cent of the children 'experienced at least one significant adversity, including natural or human made disasters, accidents, witnessing a traumatic episode, crime victimisation, or family adversities such as parental death, child abuse, or domestic violence' (Luecken et al., 2011, 304) and that many children experienced more than one event.

Resilience in adolescents can be compromised by maltreatment during their childhood, maltreatment that persists into their teenage years or both (Trickett et al., 2011, 3). Much of the research suggests that most children encounter potential hazards to resilience at least once during childhood.

Effects of maltreatment

Children and adolescents who have suffered physical, sexual and/or psychological maltreatment often suffer a range of consequences. Trickett et al. (2011, 10) suggest that when children are mistreated, for example in the context of physical or sexual abuse, they are more likely to develop externalising and internalising problems as well as post-traumatic stress disorder (PTSD) and attention-deficit hyperactivity disorder. They argue that children and adolescents who have experienced maltreatment tend to experience more emotional conflict in the context of their friendships and to 'display less positive affect in activities within friendship dyads', as well having 'lower peer status' and being rated by their peers as 'more aggressive and less cooperative' than children who have not been maltreated (Trickett et al., 2011, 6). They also comment that maltreated children are 'significantly more disliked, physically and verbally aggressive, withdrawn, and less pro-social than . . . comparison group children' (Trickett et al., 2011, 6).

Given that positive relationships with peers are an important predictor of resilience, the absence of such relationships can clearly be identified as a hazard. Adolescents who have suffered maltreatment in childhood are more likely to become involved in 'antisocial and delinquent behaviour' if they associate with delinquent peers (Trickett et al., 2011, 9). These difficulties with friendships in adolescence often persist into adulthood, where they can manifest as problems in romantic and other important relationships (Trickett et al., 2011, 10). The age at which the abuse or maltreatment takes place is relevant to levels of resilience in children and adolescents. Some studies suggest that problems such as PTSD and major depression are likely to be worse when abuse takes place before the age of 12 (Luecken et al., 2011, 308). Both sexual and physical abuse can be associated, in girls, with a greater likelihood of teen pregnancy, in itself a significant hazard. In boys, maltreatment is more likely to be associated with 'physically, sexually, and verbally abusive behaviors' and with the use of 'threatening behaviors or physical abuse against their dating partners' (Trickett et al., 2011, 12).

In his recent follow-up research, Nelson et al. (2013) studied a group of Romanian children who had grown up in institutions, and compared them with a group who had grown up in foster care and a group that had grown up in families. They found significant neurological differences between the groups. For example, these children responded very differently when they were shown images of their caregiver and of a stranger, and children raised in institutions demonstrated greatly reduced intellectual performance. Since the work of John Bowlby et al., there has been demonstrable evidence of the damage that, for example, institutionalisation can impose on the psychological well-being of the developing child and his or her capacity to develop resilience. Unfortunately, the world has continued to provide us with numerous examples of damaging care practices within both public and private spheres of care and education.

Activity 3.2

Of the attachment behaviours of children who have grown up in institutions, Nelson et al. note:

> There is a large literature on the effects of institutionalisation on children's socio-emotional behaviour, with all of these studies having been completed on children who have been adopted or placed into families after a history of early deprivation. The most stable and persistent finding in children who have experienced early . . . institutionalisation is their display of social disinhibition, also termed indiscriminate sociability, indiscriminate friendliness, and disinhibited attachment disorder. This pattern of behaviour has been characterised by an undiscriminating social approach to others, lack of awareness of social boundaries, and difficulty in identifying or responding to social cues about what is socially appropriate when engaging with other people. (Nelson et al., 2013, 161)

Discussion

With reference to the extract from Nelson et al., explore how social disinhibition can hinder building the attributes of resilience.

Of the experiences of children raised in deprived institutional settings, Rutter comments that they can experience outcomes 'as diverse as disinhibited attachment, cognitive impairment, quasi-autistic patterns, and inattention/overactivity that persist for more than half a dozen years after the children have been removed from the risk environment and placed in generally well-functioning adoptive families' (Rutter, 2005, 14).

Michael Rutter also points to the startling levels of resilience that can be observed in children who have experienced extreme deprivation and institutionalised care. Also referring to the case of Romanian orphans, he notes of a group of children who were adopted by British families that although many were classified as demonstrating considerable levels of retardation at the point of their arrival in Britain, many of them made dramatic, and relatively rapid, cognitive gains (Rutter, 1999b, 122).

Vignette 3.3

Maya came to the UK at age three to live with her new adoptive parents, Roger and Diane. Because her mother died when she was just a baby, she had been raised in an orphanage. Maya's home country was a very poor one, and the orphanage was underfunded and understaffed. All the people working there did their very best to care for the children, but inevitably, none of the babies and toddlers got the level of attention they needed.

Roger and Diane quickly realised that although Maya had been well-nourished and cared for on a practical level, she found it quite difficult to interact with them socially. She seemed very withdrawn, was reluctant to look them in the eye and tended to retreat to a corner and sit by herself when she was hurt or afraid rather than to come to them for a cuddle. She found it difficult to interpret facial expressions, which made communicating difficult, especially because Roger and Diane don't speak her native language. They started finding out about child development and learned to their dismay that Maya's early childhood experiences may have had an impact on her neurological development. At first they were very discouraged, but then they decided that knowledge is power. Assuming that Maya's neurological development may well have been affected by her childhood of neglect, no matter how well-meaning her caregivers, surely there was something they could do to help!

Discussion

Explore how attachment theory can explain Maya's behaviour, and discuss how this understanding may help Maya's adoptive parents to help her to improve her social and emotional interaction with them and others.

Discuss how co-regulation may be utilised to support Maya's development in her new country and new culture.

Conclusion

Although some children are born with a greater psychological disposition towards resilience than others, and although too many children experience significant hazards to their development of psychological well-being at different periods in their childhood, this does not imply that there is 'nothing to be done' about either case; indeed, quite the reverse is the case. The psychological components most closely associated with building resilience suggest that these components are not age specific but can exert influence in different ways throughout childhood and adolescence. In other words, although certain qualities and circumstances in early childhood make it easier for the child to acquire skills essential to resilience, it is still possible to acquire these skills later on, given the right sort of support.

The psychological perspective of resilience is centred on the premise that good mental health during childhood and adolescence is necessary for the acquisition of effective traits of resilience. Thus, the capacity of children and adolescents to develop cognitive skills and competence over time is one of the cornerstones of the promise of resilience. That capacity and capability to learn, adapt and grow are crucial to the promise of resilience, which is there even in the most difficult cases, such as a childhood spent in deprivation, neglect or alienation.

Most importantly, this chapter has demonstrated that the main psychological components associated with resilience rely on the quality of person-to-person interactions and, as a consequence, place great emphasis on the role of significant others. Childhood and adolescence provide a wealth of opportunities for person-to-person relationships to be nurtured in a multitude of ways and with a number of different people at different times, culminating in cognitive developments that enhance capability and competence in adulthood.

CHAPTER 4

A Social Neurobiological Perspective

Introduction

Over the last decade, there has been a significant level of interest in identifying adaptive and coping mechanisms that support and foster the development of resilience. The study of resilience in childhood has more recently been extended to the study of the human brain to determine the brain structures and circuits that impact on and influence behaviour generally and, more specifically, the development of resilience.

Research has necessarily focused on early beginnings, not least because when a child is born, his or her brain is still forming. The brain continues to develop during childhood and adolescence and even throughout adult life. Every experience a child has, especially during important developmental stages, helps to mould his or her brain and, in turn, the ways in which he or she will tend to respond to stimuli throughout his or her life. In infancy, the baby's brain undergoes a period of dramatic transformation, and in childhood and adolescence, tendencies become more clearly 'laid down', setting the scene for the future adult's behavioural patterns.

Certain specific physical reactions in the human brain and body can be clearly quantified and described, and these can have very profound implications for how children and young people develop qualities of resilience, both psychological and physiological. Research increasingly shows that certain aspects of physical development are strongly associated with the development of emotional competence, and that the development of resilient attributes is itself inextricably linked with how the child's experiences impact on the development of his or her brain. Although understanding of resilience from a neurobiological perspective is still at an early stage, research over the last decade has made significant contributions to our understanding of physiological and neurological factors that influence the development of both resilient and non-resilient behaviours and attributes.

The brain, life cycle and resilience

Everything that we experience in the course of our lives, and particularly during infancy, childhood and adolescence, has the potential to influence how our brain functions, even how it is physically formed. The brain is an immensely complex organ with 'over 100 billion neurons and ten times as many glial cells, all organized into systems designed to sense, process, store, perceive and act on information from the external (e.g. visual, tactile, olfactory, auditory) and the internal (e.g. hormonal signals associated with hunger) environment. The major working units of the brain are neurons, and neurons are interconnected into networks, and networks into systems, and systems work together to mediate a set of specific functions (e.g. vision)' (Perry et al., 1995, 273). Much of this research supports the view that ability and scope to develop resilience has strong associations with brain circuitry as well as genetic factors.

Although the brain remains plastic, or capable of change, throughout the course of a lifetime, it is particularly malleable during infancy, childhood and adolescence. The individual's experiences during this time contribute to the development of neural pathways in the brain that will contribute to, or even form, behavioural responses that can last a lifetime: 'Although experience may alter the behavior of an adult, experience literally provides the organizing framework for [the developing brain of] an infant, child and adolescent' (Perry et al., 1995, 275).

The distinct periods in the life cycle of a human being can be categorised as infancy, the juvenile period, adolescence and adulthood. Each period is characterised by a particular phase of brain development, and each has influencing roles to play in shaping both ability and capability for developing resilience throughout the life cycle.

Period of infancy

When an infant is born, its brain contains many billions of neurons and synapses, or 'connections'. When the developing child experiences something, the neurons in his or her brain that respond to events emanating from the world outside the child are activated. Neurons, Siegel (2001, 69) explains, are 'the basic cells of the brain . . . long cells that contain a central nucleus and sending and receiving extensions that connect with other neurons'. Each neuron is connected to an average of 10,000 others, with about 10 billion in total. In Chapter 3, we noted Siegel's argument that when babies are born, they are 'hardwired for attachment' (Siegel, 2001, 69). Instinctively, they seek to form close attachments with their caregiver. These constant bonding activities will help to develop neural pathways that deal with affect and attachment. This hardwiring will consolidate as attachment and bonding grow.

However, when this does not occur, or when children are mistreated, the healthy development of the brain can be interfered with, causing damage that can present as permanent and significant problems often reflected in non-resilient behaviours. Cicchetti and Rogosch (2001, 785) state that the brains of children in this situation demonstrate neuronal loss in the hippocampus and abnormalities in synaptic pruning, among other problems. The attendant problems these children may have with attachment and relationships will be a hazard to their developing resilience in their own lives, for example affecting their ability to develop positive and lasting reciprocal relationships.

During this very early period of brain development, the brain is extremely 'plastic', which refers to the fact that it is still malleable and changing and highly responsive to anything that it experiences. During the periods of greater brain plasticity, it is easiest to learn and to lay down behaviours and norms that will foster qualities of resilience. The human infant, Schore says, is like any other living system insofar as it 'is open to and interactive with its environment. The human infant . . . actively seeks environmental input, adjusts to the variations of this input, transforms it with its organizing properties, and incorporates it into its developing form' (Schore, 1997, 597). Maternal behaviour, Schore says, is the primary source of information for the developing baby, and 'functions as an agent of natural selection that shapes the trajectory of the infant's emerging self' (Schore, 1997, 607). These findings promote contemporary values of child-rearing wherein key factors (Table 4.1), including positive family functions and connections, are considered essential for young children to begin to develop the effective neurological functioning that is crucial for building skills of resilience.

Table 4.1 Key factors during infancy

Researchers	Key factors
Schore (1997)	The quality of the relationship a baby has with care givers can impact on brain development.
Cicchetti and Rogosch (1997)	Babies actively seek interaction with their caregivers, and the child's development of 'self' evolves in the context of these relationships and interactions. Babies and young children who do not receive affectionate interaction and care from their caregivers can experience neuronal loss, with consequences for their own later abilities to form attachments and bonds.
Anand and Scalzo (2000)	Adverse experiences in infancy can lead to abnormal brain development, with consequences for behaviour in later years. Infants' brains are particularly susceptible to damage from adverse experiences. Problems including pain, infection and a lack of attachment to the mother can all result in 'multiple alterations' in the developing brain.
Siegel (2001)	Babies are born with billions of synapses, or connections, between neurons in the brain. When a baby has an experience of any kind, the neurons in his or her brain respond to what is happening and activate connections.
Johnson (2001)	Human infants are born with relatively underdeveloped brains, so they are particularly susceptible to the things that happen after birth. Because the human brain is so underdeveloped and malleable, the experiences of the infant have a particularly marked impact on brain development. Babies are born with the ability to respond to the stimuli in their environment, and the ways in which they interact with stimuli influence how their brain develops during infancy and beyond.

Researchers	Key factors
Davies (2002)	Poor-quality family or institutional care can impact negatively on neurological development. Children who have been subjected to inadequate family stimuli or have been brought up in institutional care, especially from infancy (as in Romania), have been shown to have brains that have developed differently to normal, healthy brains.
Herba and Phillips (2004)	The ability to understand emotion is acquired in early infancy. In infancy, children start to learn how to recognize emotions and respond to them, and the experiences they have in early childhood impact on how they will respond to emotional cues over time. Those who have experienced abuse or neglect are likely to over-respond when they perceive aggression, etc., in their environment.
Grossmann and Johnson (2007)	We can understand more about how adults interact in social environments by understanding how their social abilities are informed by early childhood experiences. During infancy, the human brain learns about the social environment; it is specifically adapted to develop in a social context, and the social environment in which infancy is spent has a great deal to do with the specialisations that can be seen in the adult cerebral cortex, with implications for perceiving human emotions and actions, etc.

The child's experience of early childhood and its close, unique relationship with its primary caregivers are instrumental in developing a brain that will tend to lead to more or less resilient reactions. Although people do not retain conscious memories of infancy, their experiences as babies have an enormous impact on them that goes beyond psychology to encompass the physical composition of the brain. As Siegel (2001) says:

> [A]lthough we may never recall 'explicitly' what happened to us as infants, the experiences we had with our caregivers have a powerful and lasting impact on our implicit processes. These experiences, as we have seen, involve our emotions, our behaviors, our perceptions, and our mental models of the world of others and of ourselves. Implicit memories encode our earliest forms of learning about the world. Implicit memories directly shape our here-and-now experiences without clues to their origins from past events. (Siegel, 2001, 74)

In a study of the behavioural and neurological aspects involved in small children learning how to read emotion from facial expressions, Herba and Phillips (2004, 1186) point out that even babies of just a few months have been demonstrated to have the capacity to distinguish happy, sad and surprised faces, and even to be able to tell the difference between varying degrees of emotion. This is an ability that gradually improves with time.

Whereas small children rely primarily on facial cues to understand the emotions of those around them, as they grow up, they start to use information from a range of inputs:

[T]hree- to five-year-olds focused almost exclusively on facial expressions, whereas by eight or nine years of age, children relied additionally upon situational cues. Furthermore, with increasing age, children become more insightful into their own emotional lives, and demonstrate increased understanding of mixed emotions in others. (Herba and Phillips, 2004, 1187)

Herba and Phillips's research also indicates that when children are not suitably stimulated emotionally at crucial early stages, this can make it neurologically difficult for them to feel and express appropriate emotions later in life. Strongly associated with resilience is the ability to regulate emotions, to empathise and show sympathy. Factors that hinder brain growth necessary to support emotional development in the growing child are known to have long-lasting effects. Davies (2002, 425) cites brain scans carried out among the Romanian orphans that showed 'distinct functional eccentricities in various areas connected with emotion'. Davies reports that in children who have been abused, the corpus callosum, which is the bundle of nerves connecting the two halves of the brain, was found to be 40 per cent smaller than average (Davies, 2002, 432).

Vignette 4.1

Leonora has just given birth to her first child, Sam. Over the next few weeks, the baby spends most of his time asleep, but when he's about a month or so old, he starts to smile. For Leonora, that wonderful moment, seeing her baby smile for the first time, makes the tedious months of pregnancy and the painful birth more than worth it. Sam quickly realises that his smiles elicit loving attention from his mother, and smiling is soon an entrenched habit. With each reiteration of this behaviour and the corresponding expressions of love and affection from Leonora, Sam's brain lays down neuronal pathways that will help to ensure that these behaviours are repeated. Sam starts to learn other ways of attracting the sort of positive attention he desires, and little by little, he starts to become a sociable infant developing a reciprocal relationship with his caregivers.

As the months pass, Sam's infant brain continues to grow and develop, and everything he experiences during this crucial period will help to form Sam's brain and shape the sort of child and adolescent he will one day become.

Discussion

With reference to the vignette, explore care strategies that would positively contribute to the infant (aged 0–1 year old) 'laying down neuronal pathways' that would help the infant to specifically develop the foundations of good verbal and non-verbal communication skills.

From a practitioner perspective, explore the value of the early development of verbal and non-verbal communications skills as preparation for starting school at four years old. Examine how effective early communication skills relate to skills of resilience in childhood.

The juvenile period

In all social mammals, the juvenile period 'provides the extended period of brain growth and learning time necessary for reproductive success in various species' (Bogin, 1999, 118). Humans have a particularly long childhood; we are juveniles for a very considerable proportion of the life cycle. This lengthy juvenile period reflects the fact that we lead very complex lives and that a detailed and nuanced understanding of our society and our place in it is hugely important to the development of qualities of resilience and a successful adult life.

This period of growth, during which children are still largely dependent on their parents, is also when they practise and learn many skills that they will need throughout their adult lives. In many human cultures, this period of brain growth offers the opportunity to learn and internalise skills and tools that will facilitate the child's positive survival in later years, perhaps especially during difficult periods. Clearly, the emotional landscape in which the child is growing up will favour the development of certain neural pathways which will then determine the 'default' way in which he or she reacts in a given situation.

The human brain remains highly plastic throughout the juvenile period, when the brain continues to grow and develop. During this period, which is 'characterized by relatively rapid neurological development and slow physical growth and development' (Bogin, 1999, 127), children also learn and internalise vital information about risk and safety. Of course, the precise nature of risk varies considerably. In some cultures, venomous snakes and other animal predators are a real danger; in much of the world today, fast-moving vehicles and other hazards that relate to our industrialised lives are much more likely to present a danger. In each case, children learn how to approach and assess the risks that they are likely to encounter as they move through life.

Just as importantly, it is during this time that young people learn vital life skills that may be particularly relevant to their culture and social environment. They learn how to be members of a social group and how to interact with their peers and the other people they encounter in their daily lives. They learn how to interpret both subtle and overt social and emotional cues and how to negotiate the complex world of interpersonal relationships. Prosocial behaviours, such as altruism and moral interpretation, are social interactive behaviours that commonly reflect internal belief systems and importantly represent culturally based values and ethics. Development and interpretation of prosocial interactive behaviours are commonly associated with resilience and form the basis for understanding resilience as successful adaptation to environmental challenge. Resilience as successful adaptation relies on effective responses to environmental challenges, and a greater understanding of the neurobiological factors that promote and increase cognitive agility adds weight to the adaptation perspective.

In contrast, experiencing trauma during childhood that impacts adversely on brain or psychological development is often associated with a range of social and emotional problems in later life and can be a significant hazard to resilience (Table 4.2). According to Perry et al., 'Millions of children across the world, are exposed to traumatic experiences. These may be pervasive and chronic (e.g., course of conduct maltreatment such as incest, war) or time limited (e.g., natural disaster, drive-by shooting)'. In the past Perry et al. put forward a conservative estimate of the number of children in the United States exposed to a traumatic event in one year as exceeding 4 million (Perry et al., 1995, 273–4).

Activity 4.1

Commenting on the longitudinal study he carried out with Romanian orphans, Rutter reports:

> The findings provided a dramatic demonstration of the environmentally mediated risk effects of profound institutional deprivation. However, the findings also brought out another less expected feature. The effects of duration of institutional deprivation were just about as strong at age 11 years as they had been at age 6 years and, before that, at age 4 years, meaning that some environmental effects can be remarkably persistent despite very major changes in the rearing environment. The implication is that some kind of intraorganismic change, possibly a type of biological programming, may have occurred. (Rutter, 2005, 8)

Discussion

With reference to this extract from Rutter, and from a practitioner perspective, explore the consequences and opportunities for juveniles in transition between family and public care environments and vice versa.

Discuss the role of assessment strategies used in social care for identifying risk and protective factors in relation to juvenile adaptive responses.

Table 4.2 Key factors during the juvenile period

Researchers	Key factors
Perry et al. (1995, 1997)	Trauma in childhood poses a significant risk to healthy brain development. Many individuals exposed to trauma during childhood experience neurological consequences, with significant repercussions for their behaviour throughout life and for their subsequent development.
Bogin (1999)	Childhood is a crucial period for learning and brain cognitive development. Compared to other mammals, humans spend an exceptionally long period as juveniles. During this period, the brain remains highly plastic and capable of considerable change and development.
Casey et al. (2000)	The brain, and especially the prefrontal cortex, continues to develop and organise throughout childhood.

Researchers	Key factors
	Children's brains continue to develop significantly throughout the course of childhood, with the prefrontal cortex maturing at a relatively late stage, implying the continued development of functions including attention and memory in childhood and adolescence. During this period, connections (synapses) between the neurons are strengthened.
Farah et al. (2006)	Systemic poverty leads to reduced cognitive achievement, at least partly because of the impact on the child's developing neurological system. It has long been recognised that a childhood spent in poverty tends to be associated with lower measurable intelligence. The effects on brain development can impact on a range of functions, including language, memory and cognitive control.
Anda et al. (2006)	Children who suffer maltreatment in childhood tend to show changes in brain structure and function, among other problems. Adverse experiences in childhood, including abuse, maltreatment, household dysfunction and witnessing domestic violence, can all impact on the child's outcomes in the areas of affect, substance abuse, memory, and more. As a rule, the more negative experiences the child suffers, the more impairment to brain structures and functions there is likely to be.
Andersen et al. (2008)	Traumatic events during childhood can impact on neurological development. Abuse during childhood is strongly associated with the development of serious neuropsychological and neurocognitive problems that are caused at least partly by the adverse effects of abuse of brain development during this sensitive period.
Lipina and Colombo (2009)	Systemic poverty has a deleterious effect on developing brains. Children who experience systemic poverty and all of the issues associated with it, as is common in much of the developing world, tend to suffer from poor neurological development, with serious consequences for cognitive and socio-emotional development.
Thomas and Knowland (2009)	Loss of synapses through 'pruning' occurs during childhood. Babies are born with many more synapses than they will ever use. As they experience and grow, a 'pruning' process removes synapses, and connections between the synapses are strengthened.
Gu and Kanai (2014)	Genetic inheritance and experience both impact on neurological development in childhood. Adult brains vary a lot in structure, and these differences influence factors including behaviour, intelligence and health. Genetic heritage plays a big role in determining brain structure, but so do the individual's experiences since birth – environmental influences. Genes and environment interact and separately and together play a critical role in determining brain structure.

Every experience a child has makes an impact on his or her neurological development, and according to Perry, trauma can have an enormous impact:

> Depending on the severity, frequency, nature, and pattern of traumatic events, at least half of all children exposed [to trauma] may be expected to develop significant neuropsychiatric symptomatology. Children exposed to sudden, unexpected man-made violence appear to be more vulnerable – making the millions of children growing up with domestic violence or community violence at great risk for profound emotional, behavioral, physiological, cognitive, and social problems. (Perry et al., 1995, 274)

Children who experience trauma are at risk for developing exaggerated responses to more minor causes of stress in later life (Perry et al., 1995, 275) or, conversely, for becoming dissociated, internalising their emotions and becoming at elevated risk of self-harming and related problems (Perry et al., 1995, 283). Perry et al. (1995, 285) note that adults can often underestimate the impact of trauma on children, ascribing qualities of 'resilience' to them that may not really be there at all. It is often difficult to recognise a child's dissociative behaviours in the face of trauma because children tend not to respond as an adult would. However, because children's minds are malleable, in the process of coping with trauma, 'elements of their true emotional, behavioral, cognitive, and social potential can be diminished or lost forever'. The impact on their capability to develop the skills and competence of resilience may be equally diminished or severely damaged.

In particular, abuse during early childhood has been shown to 'impair the development of the corpus callosum, as well as leading to a diminished development of the brain as a whole' (Siegel, 2001, 82–3). Perry et al. note that early intervention in the case of trauma can reduce the child's likelihood of developing sensitised neural systems or displaying signs such as 'persistent hyperarousal or dissociative symptoms, or both' (Perry et al., 1995, 285).

The period of adolescence

In adolescence, the developing brain is still highly malleable, and the teenager's expanding world contains a wide range of potential protective and risk factors with respect to development. Adolescents' experiences during this period continue to impact on their neurological development. Also, normal neurological development during this period can contribute to their engaging in behaviours that themselves are potential hazards to resilience. The rapidly developing field of neurobiology is of increasing relevance to our understanding of factors that can influence the development of resilient attributes.

Adolescence is a crucial period during which the human body engages in substantial and significant growth and change. The acquisition of skills of resilience, before the rapid physical and emotional growth that takes place in adolescence, provides the foundations for well-adjusted adulthood and even contributes to the resilience of the social unit – starting with the family – and not just of the individual. It is also the period during which the human body prepares to take on the responsibilities of social and biological imperatives to find a mate and start a family.

Adolescence is characterised by rapid physical growth and by significant changes in the function and structure of the human brain. Whereas the brain has reached its full adult size by around the age of ten, the way in which the brain works changes during adolescence. Research has revealed that adolescents can use different parts of the brain to carry out the same tasks as children (Steinberg, 2011, 42). The adolescent brain retains a higher degree of plasticity than the adult's, as it is still developing and growing:

> A growing body of literature from both human and animal studies indicates that many cortical and limbic brain regions implicated in cognitive and emotional function continue to mature well into the adolescent state of maturation. For instance, frontal gray-matter volume decreases during adolescence, while hippocampal and amygdalar volumes increase. (Romeo and Karatsoreos, 2011, 269)

These normal functions of the adolescent brain have been shown to be particularly sensitive to stressors experienced by the individual, to the extent that chronic or serious stress during adolescence can cause interference with the 'normal developmental trajectory of neural circuits imperative in modulating cognitive processes and emotionality' (Romeo and Karatsoreos, 2011, 269). Studies by Romeo and Karatsoreos (2011, 276) suggest that the development of the hippocampus is especially vulnerable to disruption during stress in the case of adolescents. Adolescence is characterised by an increased need to regulate affect and behaviour; therefore, maturing adolescents demonstrate increasing capacity to attend selectively to information and to control their behaviour. However, disruption to normal brain development can have profound consequences on, for example, working memory, which is fundamental to the performance of cognitive tasks and adaptive responses.

During late childhood and adolescence, these synapses can undergo 'pruning', and the loss of neurons – according to Thomas and Knowland (2009, 17), up to half of all the synapses can be lost. Thomas and Knowland compare this process to the formation of paths through a field of grass; when the easiest, most useful route through the field has been selected, it becomes the one most travelled. With the passage of time, it becomes clearly defined, whereas all other potential routes are hidden by the grass. In this way we can understand how promoting the use of some synapses and reducing the use of others can result in a fine-tuning of the mind that results in greater gains in certain skills and disabilities. Because adolescence is also a period of substantial social development, the consequence of impaired neurological functioning (Table 4.3) also has an adverse effect on adolescents' social development, such as reducing capabilities to cope with the increasing complexities associated with peer relationships and developing a strong sense of self.

Table 4.3 Key factors during adolescence

Researchers	Key factors
Andersen (2003)	Certain periods in life are particularly sensitive and important to brain development, and adolescence is one of them. During two periods in life, just before birth and adolescence, most regions of the brain see the overproduction and elimination of synapses and receptors. These are very important periods for the development of the brain, which becomes 'wired' to meet the needs of the individual. Because adolescence is such a sensitive period for brain development, both positive and negative experiences can have a major impact on the eventual adult brain.
Sisk and Zehr (2005)	Hormonal changes during adolescence impact on neurological development. During puberty the reproductive system matures, and higher levels of 'sex hormones' are secreted. These play a role in creating neural circuits and the restructuring of the nervous system. Variations in how this process proceeds from one individual to the next can lead to long-term differences in behaviour.
Romeo and McEwen (2006)	Adolescent brains change dramatically in terms of structure and function, potentially making them particularly vulnerable to stress. The brain is particularly 'plastic' during the period of adolescence, potentially making adolescents especially vulnerable to the negative effects of stress. This also implies that adolescence might offer a range of opportunities to intervene in ways that could help to mitigate damage resulting from negative experiences during earlier developmental phases.
Casey et al. (2008)	There are important neurological inputs to risk-taking and other potentially dangerous behaviours during adolescence. Research shows that adolescents are more responsive to incentives and to the socio-emotional environment during this developmental phase. This may be due to neurological factors which imply a greater emphasis on incentive and emotional processing as compared to both children and adults.
Steinberg (2008)	Adolescence is marked by changes in the way the brain functions. Research indicates that adolescents use different parts of the brain for the same tasks, as compared to children, as part of their neurological journey towards adulthood. Adolescents are particularly prone to engaging in risk-taking behaviours such as substance abuse, violence, etc. This may be related, among other things, to the sudden increase in dopamine in the brain during this period. Higher levels of dopamine are associated with a sensation of pleasure and can be implicated in risk-taking behaviours. There is also an increase in oxytocin receptors during this developmental period.

Researchers	Key factors
Squeglia et al. (2009)	Substance abuse is common during adolescence, with serious repercussions for neurodevelopment. Many adolescents take substances such as alcohol and illegal substances, and research suggest that those who use these can demonstrate abnormalities in brain functioning, volume and quality of white matter, especially in young people with a history of relatively heavy drinking, even over just a year or two.
Bava and Tapert (2010)	Neurological factors can predispose adolescents to engage in risky behaviours, which in turn have neurological repercussions. Although the brain doesn't change much in size from late childhood, it continues to mature throughout the adolescent years. Neurological factors can make it more likely that adolescents will engage in risk-taking behaviours, some of which – such as substance abuse – can have negative consequences for their healthy neurological development throughout this period.
Romeo and Karatsoreos (2011)	The brain continues to actively develop throughout adolescence and is vulnerable to stress. The brain is far from 'finished' even in late adolescence. Throughout these years of dramatic growth and development, it continues to mature and to demonstrate significant changes. Particularly during this period of growth, the brain is vulnerable to neurological damage with significant potential repercussions.

Adolescents appear to be prone to different sorts of behaviours depending on whether or not they are with peers, and to register different neurological activity depending on the given environment. Researchers at Temple University studied how patterns of brain activity differed between adults and adolescents, and learned that when they are with peers, the reward centres of adolescent brains tend to be activated. In other words, their brains respond differently to stimuli as compared, for example, to when they are with their parents or other adults. This suggests that they might be more inclined to take risks when with their peers because they are more likely to focus on the social rewards that might accompany a risky choice rather than the potential costs to them (Steinberg, 2011).

Steinberg (2008) asserts that:

> adolescents and young adults are more likely than adults over 25 to binge drink, smoke cigarettes, have casual sex partners, engage in violent and other criminal behavior, and have fatal or serious automobile accidents, the majority of which are caused by risky driving or driving under the influence of alcohol . . . many forms of risk behavior initiated in adolescence elevate the risk for the behavior in adulthood (e.g. drug use), and because some forms of risk-taking by adolescents put individuals of other ages at risk. (Steinberg, 2008)

Steinberg believes that, in order to understand why adolescents engage in risky behaviour, despite being able to understand and recognise risk, and to devise strategies to minimise the impact of this behaviour, it is necessary to explore the neurological input to their behavioural choices. His research shows that adolescents experience emotions more intensely than children or adults. This relates to a sudden and rapid increase in dopamine in the brain in early adolescence. Dopamine is a substance that creates a feeling of pleasure. Pursuit of a 'dopamine high' can put adolescents in a very vulnerable situation that can compromise their resilience now or at a later stage. In part because of this neurological fact – the secretion of higher levels of dopamine – adolescents are more likely to favour short-term gain over the avoidance of risk. This is a contributory factor to risky sexual and other behaviour, all of which can compromise their capacity to display resilient choices. Many parents and caregivers have a great deal of (possibly unwelcome) experience of trying to control adolescents' intense emotions and thrill-seeking behaviour.

Activity 4.2

Although there may be many psychological and sociological inputs to risk-taking behaviours in adolescence, Steinberg believes that there is also a significant neurological input:

> There is strong evidence that the pubertal transition is associated with a substantial increase in sensation-seeking that is likely due to changes in reward salience and reward sensitivity resulting from a biologically-driven remodelling of dopaminergic pathways in what I have called the socio-emotional brain system. This neural transformation is accompanied by a significant increase in oxytocin receptors, also within the socio-emotional system, which in turn heightens adolescents' attentiveness to, and memory for, social information. As a consequence of these changes, relative to pre-pubertal individuals, adolescents who have gone through puberty are more inclined to take risks in order to gain rewards, an inclination that is exacerbated by the presence of peers. This increase in reward-seeking is most apparent during the first half of the adolescent decade, has its onset around the onset of puberty, and likely peaks sometime around age 15, after which it begins to decline. Behavioral manifestations of these changes are evident in a wide range of experimental and correlational studies using a diverse array of tasks and self-report instruments, are seen across many mammalian species, and are logically linked to well-documented structural and functional changes in the brain. (Steinberg, 2008)

Discussion

With reference to this chapter, explain the rationale behind the notion of 'the hormonal adolescent'.

From a practitioner perspective and with reference to increased physical and social development and increased neurobiological activity, explore a range of challenges that adolescents face in relation to risk and risk-seeking behaviour.

In combination with the many physical changes associated with puberty, adolescents also experience increased libido and a much more focused interest in sexual matters. Given that puberty tends to occur at an earlier age than was the case for previous generations (especially in girls) (Biro et al., 2012) and in combination with issues already discussed with respect to adolescents' tendency to engage in risk-taking behaviour, it is easy to see how a burgeoning sense of sexuality during adolescence can be a major hazard to resilient choices over the course of a life. Unprotected sex can lead to pregnancy or sexually transmitted disease, either of which can tip a vulnerable adolescent into an 'at risk' group for a range of social and personal problems, including poverty and chronic ill health. Physically, puberty 'consists of two distinct processes, i.e. increased secretion of adrenal androgens, known as adrenarche, which normally occurs 1–2 years before the maturation of gonadal function, known as gonadarche. Both processes contribute to observable bodily changes' (Bratburg, 2007, 15).

In current social and political arenas, a number of social problems, such as drug-taking during adolescence, teenage pregnancies, and antisocial behaviours, are commonly associated with increased risk-taking behaviours during adolescence. Thus, adolescence is viewed as an extremely vulnerable period for the development of resilience. Positive cognitive development through adolescence is associated with, for example, progressively greater self-control capabilities and effective emotional behaviours in adolescence. Effective social and emotional behaviours are accepted as cornerstone behaviours for building effective resilience in adulthood, and adolescence is perceived as the proving ground for the effective maturation of these skills. In recent years, the interplay between brain and endocrine activities and social and emotional development in adolescence has been a focus for a great deal of research. This has improved our understanding of patterns of neural activity and functional changes to the brain and, in relation to the development of resilience, improved our understanding of the challenges facing adolescents during what is a long period of human years.

The adult period

As the individual grows towards adulthood, his or her brain becomes progressively less 'plastic', or capable of change. However, although it was once believed that the adult brain was essentially incapable of significant change during adulthood, now we know that a degree of plasticity is retained up until and throughout adulthood and that this has consequences for resilience or the lack thereof:

> [T]he effects of experiences have been demonstrated for experiences in early life, middle childhood, adolescence, and adult life. Risk and protective effects are by no means confined to early life. (Rutter, 2005, 14)

An inability to recognise faces can have major implications for how well the individual will be in later life in terms of social and emotional adjustment. Poor emotional and social function is often associated with problems with the regulation of emotions such as anger management and violence (Herba and

Phillips, 2004, 1194). Siegel reports that when longitudinal attachment studies have been carried out, it seems that adults who experienced secure attachment in early childhood benefit from a number of long-term positive outcomes, whereas insecure attachment appears to be associated with 'emotional rigidity' (Table 4.4). 'Suboptimal attachment experiences', he suggests, 'may predispose a child to psychological vulnerability in part by altering the brain's neuroendocrine response to stress' (Siegel, 2001, 77).

Table 4.4 Key factors in adulthood

Researchers	Key factors
Maguire et al. (2000)	Adults' brains are capable of much more change than was once thought. Although the main periods of brain development are in infancy, childhood and adolescence, even in adulthood the brain remains capable of change and growth, a quality known as 'plasticity'.
Siegel (2001)	Positive outcomes for adults are related to childhood experiences. A difficult childhood can actually impact neurologically, by changing the way in which the brain reacts to stress and creating a suboptimal brain that has many implications for adult life.
Herba and Phillips (2004)	People learn how to recognise and respond to emotions in early childhood. Disruptions at this stage can have long-term consequences. Distinct parts of the brain are used in developing the skills of identifying and responding to emotion, which are acquired in early childhood. When childhood experience inhibits this key period of neurological development, there can be long-term repercussions that persist into adulthood.
Robinson (2008)	Issues that impact on brain development in infancy can have implications for adults. There are ramifications for the adult brain in individuals who did not receive enough maternal attention as infants. Changes to the brain from that period can result in permanent change, with consequences for adult social behaviour, attachment and the ability to deal with difficult situations.
Conrad (2011a)	Adults' brains are vulnerable to unhelpful neurological change as well as growth. Adults who experience ongoing problems such as chronic stress can experience damage to the brain, with problems including issues with memory and spatial awareness.
Herrman et al. (2011)	Stress in childhood and adolescence can cause permanent neurological change. Adults who were exposed to stress in childhood and adolescence can be more vulnerable to mood and anxiety disorders because of changes to particular areas of the brain.

Herrman et al. remark, 'Exposure to stressful events in childhood and adolescence is consistently shown to produce long-lasting alterations in the HPA axis [the hypothalamic, pituitary, adrenal axis], which may increase vulnerability to mood and anxiety disorders' (Herrman et al., 2011, 260).

Although most people find coping with stress difficult, it appears that some are much more likely than others to have dramatic, negative responses and that in many cases this has everything to do with the events that influenced the development of their brains during childhood (Schore, 1997, 620).

Neurobiology and chronic stress

It has become established knowledge that humans exhibit a remarkable amount of resilience when faced with extreme stress, with most children and young people resisting the development of psychiatric disorders. When we experience stress in childhood as well as adulthood, our adrenal glands, which are located above the kidneys, produce a hormone known as cortisol. This is a normal, natural and functional reaction. The release of cortisol in people experiencing stress – for example if they are being chased by a predator, or attacked, or are walking alone on a dark street at night and suspect that they are about to be mugged – provides them with a quick burst of energy that facilitates the fight-or-flight response and enables them to either make their best effort to get away or to stand firm and defend themselves to the best of their abilities.

Cortisol is also released in response to stress induced by, for example, intense physical exercise. This normal physical response does not compromise the health and well-being in any way; in fact, occasional periods of appropriate stress responses are good for a person's overall health. As well as the production of cortisol, the adrenal medulla of individuals suffering stress secretes adrenaline and noradrenaline, increasing blood pressure and heart rate and therefore the amount of oxygen reaching the heart and muscles. This too enhances a person's ability to either leave or stand their ground, and again, this is a normal and healthy reaction to stress.

Higher levels of oxytocin are also protective against cortisol. As discussed above, cortisol is the 'fight-or-flight' hormone that is released under stress. It has an important function in the case of acute stress but can be dangerous in chronic stress situations. For the purposes of the development of useful, supportive interpersonal relationships and responding appropriately in the face of threat – both important aspects of resilience – it is clearly important for these systems to be functioning properly in terms of both the emotional and the physical threats and opportunities the environment poses at any given time (Rutter, 2005, 14).

However, problems emerge when someone experiences chronic stress; his or her level of cortisol can remain high for prolonged periods, during which the person has no real need to fight their corner or flee the situation. This means that he or she is essentially always prepared for flight or fight, with high levels of adrenaline, elevated heartbeat and levels of oxygen to the muscles and so on, even when this is not an appropriate way for the body to respond to the given situation.

Chronic stress might be experienced, for example, by a child growing up in a home in which the parents often quarrel; in a difficult work or school environment; or because of anxiety about financial or other personal or family concerns. A vicious circle can be created; because the person is experiencing chronic stress along with all the associated physiological changes, he or she can overreact when experiencing high levels of stress, which invokes a cycle of becoming incrementally more stressed, physically and psychologically. Over time, chronic stress and the neurobiological reactions it leads to can cause serious health problems, both physical and mental, and can be a serious obstacle to the development of the social and emotional competences that will lead the individual to develop resilience.

Many studies link chronic stress during early and middle childhood to long-term consequences in adulthood:

> Among a large representative sample of US adults, stressful childhood environments (including parental death, divorce and psychopathology) remained significant risk factors for the development of subsequent mood disorders, substance abuse, and conduct disorders years after the stressor occurred . . . psychopathological consequences of childhood family adversity can persist through young adulthood and into middle age. (Luecken et al., 2011, 305)

As Herrman et al. say, 'Levels of stress associated with excessive, persistent or uncontrollable adversity, without the protection of stable adult support, are associated with disruptive effects on brain function (and multiple organ systems) . . . [and] can lead to lifelong disease and behavioural problems' (Herrman et al., 2011, 259). Children who experience high levels of stress can develop behavioural responses that are adaptive and useful in the short term, such as hypervigilance to stress, but that are less than helpful over the longer term. They can grow up experiencing difficulties with regulating their emotions, making them more vulnerable to outbursts of temper, immoderate expressions of grief, and so on. Many studies have highlighted the adolescent's elevated vulnerability to problems including depression, anxiety and drug abuse, and it is suggested that, although most adolescents take part in risky behaviour of one kind or another occasionally (Arnett, 1999, 322), they are most likely to experience these problems when they are exposed to stress (Romeo and Karatsoreos, 2011, 269).

In contrast, much has been written about the value of stress, and according to Luecken et al. (2011), exposure to a degree of stress during childhood and adolescence can facilitate the development of resilience in the form of 'coping methods'. In other words, experiencing a degree of stress offers young people the opportunity to develop valuable coping mechanisms that enable them to become resilient. Some writers have referred to this process as 'stress inoculation', and this is explored more fully in Chapter 6.

Neurobiology and the environment

Evidence increasingly shows that at least some of the factors that help to determine the degree to which we become resilient are influenced by environmental circumstances and events – including those experienced by our predecessors.

Ungar (2012, 21) states that 'resilience is triggered by aspects of the environment that bolster the expression of latent individual capacity, just as noxious environments can trigger dysfunctional self-regulatory processes'. With growing understanding of the role that the environment can play in mediating behaviour, and of how the human mind functions, increasing numbers of researchers have endeavoured to explore how the environment interacts with biology to affect behaviour.

Rutter cites a 1999 study by Michel Duyme et al. The researchers

> focused on a high-risk group, namely, children who had been removed from their parents because of abuse or neglect, and they instituted a nationwide search in France to identify an epidemiologically representative sample of children in this category who had had a psychometric assessment before the adoption and who had been adopted between the ages of 4 and 6½ years. The results were striking . . . Second, and this was the really new finding, it was shown that the degree of increase in IQ was a function of the qualities of the adoptive home into which the children were placed. That is, the increase in IQ was much greater in the case of children placed in highly advantaged homes as compared with those placed in less advantaged ones. The fact that this finding was based on within-individual change, in the context of a major change in environment, constitutes powerful evidence in support of an environmentally mediated effect stemming from variations in the characteristics of the adoptive family environment within the normal range. (Rutter, 2005, 7)

Further evidence of the fact that IQ is not entirely determined by genetic heritage comes from the Abecedarian Project (Curtis and Nelson, 2003, 471), a study which involved two groups of children from families that were either low or high risk. The group placed in an early childhood intervention programme demonstrated mean IQ scores of 101 at the age of three, in comparison with the control group, in which the mean was just 85. The project indicated that the children at greatest risk were the ones who benefitted the most from the programme: on retesting of the early intervention group, they were found to have IQs 'on average, 21 IQ points higher than the control children at 4½ years of age . . . in contrast to the mean gain of approximately 8 IQ points for the intervention sample as a whole' (Curtis and Nelson, 2003, 472). Given the strong correlation between improved environments and higher levels of resilience, understanding the influence of biology and the interplay with different environments is clearly of great importance.

For children and adolescents, the use of imitation as a form of social interaction is prevalent in both relationships with peers and with significant adults. Imitation is an important aspect of human behaviours, facilitating learning, especially that which is associated with transmission of culture and social norms. According to Iacoboni et al. (2014), the functional processes implemented during imitation are more heavily oriented toward a motor representation of actions rather than a visual representation. This is theoretically important because it reveals that the imitation process, which we rely on during childhood, is embodied or anchored to the motor and body parts representations of the cortex. Imitation, co-regulation and modelling are all strategies that are utilised from infancy to adulthood. However, this research demonstrates the importance of the neurobiological foundations of imitation.

According to these findings, behavioural data suggests a strong correlation between the tendency to imitate and the capacity to empathise and effectively read facial and non-verbal interactions. The resilient child is not only dependent on interactions that allow him or her to imitate others but also on interactive learning that leads to the development of effective social and emotional capacity (see Chapter 3). Iacobani (2009) reports that brain imagery suggests that diminished capacity in the frontal lobe of the brain may be crucial for inhibiting automatic imitation and modelling. Children and adolescents with a diminished capacity to imitate or model behaviour are at a disadvantage in relation to developing the skills and behaviours of resilience, primarily because their capacity to build skills in empathy, social cognition and importantly goal-oriented behaviours may be seriously inhibited. Thus, impaired brain function can crucially impact on levels of engagement with behaviours and attitudes associated with, for example, co-regulation activities, as explored in Chapter 3.

This research into functional brain activity is important to inform our understanding of developing resilient behaviour and attributes, but crucial for understanding the development of these behaviours and attributes through the human life cycle. Importantly, research into neurobiological inhibitors or enhancers to resilient behaviours will provide essential knowledge to continue the identification of risk and protective factors during childhood.

Conclusion

Although we know more about the structure of the brain and how it interacts with our endocrine system that ever before, this remains an area of study in which a great deal remains undiscovered. Nonetheless, our growing knowledge in this area offers us many opportunities to develop not only our understanding of how healthy brain development can be disrupted, leading to major problems with the resilience for those affected, but also the ways in which we can help neurologically damaged individuals to acquire resilience despite what can be significant risks to them. Moreover, when we understand that positive attachment in childhood has a direct effect on the healthy development of the child's brain, we can envision and put into place systems and provisions that are more likely to enable this attachment to take place. Although this knowledge has profound implications for everyone, perhaps these results are most significant for children growing up in more difficult circumstances. Similarly, understanding the neurological implications of trauma and stress can help us to devise strategies that will help to mitigate the negative effects of these throughout childhood and adolescence.

Given that the neurobiology of each and every individual is influenced in a wide range by his or her physical and social environment, understanding how the brain and the endocrine systems change and adapt to diverse circumstances is essential to acquiring a real understanding of resilience. However, it is already evident that the implications for our understanding the positive and negative contributions of neurobiological to the development of resilience are profound, perhaps especially the knowledge that exposure to issues such as deprivation and stress can have consequences not only for the individual who experiences them directly but also for future generations. As we learn more about the neurobiological mechanisms that hinder or foster resilience in childhood, it has also become important to continue this research, recognising, of course, the ethical challenges of conducting neurobiological research on humans.

CHAPTER 5

Significance of Ecological Environments

Introduction

Of course, young people's lives are not just lived in the context of a small, intimate circle of family members and caregivers. From infancy, they have to learn how to be within the context of broader society, which is a realm rich in both risk and opportunity in terms of resilience.

Human beings are social creatures, and in sociological terms we have evolved to live in 'tribal' situations – that is, in a state of mutual interdependence with one another. We develop and learn in a social context and operate within a social environment throughout our lives. Human development 'takes place in a socio-historical context' (Schoon, 2006, 18). Thus, interactions that people have with others play a significant role in fostering or hindering the development of social skills and social competence. Actions and interactions take place against a backdrop of social norms, general, local and familial, and in particular sociological and historical contexts that are not static but in a state of continuous evolution.

Understanding how resilience can be developed means understanding more than just the individual's inner world and their relationship with their family and close caregivers. Children are born into societies, and they develop as social selves throughout childhood and into adulthood. Opportunities (or lack of them) to build resilience only have meaning when they are considered in this broader social context. Indeed, the very concept of 'resilience' has little meaning outside the context of social interactions.

This chapter provides an application of Bronfenbrenner's social ecology model to explore the complex interaction between the child/young person and his or her environment in order to reflect on barriers and enablers for developing the skills and attributes of resilience. The definition of the ecological environment adopted in this chapter is drawn from Bronfenbrenner's classic definition 'that the ecological environment is conceived as a set of nested structures, each inside the next, like a set of Russian dolls' (Bronfenbrenner, 1979, 3). Although the Russian-born Bronfenbrenner was known to be a psychologist, he is also credited with creating the interdisciplinary field of human ecology and, more specifically, child development. In this chapter, this social ecological perspective provides a theoretical framework to explore how complex environmental factors may enable and or hinder the personal development of skills of resilience in childhood. This approach facilitates an analysis of the impact and influence of the larger cultural and social world on children's and young people's potential to build the skills of resilience. This conceptualisation recognises Bronfenbrenner's (1979) ecological systems approach and its value in framing an analysis of barriers and enablers for developing social competence in children and young people. This chapter also explores how this enhancement and or hindrance can be transmitted across generations and social communities.

The ecological environment

Before Bronfenbrenner, child psychologists studied the child; sociologists examined family; anthropologists, the society; economists, the economic framework of the times; and political scientists, the governing. In his seminal work, Bronfenbrenner (1979, 7–8) identified an interdisciplinary social ecology model based on five distinct environmental levels (four original levels and one added later). This presented, for the first time, the now commonly accepted view that interactions and interrelationships, whether at the closest or at the most distal of human interactions, did not exist in a social vacuum. Bronfenbrenner established, with his characterisation of a set of Russian dolls, that within each environmental level, the growing child or adolescent's social development is shaped by interactions, positive and negative influences, and the meanings that they take from these interactions and influences.

Bronfenbrenner's (1979) ecological systems model consisted of four environmental levels – the microlevel, the mesolevel, the exolevel and the macrolevel – and in 1986, Bronfenbrenner added a fifth environmental system – the chronolevel.

In Bronfenbrenner's perspective, each system impacts differently and cumulatively on the development of an individual. Figure 5.1 outlines the

Figure 5.1 The socioecological approach

conceptualisation of Bronfenbrenner's systems approach adopted in this chapter. This chapter places emphasis on environmental processes and interactions with the social individual. It recognises Bronfenbrenner's 'Process-Person-Context-Time' model in an exploration of the development of resilience as a process over time and in response to emerging and evolving contexts. This chapter reflects the perception that ecological systems are both naturally 'developmentally generative' (promoting development) as well as naturally 'developmentally disruptive' (preventing development).

Bronfenbrenner's ecological systems (Onwuegbuzie et al., 2013, 4) are:

- The **microlevel** involves the immediate level with which the child/adolescent closely interacts, such as classroom, playground, recreation centre, home, friend's home, neighbour's home and religious institution. This is composed of the groups and institutions that have the most direct impact on the child in his or her most informative years and includes immediate and extended family and close friends. Bronfenbrenner (1979, 22) defined the microlevel as a pattern of activities, roles and immediate interpersonal relations experienced by the developing child in a given setting with particular physical and material characteristics.
- The **mesolevel** refers to relations among the microlevel and/or connections among contexts such as relationships between family experiences and school experiences, between school experiences and neighbourhood experiences, and between family experiences and peer experiences. This level is composed of the relationships between the family and, for example, schools, or other organisations such as church or faith-based or community organisations. Peer relationships also play a significant role in relations and interactions as children and adolescents extend their circle of interactions, participation and influence. Bronfenbrenner (1979, 25) defined this level as the interrelations among two or more settings in which the developing child actively participates.
- The **exolevel** can be characterised as links between the child's family and social settings or organisations in which the child or would not normally be expected to play an active role (at least not in Western societies), such as employer organisations and/or local law and order professionals. Although this level may have limited direct contact with some children and young people, the influence on personal and social development can be weighty. Bronfenbrenner (1979, 25) defined this level as one or more settings that do not involve the developing child as an active participant, but in which events occur that affect or are affected by what happens in the setting.
- The **macrolevel** incorporates broader cultural and governance issues. This level of interaction reflects the many cultural influences outside of the child's control but which will impact very heavily on his or her development and understanding of the social environment, including influences relating to economic status of the family, communities, community governance, ethnicity and/or religious identity. The macrolevel is an overarching system of influence which includes ethnic and cultural influences as well as economic and political policy. According to Bronfenbrenner, this level

refers to consistencies in the form and content of lower-order levels (micro-, meso-, and exo-) that exist, or could exist at the level of the subculture or the culture as a whole, along with any belief systems or ideology underlying such inconsistencies (1979, 26).

- The **chronolevel** was added by Bronfenbrenner after his initial development of the concepts above and refers to actions and interactions that happen during one's lifetime and that continue to have an influence on the quality of life long after the actual event. This level might include personal and individual life events such as bereavement, parents' divorce or personal tragedies such as abuse, neglect or famine and war, which are known to continue to affect social and emotional behaviour later in life. Bronfenbrenner (1986) characterised this level as changes which exert influences over time within the child or young person him- or herself and the environment, and the dynamic relationship between the two.

As children and adolescents mature and become increasingly aware of the world around them, they interact with a wider array of people and circumstances. Growing children's social development will be influenced at each level, and each level will be influenced by the other levels and by the children and or adolescents themselves as they engage with an increasing complex environment. The five social ecological systems as influential social environments are explored below in more detail.

Vignette 5.1

Navita is a 12-year-old girl of African ethnicity, with moderate mental impairment and some behavioural problems. She lives with her parents in Birmingham, England, and goes to a special educational needs school about 30 minutes away from home. Her parents are both employed, are active within their community, attend an Anglican church regularly and are keen for their daughter to be able to be as independent as possible and to be able to go to work when she grows up. Navita describes herself as a tomboy, enjoys running and high jump and wants to be a PE teacher when she grows up. Although her parents and her sister and brother are very positive and hopeful about Navita and her ability to be independent, their views are not shared by the rest of their extended family. They are a close family group, and Navita has four sets of cousins who all attend mainstream schools and are doing well. Navita and her mother are particularly close to two of her aunts – neither of whom works – who think that Navita should not be encouraged to be independent outside of the family environment. Navita also has a very close relationship with her eldest cousin (Cata) (who has lived next door to Navita since she was a baby) and who, in three months time, will be moving to the US to go to university. Navita has not yet quite understood that she will not be able to see Cata regularly.

Discussion

With reference to Bronfenbrenner's ecological systems, map out Navita's socioecological environment. Explore opportunities and vulnerabilities within her environment and the importance of links between the different systems within her environment.

From a practitioner perspective, explore the ways in which advocacy and educational services may be able to support Navita to develop appropriate skills and attributes of resilience that would help her to achieve her aspiration to be a PE teacher.

The microlevel

As we have seen in Chapter 3, children are born pre-programmed to seek social contact and interactions with others. For example, Nagy reported that 'neonates discriminate between and differentially imitate the fine finger movements of a model. When the experimenter raised her index finger babies raised their index fingers' (Nagy, 2011). In this imitative behaviour, even very small babies are clearly indicating their interest in interacting with others in a social way and in creating the sort of social and emotional bonds that can be a significant protective factor throughout life. Having established a firm relationship in the home with a caregiver or caregivers, children then start to relate to bigger groups, such as those they find in early years care and education settings. In these environments, as well as at home with their families, they can start to learn the social skills that they will need as they move through life.

Acquiring social skills early in life is a very important ingredient in fostering the friendships that will facilitate resilience later on (Dowling, 2010). Dowling reports that:

> studies suggest that the first six or seven years of development are critical for the development of key interpersonal social skills. By four years a child should easily be able to deal with several peer relationships. (Dowling, 2010, 36)

In childhood, most people start learning how to 'deploy their talents' within the safe environment of the family. This provides children with their first experiences of social interaction. The microlevel represents the crucible in which the child forges his or her first close personal relationships, and the family's circumstances – economic well-being, general harmony, ethnicity – influence the nature, extent and scope of both social skills and social competence. The microlevel with which the child or adolescent grows up, and the quality of relationships with others, play a very important role in developing strategies that will help them to develop the fundamentals of resilience (Table 5.1).

Early theory and research on family functioning in the social sciences and psychiatry sought to define 'the normal family' in terms of a universal set of traits or a singular family form, in the model of the intact nuclear family with traditional gender roles. Observations of typical middle-class, white suburban families in the 1950s became the standard deemed essential for healthy child development, with deviant family patterns assumed to be 'pathogenic' (Walsh, 1996, 5). However, subsequent research has shown that the way the family

Table 5.1 Example characteristics at the microlevel

Environment	Factors	Example characteristics
Microlevel	Family, extended family and close friends	• Babies actively seek to engage and imitate their caregivers. • Having established attachment at home, children can start to form bonds within a wider circle, such as a crèche or other social environment. • The early acquisition of social skills mirrors the formation of relationships in later life. • Emotional bonds formed in childhood can be a protective factor throughout life. • The first six or seven years of a child's life represent a critical period for the acquisition of important social and affectional skills. • The potential disadvantages of a childhood spent in difficult economic circumstances are mitigated by the formation of close bonds in early life. • The way in which a family functions, rather than the extent to which it conforms to social ideals or norms, is what really matters. • How the family connects to the community can exert either positive or negative influences. • Children without close familial bonds can still establish attachment with alternative caring or mentoring figures.

functions with the microlevel, rather than the extent to which it adheres to cultural norms (perceived or actual), has much more to do with how resilient it is as a unit and how well it fosters the growth of resilience in its members (Walsh, 1996, 5). Studies have indicated that when children do not have a strong social and interactive relationship with parents, 'competence can often be linked to surrogate caregiving figures who can serve a mentoring role' (Atwool, 2006, 322).

> **Vignette 5.2**
>
> Spiros, a child of Greek Cypriot origins living in London, is attending a programme in his area intended to provide extra support to families on low incomes. Spiros's family certainly qualify for support. Neither of his parents works. They were both just 18 years old when he was born, and now that he is five, they are still very young. Spiros's dad had started a plumbing course with the idea of getting more qualifications, but he won't be able to earn a good wage for at least two years. His mother used to work on and off at a McDonald's franchise, but that didn't bring in a lot of money, and now she is expecting twins and suffering

from symphysis pubis dysfunction (SPD), so she is not able to work at all. Spiros has often turned up at his early years setting wearing very shabby, dirty clothes, and he often appears quite grubby himself, which the caregivers consider to be a 'red flag'. His behaviour is deteriorating. Staff have noticed that when he wants something either from staff or other children, he throws a tantrum instead of asking for what he wants. The child care setting has referred him to the programme's social worker for assessment.

After meeting with Spiros and his parents, the social worker had a follow-up meeting with the programme's caregivers and director. She was delighted to report that Spiros is a happy, healthy and very well-adjusted little boy. His parents are not the world's greatest housekeepers, especially since his mum has developed SPD, but they take excellent care of him, and he is also much loved and cherished by his extended family.

Discussion

With reference to the vignette, describe the characteristics of Spiros's microlevel. Explore opportunities and vulnerabilities within the environment and any potential impact on Spiros's ability to develop social and emotional competence.

From a practitioner perspective, identify what extra support for the family might help improve his childhood experience, and examine priorities for Spiros to help him to develop appropriate social and emotional skills for his age.

The mesolevel

As children grow and learn, they move progressively towards a situation in which they have many more social interactions outside the family, with various people and institutions within their communities. At the mesolevel, children first begin to actively engage with external influences, including schools and peer groups. A study carried out in Finland by Kärkkäinen et al. (2009, 414–15) indicated that, although schools tend to communicate with parents on the subject of children's academic progress, parents tend to be less well informed on the matter of their level of resilience. Yet the school is a very important arena, posing both opportunities for and challenges to resilience. According to Schoon (2006, 145), 'Affirmative school experiences can promote feelings of self-esteem and self-efficacy, which in turn might stimulate the individual to persevere in difficult circumstances and to maintain a positive outlook on life' (Table 5.2).

Rutter (2012, 38) points out that pupils spend approximately 15,000 hours at school during the course of their education, making this a very important aspect of their social experience and very relevant to an understanding of resilience, and to efforts to foster the qualities of resilience.

> Comparison of effective and less effective schools (as judged by pupil success) showed the value of an appropriate academic emphasis and of high expectations, but the findings also pointed to the crucial role of social experiences. Children fared better when treated well, given responsibility and multiple opportunities for success in varied fields, and the teachers provided models of conscientious behaviour and an interest in a positive

Table 5.2 Example characteristics at the mesolevel

Environment	Factors	Example characteristics
Mesolevel	Relationships from an expanding circle based primarily on school and peer interactions	• As children grow up, their social circle widens progressively. • Certain elements in children's lives, such as school and peer groups, become very important to their future development and to outcomes in adulthood. • Schools, where children spend so much of their time, are not just about academic learning but also the acquisition of social skills. • Children's experience of education can have a positive or a negative effect on their life chances. • Teachers can have a great impact on a child's development. Their expectations for the child can impact on how well he or she will do. • Positive experiences at school can help to mitigate negative experiences children may have elsewhere in their lives. • For young people who are enduring ongoing adverse circumstances, a positive relationship with a teacher can have a lasting mitigating effect. • Peer group relationships are hugely influential for the development of social skills across phases of development. • Membership of a dysfunctional peer group can lead to a range of personal and social problems; membership of a positive and supportive peer group can have the opposite effect. • The perceptions that caregivers and other authority figures hold and the expectations that they have for children and/or adolescents can play a big role in the quality of opportunities available to children and young people.

response to pupils' work and other activities . . . The findings showed that that the school *will* affect social functioning simply because it constitutes a social group as well as a pedagogic institution. It is not a matter of schools choosing to target social functioning; rather the issue is whether the social group (both in terms of teachers and pupils and the mix of the peer group) will have a beneficial or damaging effect. (Rutter, 2012, 38)

School offers both an opportunity to develop resilience and, potentially, a challenge to it. As Martin and Marsh (2009, 354) say, 'Although there are many students who perform poorly and continue to perform poorly there is a significant number of other students who manage to turn around their academic fortunes by overcoming initial problems and disadvantage.' Morrison et al. comment that 'cognitive and affective bonds to school may reduce the incidence of negative developmental outcomes and enhance academic and social-emotional outcomes' (2006, 20).

Theron and Engelbrecht carried out research with a group of South African adolescents that included the importance of teachers 'as active role-players that nurture young people's coping under adversity' (Theron and Engelbrecht, 2012, 265). They suggest:

> Support from teachers is positively correlated with youths' adaptive academic and behavioral functioning at school and with the likelihood of school success: typically, youth who like and trust teachers, and who are liked and trusted by their teachers, are more motivated and better supported to engage at school, behave prosocially and succeed academically. (Theron and Engelbrecht, 2012, 266)

Teachers' views on the many aspects of children's home life, ethnic and cultural background, and so on, are influenced by how their many interactions with them unfold (Shim, 2012, 211). Teachers' own views and prejudices on how well the child is likely to do can impact significantly on the child's actual performance. For example, teachers' expectations for students from diverse ethnic minorities can be very different to their expectations for students from majority populations (Shim, 2012, 214), and these can become a self-fulfilling prophecy.

Besides schools and teachers, children and adolescents typically have prolonged and intense interactions with their peer groups. These relationships are potentially either supportive or can have negative implications for the development of the individual, depending on the quality and nature of those relationships.

Particularly in Western society, individuality is presented as a prized quality, so as children start to move through their teenage years, they tend to distance themselves progressively more from their families, with the result that their peer groups grow in relative importance. In this way, adolescents can become more similar to each other within their peer groups, and more different to their parents; in fact, substantial intergenerational and even cultural differences can emerge (Arnon et al., 2008). For adolescents, acceptance and respect from their peer group are very important. Thus, the nature of the relationships within their group of friends is hugely influential in terms of the types of skills and attitudes they develop. Arnon et al. (2008) suggest:

> Peer groups seem to be very important in helping teenagers in the transitional phase of examining and developing their own adult identity – not rejecting adult socialization agents but operating with them. (Arnon et al., 2008, 391)

Considering the huge role that peer groups play in the lives of adolescents, their capacity to enhance or compromise the skills of resilience is of great significance. Rutter commented on the capacity of certain peer groups to seriously impact on resilience not just in adolescence but throughout adult life:

> Membership of a delinquent peer group not only makes it more likely that children will continue with their antisocial activities, but it also increases the likelihood that they will marry/cohabit with, and have children by, a partner from a similar high risk background who also shows antisocial behaviour. (Rutter, 1999b, 128)

Zimmerman and Brenner (2010, 296) identify relationships within the peer group as particularly important for adolescents who do not have a great deal of support from their parents 'because it may compensate for the absence of parental promotive resources'. This hypothesis has been borne out by various studies. For example, one investigation revealed that 'participation in school and church activities reduced cigarette use among adolescents and mitigated the harmful effects of living in disadvantaged neighbourhoods' (Zimmerman and Brenner, 2010, 296). Although adolescence is a period of increasing independence and autonomy, adolescents remain very susceptible to parental and community influence. This can be a difficult period in their lives, but it also represents an opportunity to build coping and mentoring mechanisms and social networks.

> ### Vignette 5.3
>
> Sean is a 14-year-old boy growing up in an inner-city community. His parents, who were very young when he was born, separated when he was ten, after a difficult relationship characterised by alcohol abuse and outbreaks of violence. In his primary years, Sean struggled with 'acting out' behaviour at school and was often disciplined. He was frequently poorly dressed for the weather, and his parents rarely made it to parent-teacher events. Sean's teachers feared that he was likely to end up leaving school early, and the family's social worker worried that he was at risk of abusing alcohol and/or other substances.
>
> From around the age of 11, however, things started to change for Sean. He started to find it easier to control his unruly temper. As a result, his behaviour at school improved, and so did his academic performance. His relationships with both his classmates and his teachers are now generally positive, and he has started thinking about what he would like to do with the rest of his life. Sean's family is still being monitored by social services, but his behaviour and prospects are not currently a major concern; he's doing well.
>
> **Discussion**
>
> With reference to the vignette, compare the nature and quality of experiences at both the microlevel and the mesolevel that may be dominant in Sean's childhood experience.
>
> Explore the role and influence of professionals and practitioners within details of the case study, and explore the factors may have helped to improve Sean's childhood experience after the age of 11 years.

The exolevel

Although a single child or adolescent does not necessarily have a direct impact on his or her broader context or culture, the latter has a very significant impact on him or her. The word 'community' is used a lot, but it's important to achieve clarity around exactly what it means, and what the implications of community are, in sociological terms. Arnon et al. (2008, 376) refer to the 'classic definition' of community as having three principal dimensions: 'a locality or territory; a social system and structure with economic, political, cultural and social institutions, functions and interactions; social relationships and symbols which provide feelings of solidarity, cohesion, trust, unity, security and significance'. However, they note that communities can also be a source of feelings of 'alienation and social pressure' which the individual can experience as unwelcome.

At their best, communities can offer considerable social capital to children and young people (Arnon et al., 2008, 376). Children can derive qualities of resilience from their communities, even when they appear on the face of things to be in a difficult situation. Sociopsychological qualities such as a sense of pride in one's culture and history and a strong sense of community values can, for example, help to foster self-confidence. In this way, resilience can be understood as a process that results from individuals interacting with their environment and community in ways which enable them to build wide-ranging personal and social attributes and identities (Howard and Johnson, 2000). Community spirit or the lack thereof is also relevant in terms of fostering or inhibiting physical, emotional and social health in its inhabitants (Table 5.3).

Table 5.3 Example characteristics at the exolevel

Environment	Factors	Example characteristics
Exolevel	Extends to the wider community to embrace areas in which the child may not play an active role but which can still impose significant influences	• The broader culture or competing cultures within which a child grows up can have a major impact. • Communities can provide support and a sense of belonging as well as a sense of identity. • Communities can also provide a sense of alienation and of not belonging. • When the community is experienced as a positive place, it can provide support which helps to foster resilience even in people enduring adversity. • Communities that have strong support networks tend to foster resilience through social capital across memberships. • Relatively elusive factors such as 'community spirit' (or the lack thereof) can have a big impact on residents' experiences of life. • Young people who grow up in 'disadvantaged areas' may face considerable difficulties, but the potential hazards implicit in this situation can be mitigated by e.g. positive role models and peer relationships. • A positive community is one which is supportive to individuals and families as well as to local organisations. • A sense of meaning and being able to feel part of a community is an important source of strength, even in disadvantaged communities.

A study of teenagers in an Israeli town explored the role of community in building resilience in two groups: religious and non-religious adolescents.

[A]s with the family and the school systems, competent communities are characterized by the triad of protective factors: caring and support, high expectations, and participation. Moreover, communities exert not only a direct influence on the lives of youth but, perhaps even more importantly, exert a profound influence on the 'lives' of the families and schools within their domain and, thus, indirectly powerfully affect the outcome for children and youth. A competent community, therefore, must support its families and schools, have high expectations and clear norms for its families and schools, and encourage the active participation and collaboration of its families and schools in the life and work of the community. (Benard, 1991)

Vignette 5.4

Dolphin Community Centre is a social and youth centre that serves a deprived inner-city community. It offers sports for young people, a mother and toddler group, and activities for older residents, including bingo and a music night. In response to a local survey that revealed extremely high drop-out levels at school, it carried out its own local survey and found out that many of the local children were not having an adequate breakfast before starting school and that many of them found it difficult to find a quiet space to do their homework. In response it set up a 'breakfast club' at which a range of healthy options were served to children shortly before school and a 'homework club' in which a quiet space was provided for children who wanted to concentrate on their work. Although poverty was a contributing factor to the breakfast issue, a far bigger one was the chaos that characterised so many of the children's lives. The breakfast club offered a healthy meal, and it also provided some structure in the kids' day. The homework club made it easier for hard-working students to focus on their books and also provided some much-needed structure. Three years after the clubs started, school retention rates in the immediate area have increased by 15 per cent.

Discussion

The clubs discussed in the vignette provide some structure in the children's otherwise chaotic lives. From a practitioner perspective, discuss the role of structure, social patterns and social networks in helping children and young people to develop resilience.

Discuss approaches to 'engagement' that would support young people to develop roles and responsibilities within the community context.

According to a study carried out in Chicago in 2007 by Sampson, Raudenbush and Earls and discussed by Rutter (2012):

[C]rime was highest in geographical areas showing social disorganization and a lack of collective efficacy. In other words, area differences in crime were not mainly a result of noxious influences pushing individuals into crime but rather reflected a lack of a positive social ethos in the community that, when it was present, protected individuals in a high risk area from engaging in crime. (Rutter, 2012, 37)

Much of this research suggests that there is often a strong association between sociological factors, such as the level of crime and antisocial behaviour in a neighbourhood, and the happiness and level of successful coping factors among its residents. Fox reports a study by Diener and Lucas (2000, cited in Fox, 2008, 327) that showed that 'if a person living in a high crime area or in a very poor neighbourhood becomes actively involved in community politics to improve their area, they may be happier because their life has a deeper meaning even though the objective factors of their life may be fairly grim'.

The macrolevel

The broader culture in which children and adolescents grow up and learn can have a significant impact on their sociopsychological development. Consider, for example, the messages acquired by children growing up in a society in which gender rules are dramatically different for men and women, such as in Afghanistan. Also, consider the difference between being a member of a dominant majority in society and of an ethnic minority. Although neither experience is intrinsically 'worse' or 'better', they are likely to be very different.

According to Bronfenbrenner (1979, 258), although all cultures and subcultures are different, they are 'relatively homogeneous internally' in terms of the types of settings in them, the types of settings that people experience at different periods of their lives, and in the way activities, roles and relations are organised within each setting. In each society, the ways in which a society is internally organised is typically supported by that society's commonly held values. Moreover, social pressures are likely to be brought to bear on people within that society to conform to these social norms and values (Table 5.4).

The macrolevel should not be understood as a fixed system, as it 'encompasses the blueprint of the wider environment not only as it is but also as it might become if the present social order were altered' (Bronfenbrenner, 1979, 289). The interaction between the macrolevel and the individual is complex, and the connection between influences and outcomes is not always completely straightforward. Not least, 'experiences in one setting carry over into other settings, often over extended periods of time' (Bronfenbrenner, 1979, 284). In some cases, the negative effects of growing up in a deprived environment do not clearly impact in childhood, but at a later stage of life (Bronfenbrenner, 1979, 285).

Those working at the coalface of the efforts to build the skills of resilience in children, young people and their families (social workers, psychologists, educators, etc.) often focus on specific risks that appear to be inherent to the individual and/or their families, for example, on certain weaknesses or hazards in the family, or as a minority within a given culture. However, failing to appreciate the wider circumstances of the culture, society and economic environment in which they live makes it impossible to see the whole picture.

Table 5.4 Example characteristics at the macrolevel

Environment	Factors	Example characteristics
Macrolevel	Legal and moral norms and values, economic and employment influences	• The nature of wider society, and norms that dominate at this level, influence the political and moral culture. • Factors such as diverse norms for genders or being a member of the majority or a minority group can determine the nature and scope of interactions. • Although cultures may differ, they are all structured around dominant events and values exerting different influences at different times during children's formative years. • Members of communities and cultures, including children, come under pressure to conform to social, legal and moral norms. • Social norms can change, and so can the sort of pressures and influences brought to bear on members, including children. • The macrolevel can undergo fundamental shifts in time and priorities; things don't always stay the same, e.g. war or financial and economic changes. • Although this level can have a big impact on individual life chances, the nature of this impact may be difficult to quantify. • The effects of how the macrolevel impacts on the individual in one area of life can 'spill over' to other areas too – i.e. can be cumulative. • The effects of trauma emanating from the macrolevel may not be felt during an early phase of life, but at a later stage in life. • Focusing on risks to the individual without considering consequences of the wider community-based events and interactions could result in a partial picture.

The chronolevel

Not originally conceived of by Bronfenbrenner, the chronolevel was added to his initial ecological model at a later date (Bronfenbrenner, 1986). The chronolevel recognises that individuals and environments change over time, and by adding this system, Bronfenbrenner introduced historical circumstances into his original model. He recognised that social continuities and changes occur over time through the course of a life, and draws attention to the impact that this is likely to have on all the other systems.

Longitudinal studies follow subjects throughout lengthy periods of time, and trends can be observed among populations that are relevant to the study of resilience and how it is variously manifested during easier and more difficult times (Bronfenbrenner, 1986). The effects of disasters on children can include a wide range of issues, including, for example, personal abuse and/or neglect, family dysfunction and/or community trauma (Barnard and Morland, 1999, 26–7).

During the course of childhood, children pass through periods that represent particular challenges. For example, children may experience periods in which parents are unemployed, a breakdown of parental relationships, the birth of a demanding sibling or an older sister or brother's unruliness during adolescence. All of these situations can pose challenges. Similarly, the experience of personal serious illness, abuse, neglect or war may have a direct and long-term impact irrespective of the age of the child or adolescent and the degree to which he or she understands what is happening at the time of the event(s).

More recently, the long-term consequences of bullying or sexual or physical abuse have received a great deal of attention and have been identified as a significant long-term problem (Barboza et al., 2009, 101). They can be seen as relating to more than one level – the macrolevel insofar as the behaviour is likely to be supported by aspects of the wider culture, and the chronolevel because it is likely not only to be experienced during a specific period of the individual's life but also to continue to have an impact along chronological timelines.

There are also times when whole communities and societies are under stress, such as during times of unemployment, recession, famine and war. Although the concept of resilience does not apply only to difficult periods in the life of an individual or society, these are the times when the impact on quality of life is most profound. Although it would be understandable if the communities 'fell apart', they are able to draw on their personal and collective resources to resolve or improve their situation (Table 5.5).

Being involved in such an event, even if only in a secondary or indirect way, can have a profound impact not just on the community or even the societal level but also on the future progress of the individual. After the initial trauma of the event, the way in which those involved continue to respond can have significant implications. For example, Barnard and Morland (1999) state:

> In the aftermath of a disaster, after the initial shock, there can be a real sense of the community working together, and a sense of comradeship or community spirit. For some people, it is as if something positive is found in the shared experience. It is possible to see expressions of idealism and altruism. As a sense of normality establishes itself and other factors in everyday life re-impose themselves, this community spirit can be diminished as people's attention moves away from the key event and toward other, individual events. The resultant loss of idealism can lead to disillusionment, and despair or anger may then be expressed. (Barnard and Morland, 1999, 25)

The experience of economic instability, or the reverse, can have long-term consequences for the child or adolescent, with impacts on a wide range of factors such as the age at which the person enters the workforce, the sort of relationship he or she develops with parents, other authority figures, and with peers, and so on. Also relevant is the age at which these dramatic events occur and the social class or status of the family in which the child is growing up (Bronfenbrenner, 1979, 174).

Table 5.5 Example characteristics at the chronolevel

Environment	Factors	Example characteristics
Chronolevel	Events that happen with the passage of time, at both individual and societal levels	• Certain periods of life can pose particular challenges over time. • These events could include the birth of a sibling, the death of a parent, illness or any of a huge variety of societal changes. • Stressful episodes such as being the target of bullies etc. could have long-term consequences. • Events at societal level might not impact directly on the individual in question, but still be problematic for him or her, such as being in a country that is the subject of a terror attack or at war, even without experiencing any violence directly. • Events can impact on a whole society or community as well as on a smaller scale – such as financial or employment crisis. • Social shifts such as changes in the relationships between the genders, political and cultural changes, and so forth, can all have long-term impact on children. • When things change, individuals tend to respond by realigning their norms and behaviours until they are more consistent with the new circumstances – not always successfully. • Far-reaching factors, such as economic ebbs and flows, can have profound effects on communities, including children. • The age the person is when a dramatic event takes place may be relevant to how he or she reacts to and/or recovers from this and future events. • The socio-economic background of the person is relevant to how he or she will be able to react and the resources that the person will be able to draw on.

Vignette 5.5

Hassanatu Sanya is growing up in Sierra Leone. She lives with both parents, her maternal grandmother and three younger siblings. The family is reasonably well off by local standards, and her parents pay for her to attend a good secondary school in their area. Although the area is predominately Muslim, her family are evangelical Christians, and they are regular attendees at a local church; their faith is very important to them, as is their tribal identity. Although Hassanatu speaks both Krio (which is widely spoken throughout the country) and English, in the home she speaks a tribal language with her parents and grandmother.

Sierra Leone went through a civil war in the 1990s, and the scars of war are still very visible. There are still broken-down houses in Hassanatu's hometown, and many of the local men won't talk about the war at all. Quite a few of them were forced to act as child soldiers and are still dealing with very difficult memories. Everyone knows about this, but nobody wants to talk about it.

Discussion

With reference to the vignette, explore the nature and quality of Hassanatu's experiences by examining the influences and interactions dominant in Hassanatu's childhood across the five environmental systems (see Figure 5.1).

Examine the extent to which events that have occurred within the chronolevel will impact on Hassanatu's life chances and her prospects for a positive future and for developing a resilient personality as an adult.

The impact of social disadvantage

Although absolute poverty has been declining across the Western world in recent decades, many countries have been experiencing growing levels of inequality and what Schoon refers to as 'the increasing marginalisation of less privileged individuals and relatively disadvantaged groups' (Schoon, 2006, 5). It has been established in many studies (Schoon, 2006; Doyle, 2012; Creasey and Jarvis, 2013a; Kliewer et al., 2013) that experiencing socio-economic disadvantage persistently throughout life gives a clear indicator of the likelihood of experiencing problems with adjustment, not just in childhood but throughout adulthood as well:

> Children growing up in socio-economically disadvantaged families are at increased risk for a wide range of adverse outcomes including poor academic achievement and adjustment problems in later life, as reflected in own occupational attainment, social position and poor health. (Schoon, 2006, 57)

Poverty is, unsurprisingly, a significant risk factor with respect to the development of resilience:

> Growing up in poverty can affect a child's early skill development leading to greater vulnerability at school entry, poorer cognitive skills, less developed social skills, as well as more emotional and behavioural problems. In addition, such early developmental difficulties can also affect major long term personal and family achievement. (Doyle, 2012, 2)

Vignette 5.6

Marguerite came to the attention of social services when she was picked up by the police after being found, heavily intoxicated, on an unfinished housing estate a couple of miles away from her home. They brought her to the hospital, and social services were called. It turned out that Marguerite had been drinking with friends, all of whom had wandered off home when it got late, leaving her to 'sleep it off'.

Marguerite's mother, who was raising her alone because her husband was in prison, was doing her best, but, as she pointed out, the area they lived in was awful for kids. There were no facilities for sports or leisure, and drug and alcohol abuse were rampant. The flat they lived in was damp and depressing, and Marguerite didn't like spending time there. As much as she could, she only came home to sleep. The local school, which Marguerite attended, was a difficult place. Most of the students were low achievers, and that was all most of the teachers expected of them. The headmaster said that a day when nobody got injured was a good day.

This was a very difficult case. Marguerite and her mother would clearly have benefitted from moving elsewhere – but then so would everyone in their area, and that just wasn't possible. Marguerite promised to attend group therapy for young people dealing with addiction, and her mother promised to do her best to be supportive. Marguerite's mother was doing her best, so there was no point in putting Marguerite into care, but the family's circumstances were objectively very hard. To secure a better future for Marguerite, it would be necessary to look beyond her small family unit.

Discussion

Use Figure 5.1 to develop a holistic profile of the socioecological environment around Marguerite and her mother. Explore the role of the cumulative effects of disadvantage in this case study.

Marguerite seems to live in a community with many social problems – how can current social and education policies within the exolevel and macrolevel help Marguerite and her mother to change aspects of their lives?

In many societies, much attention has been directed at dysfunctional families and disadvantaged communities, which are perceived to pose very significant hazards to resilience in childhood and adolescence, and throughout an individual's life. As Cicchetti and Rogosch (2001, 783) say, impoverished communities typically 'provide fewer opportunities for positive experiences and growth outside the family than are expected from an environment that can help to promote normal developmental outcomes'.

This increased risk of adverse outcomes is also perceived as a strong indication of poor resilience in the face of adversity (Sameroff and Seifer, 1990; Sameroff et al., 1998; Appleyard et al., 2005; Schoon, 2006). Sociologist Pierre Bourdieu (in Steinmetz, 2011, 56) argues that communities perpetuate intergenerational norms and values which, in the case of disadvantaged communities, can impede children's development, including how they build resilience.

Bourdieu coined the term 'habitus', which he describes as 'a system of durable, transposable dispositions' that is 'progressively inscribed in people's minds' (1984, 471, in Shim, 2012, 211). He argues that in the course of the interactions between the individual person and social structures outside this person, he or she develops specific versions of 'social fields' that include education, social class and so on. The individual's 'habitus', or 'social fields', has an impact on the things he or she does, as well as on the way the person sees the world and the people in it; habitus incorporates the person's individual history and his or her heritage, composed of family, class, race and ethnicity. Bourdieu compared habitus to language, insofar as 'it regulates the range of possible practices without actually selecting specific practices, just as linguistic forms may limit individual utterances without in any way determining which of the infinite number of possible sentences or combinations of words are actually spoken at any given moment' (Steinmetz, 2011, 51).

Adopting Bourdieu's principle, children and young people from disadvantaged communities are socialised into and internalise a particular group 'habitus' – resulting, for example, in these young people not striving for academic achievement because they have internalised and accepted a lack of cultural capital and limited opportunities. The opposite can occur for young people from more privileged backgrounds. Thus, habitus can be understood as a predisposing factor for either a lack or an abundance of resilience. Bourdieu also introduced and discussed the concept of cultural capital (Steinmetz, 2011, 56), which we can understand as the compound of social relationships, cultural knowledge and mores that provide an advantage to the person who is in possession of them – and a disadvantage to the person who is not.

In particular, neighbourhood-wide poverty poses a significant hazard to adolescents in terms of resilience. 'As neighbourhood poverty increases,' write Creasey and Jarvis (2013b, 5), 'so do resident perceptions of social isolation and local violence. The concentration of poverty – whether it is rural or urban – also results in low levels of community and personal resources that creates problems for schools and extracurricular activities that rely on such resources to properly function.' Further, adolescents see little evidence for success, as there are few viable jobs, and limited positive role models in the neighbourhood. Communities that are unsafe (or are perceived by the residents to be unsafe) are noxious to children and young people's physical as well as emotional health: '[I]f it is 'too dangerous to go outside' then personal safety and daily survival may trump the importance of school, physical fitness and other activities important to children and adolescents' (Creasey and Jarvis, 2013b, 6).

Creasey and Jarvis (2013b, 5) identify high levels of community turnover as a hazard to communities and the young people who live in them. High turnover tends to result, for example, from increases in home foreclosures, as has occurred in recent years during the economic crisis. In such situations, young families are often driven out of communities, causing disruption in terms of education, friendships and social networks, as well as personal upset and grief. Moving house often is a significant hazard to young people, with a much greater impact on children and adolescents from lower-income families:

> High-income children who only moved once during their adolescent years were more likely to attend college than those who had not moved, but they were less likely to graduate high school or attend college if they moved twice or more. Children from low-income families experienced negative effects with only one move, cutting the probability of college attendance in half and reducing schooling completed by 0.72 years. (Allison et al., 2013, 31)

Zimmerman and Brenner (2010, 291) comment that 'the neighborhood is the larger social context in which youth, families and peers interact'. The risks to adolescents of living in disadvantaged communities are considerable:

> Families living in these communities are likely to experience chronic stress, and parents under stress are more likely to express less warmth to their children, to monitor less, and to provide poorer discipline than parents living in less stressful

environments. In addition, youth living in disadvantaged neighborhoods are more likely to be exposed to and to associate with deviant peers, which may increase their risk and decrease their protective resources. (Zimmerman and Brenner, 2010, 291)

Unsurprisingly, young people who are growing up in disadvantaged neighbourhoods are exposed to multiple hazards to resilience. Various researchers have suggested that the number of risks is a better indicator of negative well-being than the type of risk (Zimmerman and Brenner, 2010, 292; Kliewer et al., 2013, 92). Adolescents who live in disadvantaged neighbourhoods are more likely to exhibit poor resilience – engaging in risk-taking behaviour, including violence, alcohol and drug abuse, antisocial behaviour and more – all of which are associated with a range of other problems, including aggression, difficulty performing academically and social problems throughout the course of their lives (Zimmerman and Brenner, 2010, 295).

Children in public care

In his work on children and adolescents in care, Gilligan has spoken at length on the importance of 'connection' between young people and important adults in their lives. Although children inevitably face a certain amount of stress when they are removed from their homes and placed in public care, the disruption to their lives (and hence the level of risk they face) can be minimised by taking care to keep some connection with their families intact, even if contact with their biological parents is not possible, and by acknowledging and accommodating links to supportive communities (Gilligan, 2009, 38–9).

One of the greatest hazards to resilience in children and young people is disengagement from the support networks that would otherwise help them to develop important coping qualities. When families experience complete breakdown, or for other reasons, children and young people often have to spend time in care. This in itself has been identified as a significant risk to resilience. Of children in care, in 2004 Dearden reported that:

- fewer than 20 per cent go on to further education and fewer than 1 in 100 go to university compared to 68 per cent of the general population;
- children in care are ten times more likely to be excluded than their peers, with as many as 30 per cent being out of mainstream education because of either truancy or exclusion;
- between 50 and 80 per cent are unemployed between the ages of 16 and 25;
- up to 50 per cent of those placed by the courts in secure accommodation come from a looked-after background; and
- 40 per cent of teenage girls in prison custody have been in care. (Dearden, 2004, 187)

Because children often move from one care home to another, their education can be significantly disrupted (Dearden, 2004, 190). In some cases, care workers were reported not to be supportive of children's plans to attend school (Dearden, 2004, 190), presumably because they had low expectations of the children's capacity to perform well. Table 5.6 explores consequences for children in public care using the socioecological approach outlined in Figure 5.1.

Table 5.6 Socioecological environments and children in public care

Environments	Factors	Descriptors (negative and positive)
Microlevel	Relationships with care-givers, family, and public services	Looked-after children are likely to experience consider-able disruption, initially when they are removed from their family of origin, and subsequently in what may be many moves between foster homes and/or institutions, with disruption to their relationships with friends and neigh-bours, and in their social interactions with sporting and young people's organisations, etc. Relationships with public services can define and determine childhood experience.
Mesolevel	Relationships with schools, peers, local organisations and public services	When young people's lives are disrupted by frequent moves, the relationships between, for example, their caregivers and their teachers, may not always be consist-ent. It may be hard for them to consistently attend specific organisations (sports groups, church, etc.), and communi-cation between these factors may be patchy and uneven. Relationships with public services can define and deter-mine childhood experience.
Exolevel	Community engagement and influence	Issues such as the physical environment in which the young person is being looked after, the good or difficult relation-ship between foster parents or carers in an institution, and the degree of acceptance a community has for the presence of a home for looked-after children all impact on them. Relationships with public services can define and determine childhood experience, and individual access to wider societal opportunities may depend on effectiveness of public care.
Macrolevel	Wider society and political values	Events that are taking places in the broader society can have a significant impact on looked-after children. In an economic downturn, for example, the institutions in which they live or the foster parents with whom they live may experience a reduction in funding, with consequences for their wards. Changes in government policy can also impact on young people who are being looked after, with the potential for both positive and negative outcomes. Relationships with public services define and determine childhood experience, and policy determinants will change over time.
Chronolevel	Defining events over time, at both individual and societal levels	Looked-after children are likely to experience dramatic events in the course of their lives, starting with the event or events that led them to be taken into care in the first instance. Further events may involve moving between homes or institutions, with attendant issues around chang-ing schools, etc. Children may at some stage move back to their own families or experience losing an important caregiver when they are moved to another institution. Relationships with public services define and determine childhood experience, and events over time contribute to cumulative consequences – positive and/or negative.

Many of the hazards associated with the public care system can be mitigated if the child in question is offered stability and continuity; is assisted in achieving a good level of literacy; has a parent or caregiver who values education highly and presents it as providing a route to a good standard of living; and if they have friends who are not in care and are doing well at school (Dearden, 2004, 188).

Repeated studies (Dearden, 2004; Gilligan, 2009) have noted that although overall success at school tends to be lower among children from disadvantaged backgrounds, some students are very resilient; they thrive and do well despite their apparently difficult circumstances. In one study of adolescents being brought up in institutional care, it was shown that 'positive school experiences made it more likely that young people would develop a tendency to show planning in relation to life decisions concerning both marriage and careers', presumably because their experience of school gave them greater confidence in dealing with new challenges (Rutter, 1999b, 131).

Conclusion

Resilience resides within individuals, but it can be fostered or hampered as much by everyday experiences as well as the long-term consequences of past events. In turn, their resilience or lack thereof will potentially impact on everyone they come into contact with as they make their journey through life. As they start to grow up and to venture beyond the tight circle of immediate caregivers and close relatives and friends, the number of potential influences and experiences starts to multiply exponentially.

Looking at the many potential influences on a child's or adolescent's life, let alone attempting to identify and enumerate them, can seem overwhelming. Exploring these influences with Bronfenbrenner's schema, which identifies a discrete number of categories, can make it easier to understand how the various realms of influence can all impact on children, regardless of their social background. By considering these realms of influence, or 'levels', in the context of the child's individual aptitudes and experiences, it becomes easier to understand the tapestry of influences and how these impact on the individual and interact with each other.

Although all young people experience a wide range of social spheres and influences, each of which has the potential to impact enormously on their capacity to be resilient and understanding, young people whose circumstances are less than ideal, such as those who are growing up in care, face a much more complicated set of circumstances. For them, the people, organisations and diverse influences that impact on their lives may change frequently as they move from one place to another, making it difficult for them to form permanent relationships with many people or places. Understanding this, it becomes easier to envision the risks to resilience that can become both recurring and permanent.

PART III

PROMISE AND PRACTICE

CHAPTER 6

Routes to Resilience

Introduction

Various strategies for building resilience have been proposed based on perceptions about how personalities, skills, competence and ability can be influenced, shaped and honed. What is common across most of these strategies is the acceptance that building resilience is not a single event. Rather, it relies on a capacity for effective responses to complex situational and structural factors over a sustained period of time.

The inputs to resilience are not always obvious; exposure to moderate levels of stress or surmountable challenges, for example, can help to develop important coping mechanisms that will provide crucial qualities of resilience throughout life. Conversely, those who have never encountered any stress at all may struggle badly when they have to manage challenging periods in their lives.

The quality of resilience can be fostered and encouraged by important people in one's life – not just immediate caregivers and parents but also teachers, mentors, peers and other networks of significant adults who can all provide support during a 'rough patch'. Models and strategies invariably provide frameworks for controlling emotional responses or consolidating positive social interactions. Strategies for building resilience emphasise different qualities and arguably can be built up at a different pace, especially given the complex and variable nature of individual or group circumstances. As a consequence, there are a number of different routes to developing resilience. This is not to suggest that any route to resilience is linear. The exact opposite is true. Any route to resilience is likely to involve movements up and down, back and forth, and across a number of opportunities and strategies at different times, in different sequences and with varying results. Resilience grows as the individual grows and matures – more often taking the scenic route rather than as the crow flies.

Strategies of perseverance

A persistent feature in the characterisation of resilience is its importance in the transition from childhood into adolescence and into adulthood. It is a feature of its promise that requires a level of persistence and perseverance on the part of children, parents, guardians and caregivers over a long period of time. Most of the models and strategies herald the promise of resilience only so long as we can persevere through a range of opportunities, interactions and activities as children grow into adults. Perseverance and learning are features of, for example:

- The stress inoculator
- The challenge strategy
- The compensatory strategy
- The counterbalance strategy.

The stress inoculator

Chapter 4 explored the complex impact of chronic stress on neurobiological factors and demonstrated that chronic stress during periods of growth can have long-lasting negative effects. It has been observed that children who have experienced deeply stressful environments often become adults with elevated levels of cortisol, even when the agents causing the stress aren't there anymore. There are often significant ramifications for their mental health and well-being. They are more vulnerable to feeling stressed generally and tend to default more quickly into 'flight or fight' mode than other people. They can be less adept at interpreting when they are really in a dangerous situation and when things are actually okay. They tend to overreact to perceived problems, which often leads to significant problems in terms of social interaction. This can be a significant factor that works against the quality of resilience in childhood, leading to problems such as 'having a short fuse' or displays of maladaptive behaviours. They can be more likely to resort quickly to violence. Physically, they tend to develop problems with their neuroendocrine system (referring to their nerves and hormones), their cardiovascular system (the heart, blood and all the vessels that bring the blood around the body), the gastrointestinal or digestive system, their muscles and their ability to sleep (Lundberg and Cooper, 2011, 55). All of the above clearly have serious implications for the social and emotional development of children and adolescents, but also for other children, adolescents and adults in their lives.

However, much has also been written about the value of stress, and according to Luecken et al. (2011), exposure to a degree of stress during childhood and adolescence can facilitate the development of resilience in the form of 'coping methods'. In other words, experiencing circumscribed degrees of stress offers young people the opportunity to develop valuable coping mechanisms that enable them to become resilient.

Some writers have referred to this process as 'stress inoculation' and describe it as:

> a process by which repeated stress exposure (typically mild or moderate in magnitude) may facilitate adaptive responses to future stressors. That is, in some contexts exposure to adversity early in life may be associated with better adjustment in the face of later stressors relative to individuals raised in highly protective environments. (Luecken et al., 2011, 311)

Ironically, some have suggested that one rick to resilience in childhood is actually contemporary parents' heightened awareness of hazards and the fact that many children are more intensively supervised than before, reducing their opportunities to develop risk management strategies on their own and thus making them less resilient in the long term (Newman, 2002, 2).

Rutter (1990) suggests:

> Life involves unavoidable encounters with all manners of stressors and adversities. It is not realistic to suppose that children can be so sheltered that they can avoid such encounters. Rather, protection may lie in the 'steeling' qualities that derive from success in coping with the hazards when the exposure is of a type and degree that is manageable in the context of the child's capacities and social situation. (Rutter, 1990, 203)

More recently, Rutter directly compared exposure to stress with the strengthening of the immune system through exposure to potential sources of illness:

> Good physical health is not fostered by avoiding all contact with infectious agents. Rather it is fostered by encountering such agents and dealing with them successfully (the acquisition of natural immunity) or by immunization in which a controlled dose of a modified version of the pathogen is administered . . .

Zolkoski and Bullock (2012, 2298) comment that for some children, dealing with difficult circumstances seems to 'challenge rather than exacerbate their vulnerability' and that it 'heightens a sense of self-concept rather than challenging the ability to cope'.

Vignette 6.1

Malcolm, who is 12 years old, is doing well at school and at home. Sometimes he thinks about when he was little. He and his parents lived in a big house in the country with Malcolm's maternal grandparents, who still worked on the farm. Malcolm had been very close to his grandparents, especially his grandmother. Things got hard when his granddad developed Alzheimer's and had to move into a home; Malcolm missed him terribly. Then, just a year later, his grandmother died suddenly and unexpectedly at the relatively young age of 63. For a while after, everything was very chaotic at home. Malcolm felt very lonely, and his parents were so busy caring for Granddad and taking care of the farm that they often hadn't much time to spend with him. At first it was all very hard, but little by little it started to become easier. Malcolm asked his mum if he could hang up photos of his granny and granddad, and liked that he could look at their faces every day. At first he tried to deal with his difficult feelings on his own because he could see how busy his parents were, and after a while he started to talk to someone – his teacher, Miss Moore – about the good times with his grandparents, especially the time he spent with his grandmother around the farm.

Discussion

Explore the stressors in this situation for Malcolm and his family, and consider how their responses might have improved their resilience as a family.

From a practitioner perspective, what aspects of Malcolm's family life might have helped him to react positively when he experienced difficult bereavements at an early age? What other measures of support could have been used to help Malcolm?

Thus there are indications that gains produced by stress inoculation early in life can be carried into adulthood. Some studies indicate that adults who have experienced and dealt well with causes of stress in childhood find it easier to deal with problems during adult life, including problems at work, bereavement, accidents and so on (Feder et al., 2010, 37).

The challenge strategy

Most models of resilience recognise the role of risk and vulnerability in building resilience, and it has been suggested that low levels of risk (as opposed to no risk at all) can help people to learn problem-solving skills and resourcefulness: 'The risk must be challenging enough to stimulate a response, yet must not be overpowering' (Schoon, 2006, 75). In the right circumstances, this 'response' is a learning opportunity in which the individual can tap into latent qualities of resilience and/or develop skills that will be useful in later life.

Ungar (2012, 13) comments that further opportunities to acquire resilience can come from being exposed to risk 'within controlled circumstances, rather than avoidance of risk altogether'. Essentially, exposure to a moderate degree of risk provides children and young people with the 'opportunity to overcome diversity' – to deal well with the complex and multifaceted nature of life.

In developmental terms, we can also understand the challenge model as providing opportunities for incremental learning – by learning how to deal with smaller levels of risk now, the individual will be better prepared to react in a resilient way to higher levels of risk later on (see 'Approaches to resilience' in Chapter 1). According to this model, children and young people who never encounter any challenges to their well-being may not have the opportunity to acquire coping skills and may therefore be less likely to develop qualities of resilience. For example, the child who has to deal with a challenge such as moving home and changing school may acquire useful coping skills that can be brought to bear in more difficult personal circumstances in later life.

Fergus and Zimmerman (2005) specifically promote the use of this model with adolescents:

> In this model, the association between a risk factor and an outcome is curvilinear. This suggests that exposure to low levels and high levels of a risk factor are associated with negative outcomes, but moderate levels of the risk are related to less negative (or positive) outcomes. The idea is that adolescents exposed to moderate levels of risk are confronted with enough of the risk factor to learn how to overcome it but are not exposed to so much of it that overcoming it is impossible. A vital point concerning the challenge model is that low levels of risk exposure may be beneficial because they provide children and young people with a chance to practice skills or employ resources. The risk exposure, however, must be challenging enough to elicit a coping response so the adolescent can learn from the process of overcoming the risk. (Fergus and Zimmerman, 2005, 403)

Fergus and Zimmerman go on to point out that the same factors can become either risks or opportunities in terms of developing resilience:

Too little family conflict, for example, may not prepare youth with an opportunity to learn how to cope with or solve interpersonal conflicts outside of the home. Yet too much conflict may be debilitating and lead youth to feel hopeless and distressed. A moderate amount of conflict, however, may provide youth with enough exposure to learn from the development and resolution of the conflict. They essentially learn through modeling and vicarious experience. (Fergus and Zimmerman, 2005, 403)

Richardson (2002) uses the terms 'resilient reintegration' to describe a positive outcome following the individual's reactions to the difficult circumstances in his or her life. According to him, this positive outcome occurs when the person is able to acquire some insight or growth as a result of a hazard or difficult experience, leading to his or her becoming more resilient, or more able to recognise resilient qualities within him- or herself.

The compensatory strategy

Fleming and Ledogar (2008) suggest that the 'compensatory model best explains a situation where a resilience factor counteracts or operates in an opposite direction to a risk factor'. Compensatory factors should not be confused with protective factors insofar as they can mitigate and reduce the effects of a given risk or hazard to resilience rather than providing an all-enveloping quality of protection. According to Fergus and Zimmerman (2005), compensatory factors arise from the combined influence of various different strengths and resources. In other words, adversity can be compensated for by the cumulative effect of these factors.

Zimmerman et al. (2002, 223) explain the compensatory model as consisting of the factors in an individual's life that can work to counteract or neutralise the effects or risks and hazards. They provide the example of the adolescent whose peers use alcohol, which increases the likelihood that he or she will too. However, they state: 'This negative influence, however, may be counteracted by involvement in school or community organizations.'

Zimmerman et al. explored the role of adolescents' 'natural mentors' (i.e. mentors arising from the adolescents' normal interactions in their family and community rather than mentors officially assigned by, for instance, a social worker) in providing a significant compensatory factor to potentially troubled adolescents growing up in a relatively deprived social and educational environment with multiple risks to resilience. Zimmerman et al. comment, 'Young people often attribute their safe passage through the tumultuous years of adolescence to the influence of significant nonparental adults such as teachers, extended family members, or neighbors' (Zimmerman et al., 2002, 222). They cite earlier studies carried out with adolescent African American and Latina mothers in the United States which found that the presence of a mentor in the young women's lives helped to reduce the incidence of 'depression and relationship problems, social support and satisfaction with support' (Zimmerman et al., 2002, 222). In other words, for these young women who were facing a risk to resilience in the form of premature motherhood (among other things), the presence of a mentor was an important compensatory factor that enabled them to achieve higher levels of resilience.

'Mentors' were considered to be any significant adult in the young person's life who was not an immediate family member, and who could provide him or her with support and guidance. Zimmerman et al. (2002, 231) found that young people with natural mentors reported having a much more positive attitude towards school than those without, as well as lower levels of problem behaviour. They were more likely to enjoy going to school, to consider doing well in school important, and to feel that they had the capacity to succeed. In short, the presence of a natural mentor in their lives offered a significant compensatory factor to a cohort of adolescents for whom risks included having friends with difficult behaviours, exposure to drug abuse, and other issues; young people who had natural mentors were perceived to be 'better able to maintain positive school attitudes even when they had friends whose school behaviors were negative'.

In addition, their study showed that young people in the natural mentor group maintained more positive school attitudes than did youth without natural mentors, suggesting that natural mentors may have helped these youth maintain positive attitudes toward school even in a context in which school achievement was socially discouraged' (Zimmerman et al., 2002, 234). Young people with a natural mentor also reported 'lower levels of marijuana use and nonviolent delinquency . . . higher levels of school attachment and school efficacy, and were more likely to believe in the importance of doing well in school' (Zimmerman et al., 2002, 236). Zimmerman et al.'s research suggested that the compensatory effect of natural mentors was both direct and indirect; they directly helped to reduce problem behaviours and increase a positive attitude towards school, and indirectly helped by steering adolescents away from peers whose negative attitudes posed a risk (Zimmerman et al., 2002, 238).

Vignette 6.2

Roberta, who is 15, is growing up in a depressed rural community in Wales. There is little work, her family is not well off, and there are significant social problems in the area. Roberta's parents work hard to make ends meet. They do a lot of shift work, and often Roberta is left to prepare dinner for her younger siblings. Many of Roberta's classmates are in similar situations, and some of them have 'gone off the rails'. Although Roberta has been known to cut loose once in a while, most of the time she's doing very well. She gets good marks at school, and her teachers are encouraging her to stay on and do A-levels. She thinks she might like to go into nursing or physiotherapy. Roberta doesn't know why things are okay for her when so many of her friends are struggling, but looked at from outside, a number of factors may have contributed. Roberta formed a good relationship with Mrs Grimes, her best friend's mother. Mrs Grimes always made both girls feel positive about things and gave them confidence that they would be able to do anything they wanted to do in life. Roberta and her best friend were also friendly with a group of girls who were hard-working and aspirational. Together, they are able to dream of a future in which they are grown up, working hard and doing well. When one of them is feeling down, the others rally around and offer support.

Discussion

Explore the nature of the challenges facing Roberta, and examine how complex compensatory factors have contributed to Roberta's social and emotional development.

This scenario relies on positive peer relationships. From a practitioner perspective, explore the implications for the case study if peer interactions were not of a positive nature, and examine how and what compensatory factors might be helpful in this alternative scenario.

The counterbalance strategy

Research indicates that life chances are affected by the existence of the number of risk factors in a child's life. This is known as 'cumulative risk'.

Appleyard et al. (2005) propose two models of cumulative risk:

- a threshold model that postulates that after a given number of risk factors present themselves, there is a substantial increase in poor outcomes; and
- an additive model that puts forward the idea that as risks accumulate, the likelihood of a poor outcome increases incrementally.

In contrast, Yates and Masten (2004) conceptualise the idea of cumulative risk as a selection of risks and assets, using images of a balance sheet. They argue:

> Risks and assets may counterbalance each other, such that assets may compensate for risks, yielding a kind of net risk. As cumulative risk or adversity levels rise, positive outcomes tend to decrease in frequency. (Yates and Masten, 2004, 523)

When a child experiences multiple risks, the likelihood that he or she will grow up not to display resilience increases dramatically with the addition of each risk. In Sameroff et al.'s study (1998) it was found that the risk for a number of poor outcomes was much higher for young people who had to confront eight or more risk factors, in comparison to those who faced three or fewer. Importantly, however, according to this model, when children and young people have had access to more psychosocial resources than exposure to risk – even cumulative risks – they are more likely to be resilient. Psychosocial resources (see Chapter 3) could include, for example, the ability to access feelings of optimism for the future and a generally positive self-identity.

Psychosocial resources can have a positive effect for the individual in difficult circumstances, and similarly, when no serious risks are being experienced: '[R]esource factors can have an equally beneficial effect for those exposed and those not exposed to adversity' (Schoon, 2006, 76):

> [I]ndeed, most of the well-established resource factors, such as parenting skills or self-esteem[,] show their effect in general (low adversity) conditions as well as high-risk conditions. (Schoon, 2006, 76)

Essentially, this model proposes that when the 'pros' experienced by the at-risk child or adolescent outweigh the 'cons', he or she is more likely than not to develop qualities of resilience. Fleming and Ledogar argue:

> [A]ssets or resources moderate or reduce the effects of a risk on a negative outcome. Protective factors may operate in several ways to influence outcomes. They may help to neutralize the effects of risks; they may weaken, but not completely remove them; or they may enhance the positive effect of another promotive factor in producing an outcome. (Fleming and Ledogar, 2008)

Activity 6.1

Explore the theoretical differences between the threshold model of cumulative risk and the additive models of cumulative risk.

From a practitioner perspective, explore how counterbalance strategies can be used to support children and young people in public care.

Strategies for individual development

Building resilience requires constructive interventions, and Rutter (2000, 673) argues for policies and practices that help children to acquire coping skills during childhood and beyond. He suggests that 'there needs to be a shift from a view that temperamental features are just within-the-person characteristics to an appreciation that much of their importance lies in their effects on interpersonal interactions'. Children, he argues, need to be helped to build and use personal qualities and resources in ways that are socially positive and personally constructive. Person-focused strategies include the following:

- Social adaptive behaviours
- Emotional regulation.

Social adaptive behaviours

The feeling that one is in control of a given situation is an important contributor to building self-confidence and autonomy. In response to the things that happen to and around them, children can use a diverse range of psychological mechanisms to build self-confidence, including the following:

- affiliation, when someone looks for another person to talk to;
- altruism, which encourages people to help others;
- anticipation, which encourages individuals to look forward to a better future;
- avoiding or even suppressing difficult thoughts; and
- avoiding negative thoughts and diverting from difficult memories can also be useful.

Social and emotional adaptation offers children and young people the opportunity to actively construct their own view of their personal circumstances and to engage in processes leading to problem solving and change. Thus, achieving positive outcomes (see Table 1.2) through social adaptive behaviour, especially under challenging conditions, is normally associated with good emotional adjustment.

A major feature of resilient adaptive behaviour is an ability to construct a personal view of reality through a process of experience and experimentation. Judgements about resilience are normally based on evaluative reasoning, and whether a child is judged to be resilient implies an evaluation of adaptation (internal or external or both) in his or her behaviour often over a period of time. It is important to note that determining that a particular child or young person displays resilience involves exploring his or her ability to respond to life's circumstances in a manner which leads to sustainable and constructive life chances, not just how he or she reacts when facing adverse circumstances. However, on a deeper level, resilience is about consistently making choices about one's future over a sustained period of time and within the strictures of one's society and personal circumstances. Luthar (1991, cited in Olsson et al., 2001) suggests that although children who display resilient behaviours may well experience distressing emotions, they can cope with them successfully.

Emotional regulation

Bloom Lewkowicz (2007) suggests that children's performance is often strongly linked to their emotions and is often experienced with relatively little conscious awareness. 'Without realising it,' says Bloom Lewkowicz (2007, 21), 'people are propelled by their feelings to change them, remove them or keep them. This can lead to choices that bring no result, the opposite result, or results not in a person's best interests. With increased awareness of feelings and how to respond to them, people can work towards choosing and rehearsing how they would like to feel and how to express their feelings.' With enhanced emotional intelligence come greater skills in the area of social competence and higher levels of self-esteem (Bloom Lewkowicz, 2007, 67).

Emotional intelligence, discussed in Chapter 3, can be classified using five main domains (Goleman, 1996, 43):

- Knowing one's emotions – self-awareness, that is recognising a feeling as it happens, is the cornerstone of emotional intelligence.
- Managing emotions – handling feelings so they are appropriate is an ability that builds on self-awareness.
- Motivating oneself – marshalling emotions in the service of a goal is essential for paying attention and creativity.
- Recognising emotions in others – empathy, another ability that builds on emotional awareness, is fundamental to 'people skill'.
- Handling relationships – the art of relationships is, in large part, skill in handling emotions in others.

Taken together, these domains provide the main characteristics of emotional intelligence – either individually or in combination. Much resilience research has focused on the identification of children and young people who show signs of social deficiency (see Box 1.2), and the aim of emotional regulation as a strategy is to enable children and young people to develop the ability to control and regulate their emotions and ways of interaction and reaction. In terms of interpersonal relationships and decision making, it is argued that developing strategies for social and emotional regulation (see Figure 3.1) helps to avoid excessive impulsivity and to manage underlying issues that relate to mental wellness (Kabat-Zinn and Davidson, 2011, 107–8).

Mindfulness, another emerging strategy used to control emotions, refers to the art of being 'in the moment' rather than trying to understand and analyse on an intellectual level everything that is happening in the world around us. It too is a psychological model that can be traced in some respects to Buddhist practice, but in its modern incarnation is not related to 'spiritual' matters. Increasingly, mindfulness techniques are being used as part of conventional approaches to, for example, manage stress and improve self-reflection.

One large study carried out in Iran (Parto and Besharat, 2011) focused on 717 inner-city students in late adolescence who were deemed to be 'high risk', with a mean age of 17.30. The outcome of the study confirmed the authors' hypothesis that practising mindfulness in this group was associated with positive outcomes:

> As a protective factor and a powerful supporter in the developing, strengthening and boosting of other protective factors (including self-regulation, autonomy, health and well-being) and weakening of risk factors (including psychological distress and negative affects and emotions), mindfulness can play a significant role in building health and decreasing vulnerability among adolescents. (Parto and Besharat, 2011, 581)

The research suggests that mindfulness helps those who practise it to regulate their emotions, with a range of psychological and physical effects, including the secretion of lower levels of stress hormones (see Chapter 4). Shapiro et al. identify among the many potential advantages of practising mindfulness the fact that one can learn how to 'reperceive'. 'Reperceiving' enhances cognitive, emotional and behavioural flexibility by enabling children and young people 'to see the present situation as it is in this moment and to respond accordingly, instead of with reactionary thoughts, emotions and behaviors triggered by prior habits, conditioning, and experience' (Shapiro et al., 2012, 381). This shift in perspective (making what was subject, object) has been heralded by developmental psychologists as significant for development and growth across the lifespan' (Shapiro et al., 2012, 378).

Vignette 6.3

Jason often said that he'd been 'in trouble all his life'. It was certainly true that he'd always been a handful. He was 15 now, and he was already 6 feet tall. He'd always been big and heavy for his age. As a little boy, he was rather boisterous – and his size made that a problem. Although many of the other boys in his class were just as lively, when Jason ran into someone, his sheer size meant that the person generally fell over and got hurt. It seemed to him that he was always getting into trouble, even when it wasn't his fault. Jason also had difficulties with attention and motivation. He was bright, but he got distracted very easily in school. His mind tended to drift. When he was chastised, he often overreacted. Most recently, he was threatened with expulsion from school for a number of incidents, including one in which he threw his schoolbooks clear across the classroom in anger. His parents said they didn't know what to do with him. They loved Jason, but he was difficult at home as well. Everyone worried that if he were expelled, he would drift away from education.

As a last-ditch effort, Jason was recommended to an educational psychologist to try to help him to get to grips with his problems around anger control and concentration. In conversation with Jason, his parents and teachers, the educational psychologist, Anita, established that, since he had been little, he had received much more attention for negative behaviour than positive. Because Jason was such a big presence, in more ways than one, most of the attention focused on him had been on minimising the effect he had on the people and things around him. As a result, when Jason did do well, he was often overlooked. Anita worked with his parents to develop a strategy that would see Jason getting positive reinforcement as well as negative. With Jason's permission, Anita also spoke to the school.

Anita also helped Jason by teaching him a few simple strategies to help him to be more measured in his reactions and strategies to control his temper. Jason knew that he was on his 'last chance', and he did his best to engage with the strategies Anita taught him. Over a period of months, the situation improved as Jason learnt to control his temper.

Discussion

Discuss the value of securing appropriate emotional regulation in the early years, and explore the barriers and difficulties now facing Jason as he tries to more effectively regulate his emotions.

Explore the role of the different professionals and practitioners in supporting Jason and his family in their efforts to improve his emotional responses.

Working with children and families

In many countries, child and other protection services are perennially overstretched, and children who are at risk for a range of problems may not receive all the help that they need: help that could prevent or mitigate factors that pose a serious hazard to their current and future resilience.

However, although social care and intervention are important, it is far better when families are supported in developing resilience to the point where it is not necessary to intervene in this way. Historically, child welfare programmes have focused primarily on intervening when things go terribly wrong. A child is being mistreated, abused or neglected, and there is an urgent need to remove him or her from a situation that is extremely damaging to the child. The problem is that by the stage urgent intervention of this sort becomes necessary, the child is likely to have experienced a series of events and circumstances that conspire to pose a significant hazard to resilience that will continue to be a problem for the child long after the initial emergency has been dealt with. Although having systems in place to save children from acutely dangerous circumstances is important, often by the time a rescue of this kind is necessary, the child has already had multiple experiences that can have repercussions for his or her level of resilience throughout life.

For example, many children face urgent intervention because of problems at home in the area of mental health and substance abuse. Living with a parent with either problem is a serious hazard to resilience – but so is being placed in foster or another form of temporary care (Pecora, 2012, 1123). When possible, early and better interventions (noting factors that increase risk, such as those defined in Table 1.3) for parents who are struggling can be effective in the longer term.

Social care interventions

Although the statistics on absolute poverty have improved in Western countries in recent years (Seccombe, 2002, 384), income inequality remains a big problem in many countries, including the UK and the US. Recently, US-based research indicates that 'targeted, early interventions aimed at at-risk children and their families can reduce socioeconomic disparities in children's capabilities' (Doyle, 2012, 2). In addition, rates of return are perceived to be high; benefits at both individual and societal level typically outweigh the costs of such interventions (Doyle, 2012, 3). When a cost-benefit analysis of a US 'visiting programme' that targeted high-risk families and provided them and their children with early interventions was carried out, analysts determined that it generated a return of $2.28 for each dollar invested (Doyle, 2012, 25). The range of family interventions are wide and vary in scope, and according to Doyle (2012), these have

> been found to generate long term effects for the participating parents regarding maternal employment, reduction in welfare use and government assistance, lower incidence of child abuse, and for the participating children it has resulted in improved prenatal health, improved school readiness, and fewer childhood injuries. (Doyle, 2012, 25)

However, policy planning is far from straightforward. As Rutter (2000), argues:

> In planning preventive policies, it is important to ask whether it is more useful to focus on the risks that render children vulnerable to psychopathology or on the protective factors that provide for resilience in the face of adversity. Thus, for example, should we focus on the steps needed to eliminate family conflict and breakup, or would we do better to focus on how children cope successfully with conflict and disruption of family life? (Rutter, 2000, 652)

> ### Vignette 6.4
>
> Simone was put into foster care when her mother became seriously mentally ill and her father was unable to cope. Simone had responded to her mother's illness by developing a number of self-harming behaviours, including over-eating and cutting herself. Her father worried that she was 'going the same way' and felt completely overwhelmed by the whole situation. On an interim basis, Simone was placed with a family in the same area, with the idea that she would be able to continue to see her parents and to move back into the family home when things got better.
>
> But for Simone, moving into the foster home was very hard. She felt rejected – her mother wasn't able to take care of her, and she felt her father didn't want to. Now she felt that they just didn't love her at all. Her self-harming behaviours got worse, and so did her performance at school. Although she missed her parents desperately, she was rude and sullen with them when they were together. In the foster home, she was loud and uncooperative.
>
> **Discussion**
>
> Consider Simone's reactions to her home life, her situation and the challenges to her personal development and long-term social skills
>
> From a practitioner perspective, explore the rationale for intervention in this scenario and explore the scope and range of support that is most likely to be able to turn this into a successful intervention.

Table 6.1 outlines a wide range of intervention studies that have been carried out with children and families.

Table 6.1 Interventions with children and families

Researchers	Example interventions
Bradley et al. (1994)	Interventions to improve the home environment and increase the protective factors for premature children living in poverty and facing many risks to resilience. Children in this demographic whose families participated in the intervention were more likely to show early signs of being resilient.
Gilligan (1999)	Supporting children in care by mentoring their progress in activities they enjoy such as sports or cultural activities. Mentoring young people in activities can help them to develop positive self-esteem, better mental health and social relationships, and help them transition more smoothly when the time comes to leave care.
Knitzer (2000)	Using a multifaceted approach that incorporates behavioural training in primary health care and Head Start, focusing on increasing the skills and competencies of at-risk families and integrating early childhood and family service with other social and mental health services.

Researchers	Example interventions
	The risks posed to children in the welfare system are mitigated by early interventions that are coordinated across a range of environments and approaches.
Luthar and Cicchetti (2000)	Various approaches intended to help families that are impacted by parental mental illness. Interventions that focus on modifying children's reactions, fostering resilience and identifying areas of vulnerability and protection can help to reduce the risk posed to them by a parent's mental illness.
Beardslee et al. (2003)	A family-based approach to reducing risk factors and increasing positive interactions between children and parents with mental illness, designed to enhance understanding of the condition and provide communication skills. Long-term improvements in understanding and attitudes in both parents and children, and significant benefits in resilience for children produce a reduction in risk factors and an increase in protective factors.
Pitman and Matthey (2004)	A three-day intervention to help children with a mentally ill parent or sibling understand mental illness and acquire coping skills. Children with a mentally ill parent or sibling reported that they found the intervention useful and that it made it easier for them to deal with this risk in their lives.
Pedro-Carroll (2005)	Child-focused interventions to reduce the negative impact of divorce. Programmes that focus on the risk and protective factors relating to divorce can help children by reducing their levels of anxiety, difficult behaviours, and other adjustment issues.
Greenberg (2006)	Interventions focused on prevention and that intend to reduce risk and enhance protective factors in both the children and the environments in which they interact. When children are helped to improve their levels of competence generally and in the various contexts in which they live, resilience is promoted in them.
Tein et al. (2006)	A programme to improve mental health outcomes of bereaved children carried out by mediators focusing on helping children to express and attain goals, giving them feedback, and helping them to communicate their thoughts and feelings. By participating in the programme, children's mental health was improved, with fewer negative effects, less inhibition in expressing emotion and better coping skills.
Benard (2009)	A strengths-based approach can be brought to bear on interventions that focus on both growth and problems. By focusing on the strengths inherent in any family situation, social workers can provide them with the best opportunities possible.
Lester et al. (2013)	Interventions designed to help with the specific problems faced by military children, by working to reduce hazards to psychological risk and enhance resilience, with a focus on improving family function. Risk prevention strategies with this demographic improve family functioning and reduce the levels of distress experienced by the child.

The strength-based strategy

A strengths-based approach to social care practice is predicated on the belief that 'social work practitioners who possess an understanding of individual and family resilience and the belief that resilience is a process that can be tapped within each individual and family can engage in a practice that can make a positive and powerful contribution in the lives of others' (Benard and Truebridge, 2009, 202). As such, a strengths-based approach contrasts strongly with negative interventions that are focused on what is 'wrong' and what needs to be changed:

> [V]irtually all traditional change-focused interventions maintain the belief that people need help because they have a problem – a problem that in some way sets them apart from others who are thought not to have the problem. The terminology 'having a problem' suggests that problems belong to or are inherent in people and, in some way, express an important fact about who they are. The existence of the problem provides the rationale for the existence of professional helpers and a developed language by professionals to describe the problematic areas of concern. (Hammond, 2010, 2)

According to Benard and Truebridge (2009, 203), resilience begins with belief, and beliefs are 'socially constructed judgements and evaluations that we make'. In the case of caregivers, educators and other people in positions of power who interact with children and adolescents at risk, their beliefs about their resilience or otherwise can have profound consequences. A strengths approach focuses on helping children and young people to take control of their own lives by identifying and working with the areas where they have tangible strengths and assets.

Hammond (2010, 3) identifies some of the primary aspects of a strengths-based approach:

- focus on trusting and workable relationships;
- empowering people to take a lead in their own care process;
- working in collaborative ways on mutually agreed upon goals;
- drawing upon the personal resources of motivation and hope; and
- creating sustainable change through learning and experiential growth.

With a strengths-based approach, children, young people, parents and practitioners perceive their lives not as a series of problems that needs to be 'fixed', but as a collage of opportunities and challenges with appropriate help. In this approach, families become enabled to build upon their strengths until the challenges no longer appear overwhelming.

However, the provision of social care and education is far from straightforward for practitioners, and Table 6.2 identifies a number of barriers and challenges that have been shown to inhibit the range and scope of activities and interventions.

The protective strategy

According to the protective model, factors such as a supportive family or community can help to insulate children and young people against adverse factors.

Table 6.2 Factors that inhibit practitioner activities

Researchers	Tensions
Blundo (2001)	Using a strengths-based approach often challenges caregivers' assumptions and can pose a personal challenge to them. For many social care workers, adopting a strengths perspective means rethinking the way they were trained and the way they may have worked for years. It challenges assumptions and presuppositions they may have held for years and can challenge beliefs and even cultural identity, as caregivers must start to learn how to see a client's strengths from his or her perspective.
Greybeal (2001)	Conflicts between traditional assessments of people in need of support and the use of a strengths-based approach can exist. Social care workers are often required to assess clients in a way that is based on a medical model and on a language predicated around problems and deficits. Developing a strengths-based approach in this context can be very challenging, but delivering a different assessment process can lead to a more useful, client-focused and holistic approach.
Brun and Rapp (2001)	The nature and quality of the relationship between the individual and his or her social care worker is crucial to positive outcomes in strengths-based care. Although strengths-based practice has a strong theoretical foundation and a growing body of research that supports its efficacy, a lot depends on the nature of the relationship that develops between the individual and the person or persons providing care. Depending on this relationship, care practioners' perceptions of care can vary a great deal, with ramifications for the likelihood of a successful outcome.
Allison et al. (2003)	In working with families in which children and young people have problems, social services often assume that there are certain problems and difficulties. Family therapy often focuses on addressing presumed difficulties in the areas of communication, problem solving and more, although a strengths-based approach advocates looking at strengths and building on them. When family strengths are identified before therapy has been started, a strengths perspective is more likely to succeed, especially when resilience is seen in terms of family and society rather than just the individual.
Rapp et al. (2005)	Although the strengths-based approach to social work offers great promise, there are many potential pitfalls and hurdles. A strengths-based approach is challenged on the one hand by a growing tendency to medicalise problems and on the other by the large and nebulous array of apparent choices for care and growth.
Cox (2006)	Without high levels of compliance, the outcome of the strengths-based approach can be compromised. Using a strengths approach in working with young people shifts the focus from dealing with problems to focusing on goals and strengths. This approach has tremendous potential, but for successful outcomes to be achieved, high levels of compliance are necessary. The best outcomes were associated with the highest levels of compliance, with the approach including taking care not to miss appointments.

Dulmus et al. (2012)	There is often the perception of a conflict between a focus on strengths and a focus on problems. Social care workers can be distracted from their clients' needs by their feeling that they need to opt for looking at problems rather than looking at strengths. In reality, the best social work involves keeping a focus on both strength and challenges. Effective strengths-based care and interventions do not ignore problems, but look at them while also working to build clients' strengths and capacity for positive growth.

Activity 6.2

From a practice perspective, identify strengths-based strategies and protective strategies in relation to social care practice with children and young people. In respect of these two types of strategies, consider the potential utility, the tensions and the challenges for current interagency collaboration.

In other words, during more challenging periods of the individual's life, he or she has a range of people who can be counted on for practical and emotional support.

Resnick points out that many researchers have uncovered the fact that having positive relationships with adults from outside the family (such as teachers, mentors, etc.) is an important protective factor among young people at risk (Resnick, 2000, 158). 'This sense of connectedness to adults,' Resnick says, 'is salient as a protective factor against both the 'quietly disturbed' and the 'acting out' behaviours of adolescents and has protective effects for both girls and boys across various ethnic, racial and social groups. Other protective factors have been identified as 'social skills, academic competence [and] family relationships' (Resnick, 2000, 159).

In a study carried out in Hong Kong, Sun and Shek (2013, 1172) determined that positive youth development among Chinese adolescents was associated with protective qualities including bonding, social competence, moral competence, self-efficacy and prosocial norms. However, protective factors are not always equal; they may be context-specific. Masten (2014) notes that:

early findings indicated key differences associated with good adaptation compared to maladaptation among high-risk groups of children. There was enough consistency that early reviewers (e.g., Garmezy, 1985) could summarize them in terms of child attributes (individual differences), family attributes (e.g., socioeconomic variation, parenting), and extrafamilial differences (e.g., neighborhood, school, mentors outside the family). Complexities emerged as well, including data congruent with Rutter's (1987) admonition that protective effects had to be considered in terms of function and context, and not as inherent to the 'protective factor' itself. (Masten, 2014, 9)

The protective model can be divided into a number of subcategories (Zolkoski and Bullock, 2012, 2299):

- the protective-stabilising model, when a protective factor neutralises the effects of a risk;
- the protective-reactive model, when the negative impact of a risk is moderated by how the subject reacts; and
- the protective-protective model, when one protective factor can boost the positive effect of another.

In relation to protective strategies (see Figure 1.2) that might reduce the impact of adversity on capability to build resilience, Rutter (2000, 672) proposes:

1. that therapeutic interventions with troubled families need to be concerned to help parents avoid scapegoating and drawing children into family conflict, as well as to reduce the overall level of family discord; and
2. that attention needs to be paid to the appropriate monitoring and supervision of children's experiences outside the home.

Given that outcomes for children are strongly influenced by the quality of parenting they receive, Armstrong et al. (2005, 273) argue for the principle of putting support frameworks into place to aid families in stressful circumstances or during difficult periods of their lives. This has the potential to pay enormous dividends in terms of the resilience of children of those families.

Observing that many intervention techniques are only of limited use in helping children growing up in high-risk environments, Yates et al. (2003) propose the following:

> It is essential that the varied needs of the high-risk family be addressed in order for parents to participate fully in and benefit from a relationship-based programme. Ideally, a parent intervention programme serving high-risk families should include medical, mental health, social and chemical dependency services, as well as flexibility within the programme itself to meet the unique needs of each family. (Yates et al., 2003, 257)

Conclusion

As young people move through life, they experience an ever-growing number of potential risks and opportunities in terms of developing resilience. The impact that these experiences have on them can be hard to predict. For one child, an episode of stress might be a significant hazard to resilience, whereas for another it might be a tough time that ultimately helps him or her to develop coping mechanisms that will make the child stronger in the long run; it all depends on many factors, including a child's personal qualities, the nature of his or her relationships in the family of origin, and how the child grows and develops within the various social contexts, including school, peer groups and more. Quite simply, there is no single 'one size fits all' path to resilience. It's complicated. Similarly, when a child or young person is struggling, there is no one single approach that is guaranteed to help. What is supportive, encouraging and positive for one person might not work for someone else. In developing a strategy to support a child or adolescent, professionals need to consider the entirety of the individual's situation, and strive to understand the various inputs to the resilience he or she displays, or the lack thereof. Above all, they need to understand that the path to resilience can be a circuitous one, and the journey may be rocky rather than smooth!

The above strategies have been developed on the basis of decades of research, much of which has been longitudinal, tracing the origins of resilience and the lack thereof in children and young people. One of the areas in which the state currently has the biggest remit in terms of delivering services to its citizens, and potentially enhancing resilience at every level of society, is education. As a discussion of this crucial topic warrants considerable detail, this is what we turn to next.

CHAPTER 7

Resilience – Early Years Care and Education

Introduction

From birth and throughout the early years, young children begin the process of learning about the world and their place in it. They start to become social creatures who learn how to understand themselves in the context of a growing series of relationships with other people and how they can communicate their thoughts and ideas to others. They learn about where they stand in relation to the other people in their lives and how the things they do impact on both their own experience and that of others. They begin to understand that the actions they take have social consequences and that they can initiate or engage in social contact with the people they meet. By experimenting, making mistakes and learning from them, they have embarked on the educational process that will take them through childhood and adolescence and into adulthood – and that, to some extent, will continue for the rest of their lives.

Child development in early years is explored in depth in Chapter 3 – a period during which children learn largely through imitative behaviours, observing what the other people around them are doing and trying to emulate them. They learn both how to be independent and how to rely upon others for care when they need support. They learn how to vocalise their needs, thoughts and feelings, and use their unique voice to communicate with those around them, ensuring that their wants are taken into consideration. They begin to learn how to think and conceptualise themselves as thinking, feeling people, to understand that others are also thinking, feeling people, and to comprehend how their behaviours impact on others and influence their social environment. If they are going to learn how to operate successfully on a social level (see Figure 5.1), they also need to start learning how to manage their emotions and behaviours so that these do not disrupt their relationships with others.

In this context, the sort of relationships children experience with caregivers and educators and with the other professionals they may encounter, and the extent to which they can understand, regulate and use social and emotional skills, can have a tremendous input into the qualities of resilience that they develop during these important early years and on how successfully they navigate the challenges of later childhood and adolescence, the education system and eventual transition to adulthood. The early years period in the child's life is rich with opportunities to foster and grow innate qualities of resilience and to mitigate any areas of weakness or vulnerability.

Foundations for social competence

The most basic skills required for a high level of social functioning are normally acquired in the home setting and, usually, in the context of very close relationships that most children establish with their primary caregivers, primarily the mother.

According to Bagdi and Vacca (2005), the most important thing that any parent or caregiver can do for his or her child to ensure that resilience is maximised during the crucial early years and beyond is to provide a stable core of emotional experience that assures that the child feels loved, respected and appreciated:

> [S]hared positive emotional experiences between parents and their children serve as building blocks for the development of social and emotional well-being in infants and toddlers. Furthermore, a healthy sense of well-being leads to the development of resilience, thereby supporting the child's ability to interpret, experience, manage, and cope effectively with joyous as well as distressing events in their life. (Bagdi and Vacca, 2005, 147)

In earlier chapters, we have explored the importance of a strong sense of attachment between the mother (or other primary caregiver) and the child. Although in the early years children are beginning to reach towards and interact with an incrementally bigger world, this sense of attachment remains vitally important. Landry et al. (2006, 629) stress the importance for very young children of experiencing responsiveness from their primary caregiver as they continue to grow. He argues that 'responsiveness . . . includes distinct but conceptually related behaviors that provide support for a range of cognitive and social skills'. Such responsive parenting, he suggests, could have 'positive consequences for cognitive skills and greater growth in both social and cognitive-language skills'.

Conversely, early research in resilience in children (see Chapter 2) shows that children with lower emotional and social competencies are more frequently found in families where parents express more hostile parenting, engage in more conflict and give more attention to children's negative than positive behaviours (Webster-Stratton and Reid, 2004, 97; Landry et al., 2006, 629). In other words, certain types of parenting actively contribute to suboptimal outcomes for children's behaviour and their ability to interact with other people – and this in turn can have serious consequences for their levels of academic and social competence as they grow.

But how much do social skills matter to resilience and to factors such as educational success in the early years? The answer is that they matter a great deal and that their importance goes far beyond the individual. It has long been known that the ability to comprehend and follow social rules and to conform to social rule expectations is absolutely essential to social adaptation within the family and with peers, and, Wentzel says, 'From a societal perspective, a lack of such skills can have a profound effect on the individual as well as others. For instance, antisocial children, as adults, tend to be overrepresented in groups characterized by alcoholism, unemployment, divorce, and dependence on public assistance' (Wentzel, 1991, 1).

Challenges to social competence

But not all home settings are equal, and the reality is that some children, for a variety of reasons, do much better in the area of acquiring social competence than others. The repercussions of this disparity can be seen and can grow in importance as the child proceeds along his or her journey through life (see Chapter 5).

In fact, even before they enter early years care and education, distinct differences emerge in terms of the capabilities of children from different socio-economic backgrounds (Shonkoff and Phillips, 2000, 5). The inequalities in children's cognitive abilities are substantial right from 'the starting gate'. Disadvantaged children (see Chapter 5) typically start early years care and education with significantly lower cognitive skills than their more advantaged counterparts (Burkam and Lee, 2002). As they move through the education system, often these differences become more, not less, pronounced while they are expected to start learning the abstract reasoning skills required to acquire literacy and numeracy. Although some of these disparities can arise from differences in terms of innate ability, the economic and social status of the child's household, and more, it often appears that early experiences of care and education and school generally make this inequality worse rather than better. Findings from trajectory studies (Jennings and Reingle, 2012) reaffirm the importance of understanding aggression during the early childhood period, while confirming risk factors (including male gender, low socio-economic status, maternal past antisocial behavior, maternal young age at birth of child, maternal low education, prenatal smoking, presence of young siblings, coercive parenting) associated with the long-term development of aggression. 'However, one limitation is that they do not necessarily capture heterogeneity of patterns of physical aggression in the short-term, or explain how short-term physical aggression is influenced, particularly during the critical period before school entry' (Tzoumakis et al., 2014, 409).

In quite a few cases (as many as one in eight, by some reckonings), children's behavioural issues are sufficiently severe to be considered as indicative of future mental health difficulties, including 'adverse psychosocial, educational and health outcomes in adolescence and adulthood' (Miller-Lewis et al., 2013, 2).

Researchers have identified several social indicators that suggest that children from more disadvantaged communities have a smaller range of reading books and more limited computer access in the home; they spend more time watching television and are therefore more likely to have a poor outcome in school (Jacobson, 2002, 10). In addition, children of preschool age who have witnessed violence, such as domestic violence, 'tend to have greater externalizing and internalizing behavior problems, lower social functioning, increased aggression, adverse health outcomes, and lower intellectual functioning relative to children not exposed to such violence' (Howell et al., 2010, 151). Moreover, early childhood stress, can contribute to vulnerable children falling behind academically, in part because 'the biological effects of stress undermine their ability to concentrate, remember things, and control and focus their own thinking' (Thompson, 2014, 45). Also, children aged four to twelve years who have experienced chronic stress (see Chapter 4) may become neurologically hardwired to respond to apparent threats in their environment with greater levels of vigilance and/or violent reactions, with inevitable consequences for their ability to form healthy social relationships (Thompson, 2014, 46). The consequences of a difficult background are not just sociological but can create lasting differences in the individual's physical as well as emotional responses to stressors.

For children who are actively neglected, the repercussions can be considerable:

> Early childhood is a vulnerable period for the acquisition and development of cognitive, language, and emotion regulation abilities, and therefore neglect in early childhood is of particular concern. Normal development may be disrupted by deprivation associated with neglect and can result in dysregulation of neural systems during vulnerable periods of brain development, leading to pronounced neurocognitive deficits due to maltreatment. (Spratt et al., 2012, 175)

Furthermore, children who have specific problems with their health or who suffer from a chronic health condition are also at risk of doing less well (Whiteford et al., 2013, 35). Various factors can contribute. Children who have health problems are more likely to have to spend time in hospital or at home because of their illness, which means that they will miss more days of school and that the friendships they form with their peers are likely to be interrupted. Forming friendships can be more difficult for children who are unwell compared to children who are well (Whiteford et al., 2013, 37). For children who are unwell and who need special medical treatment, the notion of feeling 'different' to the other children can be very stressful. When such health problems co-exist with other factors, such as poverty in the home, lower levels of maternal education, or ethnic minority status, the child becomes even more vulnerable. Moreover, factors of health do not exist in a social vacuum; there can be a relationship between poverty and lower levels of parental education and children's ill health. Research in Australia, for example, suggested that even when early childhood health care is available free or at an affordable cost, less educated mothers are less likely to avail of it, with possible long-term health repercussions for their children (Whiteford et al., 2013, 46).

Frequently, these differences, which are typically related to a multiplicity of issues – for example, poverty and a family in which the country's first language is not spoken – often appear to become more important as the child gets older and moves through the education system. 'There is general agreement that social stratification in educational outcomes increases as children move through school' (Burkam and Lee, 2002). Difficulties in education and interpersonal relationships are most pronounced in children who struggle in the area of social and emotional skills. Children who have difficulty in these areas when they are very young are likely to have problems and poor outcomes later on (Reebye, 2013, 16).

Young children who find it difficult to manage their emotions risk not doing well at school, and failing to understand other people's emotions can make the learning environment an overwhelming place, one from which the child might prefer to withdraw rather than engage with peers and educators in a positive way (see the importance of co-regulation in Chapter 3). In ethnically diverse communities, sometimes the social norms of the dominant culture, as represented at school, can be different to those of a minority culture. In this situation, children can be 'expected to adapt to normative expectations for behavior that are inconsistent with those espoused by their families and community'. In some cases, young children from communities that emphasise the importance of being compliant and obedient struggle with learning situations in which they are encouraged to display self-reliance and competitiveness (Wentzel, 1991, 14). Denham et al. (2012, 179) point out that the acquisition of social and emotional skills can be difficult for very young children. In early years care and education, young children are often 'required to sit still, attend, follow directions, and approach and enter group play, all of which may challenge their nascent abilities'. Many children, they say, are behind in these areas at the point at which they enter the education system. They may therefore begin to develop confrontational feelings at this very early stage as a consequence of being asked to do things (e.g. to sit quietly) that they find very difficult and extremely puzzling.

Whereas researchers previously thought that as children grow up and acquire more advanced cognitive, language and regulatory skills, they find it easier to deal with challenges and tend to grow out of 'externalizing behavior problems', more recent research has shown 'a normative developmental pathway of externalizing behavior problems that peaks at age 2 and that shows a distinct decline with age'. Thus, while it may true that most children develop adaptive skills that they can use when they encounter challenging situations, 'for some children, early-onset externalizing problems remain stable and lead to more serious maladaptive outcomes' (Calkins et al., 2007, 676). Table 1.1 (in Chapter 1) identifies six domains that promote resilience. However, in some situations these domains are significantly impeded, and Table 7.1 explores the consequences of challenging situations.

Table 7.1 Challenges to social competence

Challenges	Factors
Poverty	Growing up in poverty is associated with a wide range of factors that can impact on social competence in areas from literacy to good physical health.
Parental education	Parents' level of education, indicated by time spent in school, literacy levels and factors such as the number of books in the home, all have repercussions for children's levels of social competence.
Exposure to violence	Exposure to violence, especially chronic, repeated violence, can have serious consequences for children's development.
Chronic stress	Chronic stress, whatever the contributing factor, impacts on a child's ability to become socially competent.
Physical ill-health	Physical sickness is accompanied by a range of issues, from school absence to problems with confidence and relationship forming, all of which can have a deleterious effect.
Ethnic/linguistic minority status	Belonging to an ethnic/linguistic minority can contribute to problems at school and difficulties with integrating and relationship forming, all of which can be worsened in the presence of discrimination.

> **Vignette 7.1**
>
> Sandra is a five-year-old child from a Traveller background. Tests have shown her to be of above-average intelligence, but she is already falling behind her peers in a wide range of areas. Although Sandra comes from a loving home, she is disadvantaged in many ways. Her father is illiterate, and her mother's standard of literacy is low. For Sandra, the idea of opening a book for fun is quite strange, and there is nobody at home to support her. The family has a semi-nomadic lifestyle, travelling in their caravan from April to October, so her schooling, which has just begun, seems certain to be interrupted and sporadic at best. Moreover, Sandra suffers from asthma, which is aggravated by the damp conditions she lives in and by her frequent proximity to the family's horses. If her elder siblings' experience is anything to go by, Sandra's experience of education is likely to be characterised by frequent absences, much interruption, a conflictual relationship between her parents and the teaching staff, poor progress and an early exit.
>
> **Discussion**
>
> The vignette characterises Sandra's education opportunities as limited. From a multi-agency perspective, what (i) short-term (ii) medium-term and (iii) long-term strategies/interventions might help to improve Sandra's chances of engaging more effectively with educational activities.
>
> Explore the consequences for Sandra and her social and emotional development if her educational opportunities do not increase, and examine Sandra's experience if she were to join mainstream education at age 12.

Acquiring resilience through play

Although it is widely held that play reflects social competence, a second and stronger view of the role of play in development is that it promotes social competence (Vygotsky, 1978; Saracho and Spodek, 1998). Jean Piaget (1962) defines play as the exercise of already acquired schemes just for the pleasure of doing so. Although there are those who believe that Piaget has underestimated the power of play in development, it is also acknowledged that this emphasis on play as practical enjoyment also emphasises its role in polishing and honing social and emotional skills. As children engage with social play, they become involved in a range of interactive opportunities and cognitive routines that are crucial for their personal development of social competences and resilient skills. Play can contribute significantly to child development as a mechanism for the operation of protective factors (such as those defined in Figure 1.2).

Time spent at play, whether at home, on the playground or in an early years setting, provides a crucial opportunity for learning and acquiring the skills that are essential to resilience. Through play, whether solitary, with other children or with caregiving adults, children learn through direct experience how their actions can impact on the world around them, and can begin to exert a sense of autonomy. The cognitive stimulation offered by this sort of activity is very important for the development of many important skills, including the acquisition of language (Jaffee, 2007, 633).

Although children who grow up in poverty may be at risk of not being given sufficient time and space to play, this can be addressed in the context of early years care and education, with positive outcomes in terms of improvements in speech and language acquisition. For instance, in one US day care centre catering to children at risk, games involving rhyming and singing were shown to improve children's language skills and confidence levels on entering school (Centre for Excellence and Outcomes in Children's and Young People's Services, 2010, 24). However, teachers in some schools and institutions devoted to children's learning feel under such pressure to produce academic 'results' that relatively little time is given to allowing the children to engage in activities that are relationship building and help them to develop the emotional intelligence and networking skills that will help them to become resilient in later life (Daunic et al., 2013, 43). The importance of the sort of skills acquired through play, which include 'management of aggression and/or conflict; development of self-worth; and ability to regulate emotion and reactivity', should not be underestimated (Gokiert et al., 2014, 441).

Writing of a child growing up in poverty, with multiple risks to resilience, Wright comments of her that she never laughed and did not play with the other children in her day care centre, but simply sat by herself (Wright, 2010, 444). This situation made it very hard for the other children, and even the adults caring for them, to engage with the child, and often she was left alone. The care workers knew that Goddess was acquiring social-emotional skills when, with intensive intervention, she started learning how to play and how to laugh (Wright, 2010, 458). With the ability to play came a range of other important skills: 'Soon she received more positive attention from her teachers and peers, allowing her to build more social-emotional skills through her interactions with them' (Wright, 2010, 462).

Play, importantly, also reflects social competence in relation to peer groups and peer relationships. Thus, the quality of children's play and the development of appropriate skills will be directly linked to the quality of the play environment, the quality of each child's social capabilities and the quality of opportunities to model resilient skills and social communications.

Early years education

Early years care and education provides a valuable, even unparalleled, opportunity to help mitigate these differences and the extra vulnerability of some children during this developmentally sensitive period of a child's life. It can also provide young children with the skills of resilience that will help them in later childhood, as well as a better educational outcome and a better basis for forming positive peer relationships and friendships.

The period of early years and early school is a 'strategic time to intervene directly with children and an optimal time to facilitate social competence and reduce their aggressive behaviors before these behaviors and reputations develop into permanent patterns' (Webster-Stratton and Reid, 2004, 98). As Webster-Stratton and Reid (2004, 96) point out, 'Preventing, reducing, and halting aggressive behavior at school entry, when children's behavior is most malleable, is a beneficial and cost-effective means of interrupting the progression from early conduct problems to later delinquency and academic failure.'

Although early years care and education and primary school may never completely eliminate inequalities (see Chapter 5), the child's experience of school certainly should not magnify them – and it has the capacity to significantly reduce them (Burkam and Lee, 2002), even if at the current time this does not always happen. The early years period is a very sensitive time in terms of childhood development. It is a period of significant brain development (see Chapter 4) and one in which neural pathways are laid down that facilitate certain behaviours over the course of the child's future experience.

Early years programmes (such as Head Start and Sure Start, explored in Chapter 2) that focus on providing excellent care and interactional and educational environments to children who have been identified as at risk of failing to develop good skills around emotional regulation are likely to have a positive effect on these children's educational outcomes later on (Bodrova and Leong, 2008, 2). People working in the area of the provision of early childhood care and education have a particular role in fostering resilience among very young children and their families.

Those children who do understand others' emotions are in a better position to develop positive peer relationships as well as to avoid either instigating or

Activity 7.1

Early childhood providers are in a unique position in working with and supporting families. A responsive and collaborative approach among early childhood providers and parents is therefore warranted... collaborative work between early childhood providers, educators and parents leads to better outcomes for all involved, including but not limited to fewer conduct problems for children, increased parenting skills for mothers and better classroom management skills for teachers (Bagdi and Vacca, 2005, 148).

Tasks

From an early years setting perspective, explore strategies and approaches that can be used in collaboration with parents for integrating play into the early years curriculum for the purpose of developing skills of resilience.

From a peer relationship perspective, explore a range of practice strategies that early years settings can draw on to structure 'a responsive and collaborative approach' to building the skills of resilience in the early years.

being the target of aggression. An understanding of emotion is also strongly linked with a better academic performance later on; one study showed that children aged five who demonstrated strong skills in this area had a better academic performance four years later, aged nine (Denham et al., 2012, 180).

Fostering self-regulation and self-concept

Professional caregivers and teachers cannot control the child's home or environment, but they can help him or her to develop skills around managing his or her own behaviour and to develop a positive concept of self. A core skill that can be mastered during the early years is self-regulation, which has been described as a 'deep, internal mechanism that enables children as well as adults to engage in mindful, intentional, and thoughtful behaviors' (Bodrova and Leong, 2008, 1). Figueroa Sanchez (2008) has referred to these skills as 'emotional literacy' and suggests that any academic and other achievements expected from the young person later on are best constructed on a bedrock of emotional literacy:

> Giving young children the appropriate vocabulary and role-modeling behaviors to use in conflict or stressful situations will help to create a working classroom community in which the learning environment embraces children's voices . . . children are more likely to learn important cognitive skills when they are confident and engage in interactions with other children as well as with adults. (Figueroa-Sanchez, 2008, 301–2)

There are two aspects to self-regulation: children who have mastered the skill are able to stop doing something when they feel the impulse to (e.g. not to grab a toy that another child is playing with, just because they would like to play with it themselves) or to do something even when they don't particularly feel like it (e.g. remembering to put up their hand when they want to ask a question, or letting a classmate take a turn ahead of them). The mastery of these crucial skills in and of themselves creates a situation in which the tasks the child is asked to achieve at school become much more manageable.

Children who have mastered self-regulation (see Figure 3.3) are able to think ahead and figure out which of a range of possible responses to the things going on around them is the most appropriate in any given situation. Whereas many children know in theory that they shouldn't grab, should wait their turn, and so forth, the ability to consistently put this information into practice can indicate resilience in the context of early childhood.

The importance of self-regulation should not be underestimated; in fact, high levels of self-regulation provide a better indicator of children's future performance in the areas of reading and mathematics than IQ scores (Bodrova and Leong, 2008, 1), whereas children who have not mastered self-regulation and display 'antisocial and aggressive behavior' in the early part of their education are much more likely than others to drop out at secondary level (Wentzel, 1991, 8). Timely interventions at this stage, including 'teaching children appropriate social responses to instruction such as attending, following instructions, and volunteering answers can lead to significant and stable gains in academic achievement' (Wentzel, 1991, 8). Research has shown that children who experience rejection by peers and teachers (often because of antisocial and aggressive behaviour) in the early years of their education are likely to be at serious risk of academic failure.

Longitudinal studies of young children growing up in poverty and considered to be at risk have found that toddlers with better emotional regulation and the ambition to concentrate and persist with tasks are likely to display fewer behavioural problems even three or four years later, and that this is the case even among children who have witnessed domestic violence or experienced poverty, maternal depression, social exclusion, homelessness, and other difficult issues (Miller-Lewis et al., 2013, 2). These variables have often been found to be true of children at later stages of their education, but the research shows that factors such as a better concept of self and greater self-control even in the early years are excellent predictors of future well-being (Miller-Lewis et al., 2013, 17). Participation in high-quality early years care and education programmes outside the home can 'contribute to reduced levels of internalizing and inhibited behavior, perhaps especially if the quality of care is high and for children who are at risk of highly inhibited behavior' (Gormley et al., 2011, 2096).

Seale et al. (2013) stress that:

> Boosting positive child-adult relationships, self-concept and self-control as resources in early childhood may hold promise for helping children establish a firm foundation that will carry them forward into healthy futures, regardless of what adverse family circumstances come their way. (Seale et al., 2013, 19)

A positive self-concept fosters resilience and helps to protect resilient children from challenging circumstances (Nesheiwat and Brandwein, 2011, 9). With these skills, children are likely to display greater levels of resilience in the area of education and to be better at developing positive relationships with peers (Bagdi and Vacca, 2005, 148). Friendships in childhood are a hugely important aspect of social development:

> Through the successful formation of friendships, children learn social skills such as cooperation, sharing, and conflict management. Friendships also foster a child's sense of group belonging and begin to facilitate children's empathy skills—that is, their ability to understand another's perspective. The formation (or absence) of friendships has an enduring impact on the child's social adjustment in later life. Research has shown that peer problems such as peer isolation or rejection are predictive of a variety of problems including depression, school drop out, and other psychiatric problems in adolescence and adulthood. (Webster-Stratton and Reid, 2004, 105)

According to Bronfenbrenner's ecological theory (cited in Meyers and Hickey, 2014, 220), children develop 'through a series of transactions with a set of proximal and distal contexts in which they are embedded' (see Chapter 5 and Figure 5.1). From this point of view, it is impossible to separate the child from their social framework, and all efforts to enhance their qualities of resilience should consider the many ways in which they interact with their environment rather than a narrow focus. Table 7.2 identifies socio-environmental opportunities and factors that could impact on development in the early years.

Table 7.2 Key factors in early years education

Opportunities	Factors
Attending a well-run preschool	Early years care and education can offer children the opportunity to develop social skills in a safe, caring environment. For children dealing with difficult issues at home, such as poverty, early years settings can help to mitigate them.
Engaging in programmes designed to help emotional regulation	Children who are helped to acquire skills around emotional regulation before they enter school tend to have an enhanced ability to communicate and express their feelings in a positive way, which is a vital social skill.
Parental involvement	When early years settings work collaboratively with parents to help children acquire social skills, the outcome tends to be much better.
Transition to early care and education	The transition to early education is rich in opportunities for new interactions. However, this early move – likely to be the first transition – is also full of challenges that need to be managed by practitioners.
Multiple transitions	Children experience a number of transitions during childhood, and each presents different challenges. The quality of the child's experience of first transitions may well impact on and influence how he or she responds to subsequent transitions.
Social environment	Even before they enter early care and or education, distinct differences emerge in terms of children's capabilities. Factors such as socio-economic issues and parenting styles may also impact on transition.
Social competence	For some children, early onset externalising problems remain past age two (the age at which it normally stops) and can lead to more serious maladaptive outcomes.
Early Intervention	Can be defined as 'proactive approaches and activities that recognise potential risk factors to social and emotional development and development of resilient skills especially in relation to peer relationships'.

Strategies for early years competence

Bagdi and Vacca (2005) propose an approach that is 'family-centered, collaborative, and culturally competent', aligned around a framework of promotion, prevention and intervention, where:

Activity 7.2

The following extract suggests that the skills of resilience can emerge through a 'virtuous circle':

> The relationship between the home environment and the school environment can be circular. Ideal school environments can foster the development of good social and emotional skills in children, and school environments get better when the children have well-developed social and emotional skills. In the best situations, a 'virtuous circle' can emerge in which the child is able to bring the positive coping skills that she learns to bear on a range of circumstances both at home and at school. (Meyers and Hickey, 2014)

Task

Explore how early years settings can utilise the concept of a 'virtuous circle' to collaborate with parents and family to develop age-specific social and emotional skills.

From a practitioner perspective, explore and compare 'virtuous circle' strategies appropriate for use with individual children and for use with groups of young children.

Promotion includes approaches and activities that raise awareness regarding the importance of early brain development, nurturing early relationships, and healthy attachments on children's emotional health and well-being. Prevention can be defined as proactive approaches and activities that recognize potential risk factors for emotional wellness and accordingly construct meaningful experiences for children and families that focus on healthy relationships, skill development and resiliency. Intervention includes holistic, collaborative, child and family centered approaches and activities that provide specific, individualized supports to meet the unique needs of children and families. Interventions may include strategies and/or treatment to assist children with specific difficulties as a result of developmental, emotional, or environmental variables. (Bagdi and Vacca, 2005, 148)

Meyers and Hickey (2014, 223) describe a programme that focuses on helping young children to develop the social and emotional skills that they will need in education and in life. The 'Incredible Years Series' (http://www.incredible years.com), a programme developed specifically for children experiencing the very early years of their education, includes lessons that focus on the development of social and emotional skills, including homework to be carried out at home with caregivers and class management in school that is designed to promote awareness of emotions and prosocial behaviours. In studies, the Incredible Years programme has been shown to make a marked difference in the behaviour and social aptitude of children considered to be at risk. In one study, 'individual testing of children's cognitive social problem-solving indicated that intervention children had significantly more prosocial responses in response to conflict situations than control children'. A second programme, known as the '4Rs' (Reading, Writing, Respect and Resolution), combines teaching in the classroom with training of teachers aimed at helping them to develop their own social and emotional skills and to integrate them into their interactions with children, facilitating positive relationships between teachers and children and better academic and social outcomes (Webster-Stratton and Reid, 2004, 99).

The Early Years Foundation Stage (EYFS) framework was published in 2012 in the UK to provide an important set of standards for the development, learning and care of children from birth to age five. The EYFS framework is an assessment-based approach and is based on ongoing observations and assessment in three key areas of development (Box 7.1).

Box 7.1 The EYFS profile (Standards and Testing Agency, 2014)

The prime areas of learning:

- Communication and language
- Physical development
- Personal, social and emotional development

The specific areas of learning:

- Literacy
- Mathematics
- Understanding the world
- Expressive arts and design

Characteristics of effective learning:

- Playing
- Active learning
- Creating and thinking critically

The EYFS profile is designed, through the mechanisms of standard monitoring and assessment, to lay the foundation stones for all children to be able to progressively develop a wide range of skills through exposure to a rich learning environment. It brings together an assessment process that combines age-appropriate child development, motivating and flexible curriculum and effective organisational deployment of resources (Department for Education, 2014).

The EYFS initiative provides the opportunity for aspects of pedagogy and early years provision to be used to effectively enable young children to gain confidence in their abilities and knowledge, gain ownership of skills and attributes, and develop strong interpersonal skills with peers and adults. This initiative of learning and assessment provides a sound platform for the development of age-specific social and emotional skills (Table 1.2), ensuring that young children are supported during the journey of embedding effective skills and knowledge. One of the objectives of the

EYFS initiative is not only about education for classroom and academic skills but importantly also about the development of a wide range of both personal and interpersonal skills necessary for long-term positive outcomes. The theoretical and practical links with the development of educational resilience (and resilience more generally) in young children is undisguised (Standards and Testing Agency, 2014).

Bodrova and Leong propose four key strategies that can be utilised in kindergarten to assist children in developing these important skills (Bodrova and Leong, 2008, 2):

- Teach self-regulation to all children, not just those thought to have problems.
- Create opportunities for children to practise the rules of a certain behaviour and to apply those rules in new situations.
- Offer children visual and tangible reminders about self-regulation.
- Make play and games important parts of the curriculum.

Research shows that although all children benefit from interventions such as those described above, the ones who had the poorest skills and most difficult issues with behaviour benefitted the most (Denham et al., 2012, 186).

Early years practitioners

An important factor in working with families and caregivers to ensure the resilience of very young children is the recognition of the important work that those involved in the care of very young children do, and of their unique knowledge of the children they look after. Historically this has been a profession that has been assigned a rather low status by society (for a variety of reasons that are beyond the scope of this work); certainly it is not typically accorded the respect of a career such as speech therapy or child psychology, nor is it generally very highly paid. However, early challenges to resilience, such as delayed language acquisition or behavioural problems, are often detected first by those working in direct child care provision (Payler and Georgeson, 2013, 382), despite the fact that the expertise and knowledge of these workers is very frequently underestimated and under-respected (Payler and Georgeson, 2013, 392). This situation is compounded by the fact that those who work in early years settings frequently have limited training or experience in working in association with other professionals who have specific skills to intervene with vulnerable children (Payler and Georgeson, 2013, 394). The provision of this sort of training is clearly especially important in environments and situations in which children are likely to be particularly vulnerable (i.e. in the provision of early years care and education to very young children living in poverty, in marginalised communities, etc.). Sensitive and intelligent early years care and education can go a long way towards fostering resilience in children, including those living with disadvantage and/or trauma. Indeed, sensitive caregiving at this stage of development can help to redirect children who tend to experience 'heightened physiological responses to stressful situations' as a result of traumatic experiences at home, and thus actually impact directly on the physical expression of stress (Obradovic, 2012, 372).

Daunic et al. describe simple ways in which teachers can interact with very young children in a way that enhances not just their academic abilities but also their capacity to control and regulate emotions, and thus be more likely to enjoy positive relationships with peers, educators and family members. For example, by reading a story to the children in a class, the teacher can encourage them to discuss the emotions described and evoked by the characters and events described. If a child in the story is bullied, for example, the children listening to the story can learn to understand and discuss the sort of emotions they might be feeling. In the process, children's vocabulary, powers of reasoning and emotional skills are all enhanced. Such programmes, they say, have been demonstrated, in the context of working with children from low-income families, to lead to 'positive effects on oral language, a critical aspect of behavioural self-regulation, emergent literacy and reading comprehension' (Daunic et al., 2013, 45).

The early childhood years are a prime period for language learning and the acquisition of language, and here again the ability to regulate emotion emerges as a core skill:

> [E]motional well-being and social competence provide a strong foundation for brain development and emerging cognitive abilities . . . language learning is dependent not only on the ability to differentiate sounds and the capacity to link meaning to certain words, but also on the ability to concentrate, pay attention and engage in meaningful social interaction. These behaviours influence all areas of development. They also affect how the individual functions in later life both in personal situations and in the workplace. (Mindess et al., 2008, 56)

Research indicates that when the quality of early years care and education is high, participation in an early years programme can contribute to children displaying reduced levels of internalising and inhibited behaviour, particularly in the case of children who are 'at risk of highly inhibited behaviour' (Gormley et al., 2011, 2096).

By acquiring, understanding and practising social skills in the safe environments of the home and a nurturing early education system, even very young children can start to acquire the fundamentals of a sense of social responsibility, along with the skills they need to exercise it. Social responsibility can be defined as 'adherence to social rules and role expectations . . . that exist by virtue of social roles that define rules for group participation, as a reflection of broad social and cultural norms, or as a result of personal commitments to other individuals' (Wentzel, 1991, 2).

Assisting children in developing social skills makes it easier for them to access support within and outside their families, 'often leading to better outcomes following exposure to violence' (Howell et al., 2010, 151).

Moreover, the acquisition of social and emotion skills during this period can facilitate the acquisition of other skills as the child moves through the education system. Literacy, for example, 'includes the ability to create meaning and to apply that understanding to our own lives'. Being able to do this, in turn, means acquiring first a bedrock of 'emotional literacy', of self-understanding that grows in the context of participating in social engagement with others (Figueroa-Sanchez, 2008, 301).

Respecting the work and observations of people who work in direct care provision with very young children and providing for a greater flow of information from them to parents, teachers, social workers and the various professionals who support children enhances the likelihood that young people who are at risk in terms of resilience will get the interventions they need as early as possible. Providing early years practitioners with the vocabulary and confidence they need in order to communicate their concerns about vulnerable children is also important.

Vignette 7.2

Ana was born to very young parents in an area of social deprivation. She belongs to a minority ethnic and linguistic group. Her father has struggled with drug abuse, but he is trying to get his life on track. He is on methadone and attends group therapy as well as a back-to-work programme. Her mother suffered post-natal depression after Ana's birth and is still inclined to get 'the blues'. Ana's social worker is concerned that the little girl was not meeting her developmental milestones, although her physical health seemed to be fine. Her mother was sometimes overprotective and sometimes distracted by her own mental health issues. Anna is three years old and attends an early years setting three days a week. The setting is attached to the local community centre, and Anna attends together with 20 other one- to four-year-old children. There were no serious 'red flags' to suggest that Ana should be taken into care, but her home situation is not ideal.

Discussion

From a practitioner perspective, and with reference to the risk and challenges to Ana's social and emotional development, critically discuss opportunities for early intervention. Provide reasons for your chosen interventions.

Discuss the role of the early years practitioner in monitoring and improving Ana's capability to develop early social and emotional skills and her preparedness for primary school.

Managing transitions

The period of transition from home into an early years setting may often be accompanied by the mother returning to work after a period at home and is an important transitional period in the life of the child; it is one of a series of 'key processes that open up social and educational resources that may enhance resilient attitudes and behaviours in order to strengthen children (and parents) to deal with future demands' (Niesel and Griebel, 2005, 4). The transition to early interactions with education is a period rich with opportunity to develop both resilience and knowledge (see Chapter 5), and it is also a period full of challenges, as a result of which 'under adverse conditions lasting difficulties can occur, leading to problematic behaviour with disadvantageous consequences for the child' (Niesel and Griebel, 2005, 4). For the very young child, who often has only known one primary caregiver before entering a formal early years setting, this can be a very challenging time.

In many cultures, the very early years see a number of such transitions: from home to early years care, possibly from early years care to early years education such as a Montessori school, and from there to 'big' primary school – which is often the most challenging of the three (Niesel and Griebel, 2005, 6). When transitions are successful, they can 'strengthen the competencies of children' (see for example Box 7.2: The PATHS Programme in Northern Ireland); whereas when there are difficulties with coping, or the child does not adjust well to the new circumstances, it is likely that subsequent transitions will be difficult (Niesel and Griebel, 2005, 6). Poorly managed transitions can lead to social-emotional difficulties during the early years, which in turn 'are often associated with later troubles in school readiness and performance, social adjustment, and health' (Gokiert et al., 2014, 441). A risk is that poorly managed transitions will predispose the child to internalising behaviours, like feeling afraid or behavioural inhibition, which can be associated as they grow up with problems, including 'the development of serious anxiety problems in middle childhood and beyond' (Gormley et al., 2011, 2096).

It can be easy for adults to overlook what a big change such transitions are. For the children in question, their very identity may experience a shift. Moving from early years settings to big school means the child is 'a big boy now' or 'a big girl now', who needs to learn how to reach out to adults other than mum or dad when he or she needs help, and to interact with other children. These children can be aided in developing resilience in this context by being supported with information about what school will be like and by being supported at school and at home as they begin to develop social, numeracy and literacy skills. Other factors, such as considering the bilocation of early years and primary schools, can ease transition and foster resilience (Gormley et al., 2011, 2097).

Box 7.2 The PATHS programme in Northern Ireland

The PATHS programme, which was designed to help children in the early years of their education to access social and emotional development in the context of Northern Ireland and in which intercommunity conflict was added to individual family issues, found that participating children 'demonstrated significant improvements in social and emotional skills, attitudes and behaviour... teachers reported that pupils were demonstrating increased positive behaviour, increased self-esteem, more awareness, and better expression of how they and others are feeling'. (Sheard et al., 2012, 279)

Involving parents

As important as early years care and education is for the development of resilience in very young children, the home environment (see Chapters 3 and 5) matters hugely. Early education provides an opportunity for caregivers and educators, both informally and formally (i.e. in the context of the provision of parenting classes and feedback), to create an integrated approach to optimising social skills, emotional regulation and resilience in children (Fröhlich-Gildhoff and Rönnau-Böse, 2012, 137). Parents who are helped to acquire and utilise positive parenting techniques contribute to their children's development, including resilience. Parents who are under stress, whether this is related to poverty or other reasons, tend to respond with 'an increased use of coercive discipline techniques, behaviour that is directly implicated in increases in child problem behaviour' (Calkins et al., 2007, 677). In the early years, children 'are more likely to show overactive, noncompliant, aggressive, and impulsive behavior when their parents are displaying negative control and are uninvolved, rejecting, and harsh' (Calkins et al., 2007, 679). Moreover, these harsh parenting strategies and externalising behaviours can get locked into a self-reinforcing pattern in which the child acts out more and more and is responded to with incrementally harsher punishments (Calkins et al., 2007, 680). By working with parents to move away from these techniques, the negative impact of poverty or other aggravating factors on the child can be reduced, and this is likely to be accompanied by a reduction in unhelpful externalising behaviours. The research (see Chapter 2) indicates that a warmer, more positive relationship between children and their caregivers can provide them with a buffer against difficult factors in their environment (Calkins et al., 2007, 680).

Vignette 7.3

Martin was a physically disabled child who had started his education in a 'special school'. Despite his numerous physical issues, Martin was a very bright boy, and his parents and teachers all felt that his educational needs would be best served in mainstream education. So, at age six, Martin moved to the local primary school, where, with the help of a special assistant, he would learn alongside other children.

Although Martin had always had a very open and sunny disposition, this transition was extremely difficult for him. The other children were curious about his wheelchair and crowded around him on his first day. There was no hostility or bullying, but Martin got very angry and yelled at them all. Even after a month at the school, he didn't seem to be settling in. His behaviour at home had deteriorated, and he had started wetting the bed after having been dry for years.

Rather than sending Martin back to 'special school', his parents and teachers decided to persevere. Martin's mum suggested a day when all the kids would get to 'have a go' in his wheelchair. This was a big success. The children were able to assuage their curiosity, and Martin could see that they were really interested in how he moved around. He started to feel a little proud of how well he could manoeuvre his chair. Over time, the other kids were able to start forgetting about the chair and started seeing Martin as just another child and playmate.

Discussion

From a practitioner perspective, explore the social and emotional challenges inherent in Martin's transition from special school to mainstream school, and consider the impact on his development if these are not addressed over the long term.

Besides the strategy outlined in the vignette, examine other school- and classroom-based strategies that could be useful to ensure that Martin makes good academic progress as well as developing the social and emotional competence necessary for his new environment.

Conclusion

The early years are a period of important emotional and neurological development during which the child becomes increasingly aware of himself or herself as a social being who lives in a community of other social beings, and begins to lay down the behaviours that will help him or her to navigate the complex world of relationships, while also experiencing dramatic growth and development in both body and mind (see Chapter 3). He or she starts to venture outside the small and intimate world of the family and to interact with other children and adults in a range of formats and settings. With each interaction, skills can be learned, and behavioural tendencies are laid down. In this way, the foundational stones for the development of resilience are laid, with profound repercussions for the child's future personal and academic resilience.

Although there are many potential challenges during this crucial period, there are also many opportunities for the child to grow social and emotional skills and acquire the elements of social and academic resilience. In the case of children growing up in poverty or children from other sorts of difficult family backgrounds, there is an opportunity to provide the sort of supports that will help to address the disadvantage that is a significant hazard to their development of resilience.

With support from caregivers and educators, and a system that recognises the importance of these building blocks, children's chances of acquiring the skill set and resilience that will stand them in good stead for the rest of their lives are greatly enhanced. For early childhood interventions and early years settings that understand and take into consideration the many and complex needs of children who face hazards to resilience, the possibilities are considerable, as are the potential gains to the child, to his or her family and – by extension – to society as a whole.

CHAPTER 8

Educational Resilience in Schools

Introduction

The provision of formal education for children during the key stages of their development is integral to modern society and has become a cornerstone of how knowledge and skills are passed on to the next generation of citizens. With the exception of the small numbers of children who are home schooled, most young people around the world, and certainly in the developed world, are expected to attend compulsory education up until they are at least 17 years of age.

For many children, school is the primary setting in which they learn how to interact with people outside the family. It is where important skills associated with resilience can be learned – and it can also pose challenges to resilience. Considering the sheer numbers of hours that children and young people spend in school and the many and varied relationships they form with peers, teachers and other influences, it is important to acknowledge the central role that school plays for them (see Chapter 5). The importance of educational resilience is that it characterises how the experience of school can provide a central plank for resilience generally.

Educational resilience is certainly about learning and academic prowess, but that's not all. It's also about the relationships that young people make in the educational setting with their peers and teachers, and the social skills that they learn in the process. The development of social and academic skills is an important ingredient of resilience and more recently has been on the educational agendas of both politicians and schools. A positive and successful experience during school years can have powerful knock-on effects for the young person's ability to also access resilience in other areas of life.

This chapter emphasises that – by focusing on social skills, school and peer relationships as well as academic achievement; by expecting all students to be able to reach their full potential and assisting them in doing so; and by maintaining an atmosphere of high expectations – schools are expected to make a very valuable contribution to that promise that is resilience in later life (explored more fully in Chapter 9).

Educational resilience

Educational resilience places a great deal of emphasis on a number of interactive factors such as the presence of positive relationships between young people and adults, promoting high expectations in students and creating opportunities for students to be actively engaged in the learning process (Brown et al., 2001, xiii).

Jackson argues that acquiring a good degree of literacy is not just a potential marker of resilience, but can be a tool in developing resilience that provides children and young people with the opportunity to self-comfort and to learn on their own (Jackson, 1995, cited in Daniel and Wassell, 2002b, 36). In their 2006 study of children at risk, carried out in Crewe in the UK, Ward and Thurston suggest that a positive experience at school has

> the potential for being the stabilising influence in the lives of the majority of vulnerable children and young people. Good school attendance was cited as a protective factor for the majority of the children/young people . . . the most prevalent factor after having at least one good friend. (Ward and Thurston, 2006, 50)

Conversely, a failure to thrive academically can itself be a major hazard to resilience. Students who fail at school typically have many fewer chances to avail of opportunities offered to their peers. 'As a result,' comment Martin and Marsh (2009, 354), 'they are systematically disconnected from adaptive processes and post-school pathways and this disconnection is reflected in persistent truancy, increased substance use and abuse, employment and crime. In less dramatic circumstances, a general low-level inability to cope academically limits one's personal potential.'

In the case of students who are dealing with hazards to resilience such as poverty or a low level of parental education, DuBois (2001) proposes:

> Interventions in which the aim is to modify relevant experiences of home (e.g. parent-child relationships) or in the school (e.g. teaching strategies), could, for example, be expanded to include components that capitalise on the opportunities which such change efforts afford to enhance the self-referential views and feelings of youth concerning school and learning . . . it appears that it may be particularly useful for applied activities to focus on cultivating in youth from disadvantaged family backgrounds a strong positive sense of their abilities and aptitude as students such as would be reflected in a favourable scholastic self-concept or perceived self-efficacy for succeeding in school. (DuBois, 2001, 166)

Thus, the value of educational resilience is well established, and the opportunities inherent in education have become a policy priority throughout the Western world. Consequently, there are many working definitions of educational resilience (Box 8.1), and consistently these maintain the promise of resilience as academic achievement through perseverance over adversity.

Box 8.1 Example definitions of educational resilience

1. Educational resilience is the ability of children to thrive at school irrespective of their level of ability (Gordon and Song, 1994).
2. Educational resilience (referred to as 'academic invulnerability') refers to students who demonstrate high levels of achievement, motivation and performance despite being at risk of doing poorly and even dropping out (Alva, 1991).

3. Educational resilience is the ability of children to succeed in education despite risk factors that make it difficult for them to do so (Benard, 1991).

4. Educational resilience is displayed through 'the heightened likelihood of success in school and in other life accomplishments despite environmental adversities brought out by early traits, conditions, and experiences' (Wang et al., 1994).

5. Educational resilience is composed of a number of qualities, including motivation and goal orientation; the positive use of time, support and expectations from the family; and a positive learning environment (McMillan and Reed, 1994).

6. Educational resilience is seen when children do better than they 'ought to' considering their situation and the challenges they face (Gilligan, 1997).

The role of education

One of the early proponents of the benefits of citizenship skills for young people was John Dewey (1859–1952) (Stevenson, 2011), who believed that an education system should serve young people in terms of helping to 'foster the virtues of rationality, a participatory democracy and moral development of individual talents' (Stevenson, 2011, 74). He believed that one of the roles of schools was to encourage people from diverse backgrounds to come together and engage in dialogue, in order that students' individual as well as collective growth could be nurtured (Stevenson, 2011, 75).

Potentially, schools are perceived to be very important in terms of fostering resilience in the developing young person. Thus, if the experience of education is an unhappy one, they can do precisely the opposite of what is desired. Just as schools can provide the crucible in which resilience is forged, a poor school experience can be a hazard to resilience, as can poor relationships between students and teachers.

In the best case, 'when children are exposed to specially structured environments, such as the formal environments they experience in schools', they can, according to Thomas and Knowland (2009, 17) 'learn high-level cognitive skills that are specific to their culture'. However, they warn that in a more exam-focused culture of education, there is a risk that the development of other aspects of the students' education may be neglected, as schools' ability to help create 'critical, reflective and emotionally secure young people' becomes constrained (Stevenson, 2011, 95). Bacon et al. (2010, 50) reinforce the range of considerable research which indicates the importance of 'nurturing the wider spectrum of human competencies in order to enhance pupils' present and future wellbeing'. They also argue that 'dedicating time, energy and resources to improving the wellbeing and resilience of young people does not need to detract from other types of learning'. Furthermore, they suggest that by enabling schools to intervene early and in a targeted, focused way, it is likely that both direct and indirect costs associated with a lack of resilience would be considerably less.

The 'facts and figures' of the outcomes of a good education, or the lack thereof, are well known. Newmann (1998) comments on the picture in the United States:

Dropouts are three and a half times as likely as high school graduates to be arrested and six times as likely to be unwed parents. Dropouts are twice as likely to be unemployed and to live in poverty. In 1995, half of the heads of households on welfare and half of people in jail were dropouts . . . Children of parents without a high school education are twice as likely as their schoolmates to be non-readers. (Newmann, 1998, 88)

Frey and Walker propose that, because of the amount of time children spend at school, and because the vast majority of children attend schools, policy around resilience should focus on maximising the school's role in helping students to develop appropriate age-specific attributes, skills, competences and attitudes (Figure 1.1). To this end, Frey and Walker (2006, 86) suggest that schools can play an expansive role in:

- promoting school readiness skills for high-risk youth;
- providing early screening to identify children most at risk;
- delivering case management and wrap-around services to those who display signs of adjustment problems before second grade;
- providing seamless access to and provision of educational, health and social services through support service providers and family resource or youth service centres; and
- implementing primary prevention strategies at key developmental stages.

Lareau (2001, 96) is cautious about the extent to which schools can be relied upon. He argues that educators should be aware that there is often a much greater similarity between the cultural norms espoused by the school and those experienced by students at home in middle-class as opposed to working-class families. Because of the shared values teachers and middle-class students and their families have, teachers often 'valorize' the cultural practices of middle-class families, seeing them as ' "caring" for their children and "valuing" education' (Lareau, 2001, 96). Although inequalities in opportunity and access to education have been significantly reduced in the last 60 years, Montt (2011) argues that inequality in achievement is inherent to all educational systems and, as yet, has not been eliminated. He suggests, therefore, that the role of education as the protagonist for academic achievement across all sections of the population is far from straightforward and therefore cannot be taken for granted.

There are many features within the school systems that contribute to inhibiting equality in attainment and job opportunities, for example, children from disadvantaged backgrounds continue to be disproportionately assigned to groups with lower aspirations and resources, are more likely to experience large class sizes, are more likely to be taught by teachers who themselves have lower qualifications (Montt, 2011) and, importantly, are more likely to engage with low-achieving peers (Mayer, 2010). Lareau (2001, 96) argues that there are various cultural practices within society and some are 'selectively validated by dominant institutions' (such as schools) (see Chapter 5).

From their research into schools in underserviced communities in the United States, Creasey and Jarvis comment that they frequently have many students who receive free lunches (an indicator of low family income), and that often fewer than 10 per cent are meeting or exceeding the academic standards set by the state.

Vignette 8.1

Michael is a 12-year-old attending a large comprehensive school. Michael speaks mainly Spanish and Portuguese and has been speaking English for around three years. Michael lives with his mother and grandmother and his older brother, 15-year-old Ricardo, who goes to a special school. Ricardo and Michael are very close, and Michael looks up to Ricardo because he is tall and strong. Michael loves making Ricardo laugh. Since he started at secondary school, Michael has struggled academically, shown by his low grades and poor achievements. A teaching assistant works with Michael to develop his reading, writing and spelling. Michael is an energetic boy with a playful personality and is keen to talk to others – and shows an increasing grasp of English. His favourite subject appears to be history, as he seems to have a good memory for dates. In year 8, his history teacher began to think that Michael was probably capable of more than he was achieving. In discussion with the learning support team, Michael was given extra support for maths and history during his time in year 8. However, Michael's results have remained less than satisfactory despite the fact that the teachers think that he does understand the work. His teaching assistant has reported that she feels Michael has a real fear of success, as he thinks that his brother will not want to be with him anymore. The school has referred Michael to the school's mentorship scheme.

Discussion

Chapter 3 promotes that view that positive family attachments are important for developing appropriate skills of resilience. Explore Michael's experience, and examine the strengths and weakness of interplay between secure and insecure attachment in his case, and the impact on his educational attainment.

From a practitioner perspective, examine how the school's mentorship programme may be able to help Michael, and consider whether there are alternative strategies of support and assistance that might be effective at both improving Michael's grades and maintaining his positive relationship with his brother.

Also, such schools typically feature a high turnover of teachers as well as many teachers in 'emergency' or temporary positions (Creasey and Jarvis, 2013b, 3). The result is that the students who most need high-quality teaching – because they are already facing significant hazards to resilience – are not always receiving it. Stanton-Salazar (2001) suggests that middle-class students are better served in that they

> have what we can call very cosmopolitan networks; a set of relationships with a diverse array of people that translates into smooth access into the mainstream marketplace where privileges, institutional resources, opportunities for leisure, recreation, career mobility and political empowerment are abundant. (Stanton-Salazar, 2001, 105)

In effect, the debate about how children from disadvantaged backgrounds build the skills of educational resilience cannot be separated from the debate about the role of education systems in structural inequality.

Vignette 8.2

Hussein is a 14-year-old boy attending school in inner-city London. Although the state school is a relatively high-performing one, Hussein is not doing well. English is not his first language, and he attended the first four years of his education overseas, where he studied through Arabic. The family relocated to the UK as asylum seekers, and although his parents are highly qualified professionals, they have struggled to find adequately paid work. On top of all that, the family experienced a period of profound stress when their home country was at war and they lost family and friends, as well as witnessed violence every day. Although Hussein has not been displaying 'acting out' behaviours, he has been drifting behind since arriving at school. He prefers not to engage with teachers and other students, and often avoids even looking anyone in the eye. His demeanour is sullen and withdrawn. He does the minimum amount of work expected of him, and he is barely scraping by. His parents are distracted by their own struggles and don't realise how badly he is drifting. In fact, it's easy to overlook Hussein completely. Because he never causes any discipline problems in school and keeps to himself, he is often simply not considered.

It takes one very observant teacher to notice that all is not well with Hussein. In science class one day, instead of taking notes, Hussein just sits and stares at the wall. Mr Whitloe, who is quite new to the school, finds out that Hussein's marks, which were never great, have been slipping since he started. He suspects that Hussein is capable of much better work than he is turning in, and is also concerned about his lack of friends. Whereas all the other kids have mates that they pair off with during break and lunch times, Hussein either sits all by himself or walks around the perimeter of the school grounds, hands in pockets, staring at his feet.

Discussion

How might the trauma in Hussein's past impact on his educational resilience and what strategies might the school use to help Hussein (i) grow his self-confidence, (ii) improve his experience at school and (iii) improve his grades?

From a practitioner perspective, examine approaches and strategies that might be employed to help his parents engage effectively with the school strategies, and explore the challenges and benefits of the school and Hussein's parents working together to support Hussein.

Academic buoyancy

Martin and Marsh (2009, 356) introduce the concept of 'academic buoyancy' to describe students who cope with 'the ups and downs of everyday life as distinct from acute and chronic adversities relevant to traditional constructions of resilience'. Academic buoyancy, therefore, refers to the students' ability to cope with threats to confidence, such as result from a poor grade or experiencing stress as opposed to clinical depression; in other words, with the more usual trials and tribulations of school life. Martin and Marsh consider academic buoyancy to be 'the ongoing proactive frontline response to academic adversity', whereas 'academic resilience is the defensive backline that is invoked as necessary, if at all' (Martin and Marsh, 2009, 357). They believe that students who demonstrate academic resilience are also likely to demonstrate academic buoyancy (Martin and Marsh, 2009, 358), but that the two are not the same.

According to Martin and Marsh (2008, 54), the generally accepted definition of resilience does not adequately describe people who are dealing with 'ordinary' problems of the sort that occur normally throughout life. Successful navigation of these hurdles is, they believe, best described as 'buoyancy', a concept which they consider to align 'with recent developments in positive psychology that hypothesize about the scope for positive dimensions of individuals' lives to address aspects of their lives that are not so adaptive' (Martin and Marsh, 2008, 54). A focus on academic buoyancy, they say, 'would encompass building on strengths and emphasizing proactive rather than reactive approaches to setback and challenge. It would also emphasize key catalysts to enhanced educational outcomes' (Martin and Marsh, 2008, 54). Martin and Marsh consider academic buoyancy to be 'as the ongoing proactive frontline response to academic adversity, and academic resilience is the defensive backline that is invoked as necessary, if at all' (Figure 8.1).

According to Martin and Marsh (2008), academic buoyancy and resilience differ in terms of degree and kind:

> [W]hereas academic resilience may be relevant to chronic underachievement, academic buoyancy is relevant to the more typical experience of isolated poor grades and 'patches' of poor performance; whereas academic resilience may be relevant to overwhelming feelings of anxiety that are incapacitating, academic buoyancy is relevant more to 'typical' stress levels and daily pressures; whereas academic resilience may be relevant to debilitation in the face of chronic failure or anxiety, academic buoyancy is relevant more to threats to confidence as a result of a poor grade. In terms of differences of kind we argue that whereas academic resilience might be relevant to clinical types of affect such as anxiety and depression, academic buoyancy

Figure 8.1 Academic buoyancy v. academic resilience

is relevant more to low level stress and confidence; whereas academic resilience might be relevant to truancy and total disaffection from school, academic buoyancy is relevant more to dips in motivation and engagement; whereas academic resilience may be relevant to comprehensive and consistent alienation or opposition to teachers, academic buoyancy is more relevant to dealing with negative feedback on school-work. (Martin and Marsh, 2008, 55)

Although resilient students are likely also to be academically buoyant, the concept of resilience may not be relevant to students who display academic buoyancy. Nonetheless, many of the factors that are associated with academic resilience, including self-efficacy, a sense of purpose and a good relationship with teachers, are also likely to be associated with academic buoyancy (Martin and Marsh, 2008, 57).

Education relationships

Today there is a general understanding of the importance of secure attachment to a child's healthy psychological and physical development. However, the role of attachment in education is often overlooked, and while we cannot say that it is 'as important' as secure attachment (see Chapter 3) between a child and his or her primary caregiver(s), it can be very important and in some cases pivotal. A number of research studies demonstrate that learning and personal develop-ment gained through education relationships can establish and stabilise neural pathways such that it is subsequently more difficult to override those pathways as new information is presented (Brown et al., 2001; Bostock, 2004; Knowland and Thomas, 2014). In addition, Brown et al. (2001, 21) stress the importance of emotion in the educational process and cite research that suggests that in order for meaningful education to occur, students need to have established an emotional connection with both the process and their teachers.

Bostock (2004, 19) suggests that students can be helped to develop a sense of attachment to education when (i) they are helped to develop an intrinsic motivation to learn and (ii) when they want to learn for themselves and not because of external rewards and punishments. Furthermore, Brown et al. (2001, 22) argue that offering students tangible rewards in the form of prizes for learning can actually cause them to *lose* interest in the subject matter when the prizes are no longer given. Brown suggests that it may be far more effective for teachers to use their students' interests to help them to develop a personal attachment to the subject being taught.

According to Brown, when students feel sufficiently attached to both the matters that they are being taught about and the people teaching them, educa-tors and educational managers can transform schools into caring communities in which students are enabled to develop problem-solving and conflict-resolution skills that are important, transferable skills that they will be able to use in all areas of life. Research has shown that the benefits over time, even when the students have graduated from school, indicate 'the power of establishing resil-ience in young children as one of the most proactive strategies for meeting the adverse and fast-changing conditions of life' (Brown et al., 2001, 24).

However, many students' experience of teachers is often that although the latter may see themselves as both caring and available, many 'have little awareness of the invisible wall of ambivalence and emotional discomfort that often keeps students from approaching them for help' (Stanton-Salazar, 2001, 114). Clearly, putting 'caring' and 'attachment' centre stage in education may be pragmatic and can make a meaningful difference to the way in which children and young people are supported to develop resilience through educational experience. However, when there is a high level of turnover of staff or of changes in education, it is difficult for students to develop appropriate levels of attachment to teachers or the subjects that they are studying.

Children who are facing hazards to resilience at home can experience compensatory circumstances (see Chapter 6) at school that help them to become more resilient. Gilligan (2004, 95) demonstrated that the routines of education can be a factor that can 'preserve or restore a sense of order in the child's life and promote a sense of attachment or secure base'. Routine can include such simple issues as managing the classroom space in a predictable manner and having everyday routines around break time.

Schools also offer children and young people the opportunity to build constructive relationships with their peers, and this peer social support can be a very important factor in building resilience. Education environments provide children and young people with the chance to discover where their talents and interests lie and offer the opportunity to develop these. Constructive interactions and relationships related to their strengths and talents can contribute to the growth in self-esteem and self-confidence. Early intervention in schools often helps to create a more resilient adolescent by providing him or her with opportunities and guidance to develop and strengthen social skills (see Table 1.2) within strong peer and teacher relationships in the school context.

Vignette 8.3

Bobby is an English teenager with an Afro-Caribbean background. He loves fashion and hip-hop music, and likes to wear his hair in the latest styles. Bobby's parents both have good jobs – his mother is a paediatric nurse and his father is an accountant – and they live in a middle-class area in a provincial city. Bobby did well in primary school but started running into difficulties in secondary school. His previously good marks plummeted, and he started getting detention all the time. He also started becoming confrontational at home. At first Bobby's parents put it all down to normal teenage rebelliousness, but after they were summoned to a meeting with the headmaster, at which they learned that Bobby was 'on his last chance', they decided to get help and consulted a psychologist.

It turned out that Bobby's problems had started with one particular maths teacher. Miss Jones 'had it in for him', and it seemed that he could do nothing right. Miss Jones had accused Bobby of being a 'gang member' because of the way he wore his hair, which she said was a 'gang style'. Instead of telling anyone about his problems at school, Bobby had become resentful. It seemed that no matter how hard he tried with Miss Jones, he couldn't do anything right, so he just stopped trying. This confrontational behaviour spread to other classes, and soon he had a bad reputation among the other students and the teachers.

Although Bobby cannot be exonerated for his bad behaviour, Miss Jones's assumptions about him, clearly based on his ethnicity, certainly haven't helped. Bobby pledged to attend an anger-management course and to keep his marks up, and the headmaster arranged for Miss Jones to attend a course designed to help teachers overcome internal biases. The whole school was invited to take part in a discussion about bias, ethnicity, and mutual respect; it turned out that Bobby wasn't the only one who felt that he was being 'picked on' because of his background.

Discussion

Explore how the relationships and actions of Bobby himself, his teachers and his parents have all contributed to his progressively worsening performance at school.

Examine how stereotyping can limit the social and emotional development of adolescents, and from a practitioner perspective, explore the consequences (barriers and blockades) of perceived negative relationships and negative self-perceptions during adolescent years.

Expectations and aspirations

Facilitation that adopts an approach that includes promoting high expectations as a starting point is much more likely to help students to achieve good and better outcomes, even when they are dealing with hazards in various areas of life. An extremely important input to resilience, educational and otherwise, is found in the expectations that social care workers and other practitioners hold for and of children and young people. Overwhelmingly, when communities expect children and young people to be able to perform well, and communicate this expectation clearly, their youths respond by performing at a higher level. According to Benard (1991), low expectations for students are often self-fulfilling prophesies. Importantly, students also need to be encouraged to set high expectations for themselves, which can, in addition, help to make a huge difference in terms of their success.

In school environments in which teachers consistently have high expectations, students tend to respond by engaging more with the education process, thereby developing higher levels of academic resilience that can transfer to higher levels of resilience in other areas of life. These were classrooms 'in which teachers held high expectations, provided choice in selecting individualised and hands-on activities, and were governed by a minimum of behaviourally stated rules and had more positive motivational consequences than individual reprimands' (Hudley and Duran, 2013, 118).

Cross-cultural challenges

Society is composed of multiple 'networks' in the form of social classes and ethnic and racial groupings. According to Stanton-Salazar (2001, 104), these networks 'are socially organised and tacitly governed by a distinctive structure and a set of

Patrick was a 15-year-old boy who seemed to have been 'in trouble' all his life. From an early ADHD diagnosis to his chaotic home life in which his well-meaning parents lurched from one disaster to another, many factors had an input into his problems with emotion regulation, impulsive behaviour and tendency to lash out violently. Too many of his teachers wrote Patrick off as a 'lost cause', and he was all too ready to agree. It seemed more than likely that Patrick was destined to a life spent largely in trouble with the law.

Thankfully for Patrick, the guidance counsellor at his school felt that it was far too early to write Patrick off. At a meeting between the counsellor and Patrick and his parents, it was agreed that he could drop a few academic subjects at school (which he was failing anyway) as long as he promised to concentrate on something that he really liked doing. Patrick had a decent relationship with the woodworking teacher, Mr Chapman, who agreed that he would let Patrick sit in on other lessons and focus on woodwork as long as he kept his behaviour under control. Patrick said that he would do his best.

Patrick had a natural talent for woodwork and was already quite good at it. With the extra attention he was giving to the subject, he got even better, and the positive reinforcement he got from Mr Chapman made him feel much more positive about himself. Mr Chapman suggested that Patrick make a new bookcase for the school library, which desperately needed one. Patrick did as he asked, and for the first time in his school career was called up at assembly for a commendation. Much to the surprise of Patrick's GP and social worker, his ADHD symptoms started to recede, and he began to have better control over his unruly temper. Patrick's literacy and numeracy also improved to the point where he could start considering taking a few GCSEs. Patrick understood that if he was going to be a successful carpenter – like Mr Chapman – he would need to know how to read and write, and felt that he was up for the challenge.

Discussion

Attachment is an important aspect of Patrick's story. Mr Chapman is clearly a very important person in Patrick's life. Explore the strengths and limitations of this relationship.

From a practitioner perspective, explore strategies that could help Patrick to follow his new-found aspirations beyond Mr Chapman's class.

cultural rules permitting exchange, interdependence, and solidarity'. He suggests that in order for people to access resources and opportunities, it is important for them to experience these cultural networks as supportive and resource-full. School is often the arena in which many students encounter (and sometimes confront), for the first time, cultural networks different from their own.

Stawicki and Hirsch (2013) point out that

youth who balance the demands and expectations of academic success (defined by the majority culture) while, at the same time, maintaining pride in their own ethnic, cultural, and social group demonstrate the greatest gains in academic, social and emotional outcomes. (Stawicki and Hirsch, 2013, 22)

Considering this, it is suggested that teachers should become more fully aware of different cultural practices, including 'language, relationships and social support structures' (Stawicki and Hirsch, 2013, 23). Awareness of diverse cultural practices helps educators to help children and young people to marry higher academic aspirations with influences from diverse areas of their lives.

Stawicki and Hirsch (2013, 23) point out that 'schools that take into account the cultural context of the learning and develop assets in support of positive development have been shown to increase the academic success of their students'. They cite a study that demonstrates that such interventions have 'resulted in enhanced cognitive development and improved test scores in students and an increased confidence in teachers' (Stawicki and Hirsch, 2013, 23). Students are less likely to respond positively when they do not feel that their home culture is understood or appreciated by the people who are teaching them.

Schools can offer students the opportunity to access a range of cultural networks – without abandoning their own social and cultural backgrounds. In this context, students can learn how to access social and cultural capital that can sometimes be difficult to reach for those from less well-connected backgrounds or different cultural communities. This has been described as a secondary effect of education, rather than stemming directly from the didactic process: 'schooling not only mediates class systemic forces by directly structuring the 'pool of eligibility' available to people but also by structuring consciousness (e.g. cognitive skills, beliefs and attitudes) in ways that motivate (or inhibit) network-building behaviour' (Stanton-Salazar, 2001, 107).

In addition, according to Newmann (1998, 93), when schools are not well integrated into the community or when there is a perception of a significant cultural mismatch, situations arise whereby students' abilities to engage with their teachers and work well at school is compromised by a lack of support from across the school and home communities.

Educational resilience in disadvantaged communities

Commenting on her classic research with vulnerable children in Hawaii, Werner (1993, 509) reported that 'among the most frequently encountered positive role models in the lives of the children of Kauai, outside of the family circle, was a favorite teacher. For the resilient youngster a special teacher was not just an instructor for academic skills, but also a confidante and positive model for personal identification.'

More recently, a study carried out by Morales (2010) examined a group of 50 academically talented primarily African American students from socio-economically deprived urban backgrounds. The goal of the study was to determine which common factors, if any, underpinned the academic success of this cohort of students attending resource-poor inner-city schools. Morales (2010, 167) identified four key factors necessary for building educational resilience and personal achievement in disadvantaged communities:

Key factors for personal achievement:

- willingness/desire to move up in social class;
- caring school personnel;
- sense of obligation to one's race/ethnicity; and
- strong future orientation.

According to Morales (2010), 66 per cent of the sample reported a clear interplay between these four common protective factors. Willingness and desire to move away from a self-perception of being disadvantaged was characterised as the students' explicit longing to move up in social class and their acceptance of their perception of what it might mean to change social class (Morales, 2010, 167).

Many of the students in Morales' study identified a close relationship with a staff member at school as instrumental in their willingness to consider 'class jumping' and indicated that key qualities for teachers were 'encouraging', 'empathetic', 'supportive' and 'strict' (Morales, 2010, 168). Morales also described these teachers as mediating the different cultural milieus of the students' lives, particularly the manner of communicating at home and in the academic world: 'the mentors often served as effective cultural translators, literally and figuratively translating the academic language into words and ideas the students could understand readily' (Morales, 2010, 168). He suggests that the teachers facilitated the students in becoming essentially bicultural and negotiating this more complex world, as well as acting as academic role models for students who did not have many role models in this area:

> Essentially, they helped the students become competent in the academic culture, thus adding this cultural competency to the students' home or native culture. This demonstrated biculturalism has been identified as a particularly valuable protective factor for resilient urban students. (Morales, 2010, 172)

Additionally, below are seven protective factors which Morales suggests are key factors necessary for a social capital approach to building educational resilience in urban students (Morales, 2010, 169).

Social capital approaches for disadvantaged communities (Morales, 2010, 167):

- exposure to strong work ethic;
- capacity to persevere;
- establishing personal self-esteem;
- strong internal locus of control;
- attendance at out of zone school (i.e. a school not in the student's home (disadvantaged) area);
- supported by high parental expectations underpinned by appropriate assistance; and
- opportunity to model good interpersonal behaviour.

A key factor in this model is exposure to external sources of support from parents and other adult role models who not only demonstrated high work ethic but who were actively involved in the students' education, including helping them to access better schools outside their local neighbourhood. Morales also determined that in the case of students who had been formally identified as academically gifted and placed in schools with a focus on high achievement, this in itself had been an important factor in nurturing academic resilience in the students (Morales, 2010, 271).

Johnson (2008) argues that many of the factors at school that could be identified as contributing to students' resilience within disadvantaged areas were relatively simple, including consistency of contact between students and teachers and the ability of teachers to listen to what the students had to say – conversely, teachers who did not take the time to listen to students were identified by them as disrespectful (Johnson, 2008, 391–2). Students also identified as powerful the interventions carried out by teachers to help them out when something was going wrong, such as bullying or lack of resources (Johnson, 2008, 394).

On the basis of his study, Johnson identifies a relatively short list (Box 8.2) of pragmatic teaching practices that could make tangible differences in terms of building confidence and resilience in young people from disadvantaged backgrounds.

Box 8.2 Easy wins in professional practice that can engender educational resilience

Practitioners can:

- make themselves available and accessible to students;

- engage students by actively listening to their concerns and worries;

- take responsibility for actively teaching their students the basic reading, writing and numeracy skills needed for independent learning, even if their students have struggled in the past to master these skills;

- have empathy with, and understanding of, their students' 'tough' circumstances, yet provide them with positive strategies to deal with adversity;

- advocate for their students by mobilising existing support provisions that are available for 'at risk' students;

- actively use their power as adults and professionals to identify and oppose bullying and harassment at school;

- remember the 'human touches' that promote prosocial bonding between teachers and students. (Johnson, 2008, 395)

Howard and Johnson (2000) cite work carried out by Rutter, Maughan, Mortimore and Ouston (1979) in Britain that 'shows that another source of protective factors can be the school itself. Young people in discordant and disadvantaged homes are more likely to demonstrate resilient characteristics if they attend schools that have good academic records'. Schools that provide opportunities for children and adolescents to develop problem-solving skills and competence within a wider social setting also help students to raise their aspirations for and by themselves (Howard and Johnson, 2000).

Theron and Engelbrecht (2012) identify ways in which teachers can nurture their students' resilience, and consider these modes of behaviour as being either 'passive' or 'active'. They promote the importance of the role of teacher as advocate – especially for disadvantaged communities.

> Passive engagement includes listening, being available, communicating unconditional positive regard, or providing a safe, accepting space. More often, though, the measures taken by teachers to nurture youth resilience are active: among others, teachers overtly encourage youth to be future oriented, give advice, check on progress, affirm academic and personal competence, telephone and/or confront parents to mediate on the youth's behalf . . . (Theron and Engelbrecht, 2012, 275)

However, Brown et al. (2001) caution placing excessive emphasis on factors that are considered to identify children and young people as 'at risk' in an educational context which, he argues, can itself become an impediment to their developing educational resilience. As progressively more risk factors were identified:

> many educators came to view every child as being at risk for some kind of failure. Teachers began to describe their students' lack of success as related to specific 'risk' factors such as not doing homework, habitually coming late to school, having frequent absences, or having little or no parental contact with the school. (Brown et al., 2001, 6)

The problem with the risk model (see Chapter 1), Brown et al. contend (2001, 7), is that children from disadvantaged communities are often labelled as 'failures' before they have actually been demonstrated to be 'failing' in any area. This can create an atmosphere of low expectations that is itself damaging to their educational experience and also tends to wrongly place responsibility for students' academic success entirely on factors outside the educational environment.

Hudley and Duran (2013) note:

> Students in urban [disadvantaged] schools are often presumed to be poorly motivated. However, we begin with the reality that urban students who struggle academically are often seen as unmotivated or conduct-disordered, while struggling affluent, white children receive services (e.g. counseling, tutoring) to improve learning. (Hudley and Duran, 2013, 116)

Stevenson (2011) notes, however, that schools often 'stand accused of inflicting upon young working-class people a sense of inferiority for not having the appropriate cultural capital':

> [T]hose relatively rare working-class students who do progress in the education system are plagued by feelings of self-doubt, of being out of place and of not belonging. Indeed, many working-class people in higher education tend to choose 'local' colleges of higher education not simply because of economic reasons, but because they seem safer and there is less chance of being 'found out'. (Stevenson, 2011, 101)

Extra-curriculum and community engagement

Bacon et al. (2010, 50) point out that two-thirds of the schools in the UK now offer a range of activities after school hours to students, their families and the communities in which they live. Still, however, and especially in areas where there might be some disconnect between the educational levels and social norms of teaching staff and of the people living in the area, schools and the local community might seem to inhabit two vastly different worlds. Given that today's world has become less community focused, schools can play a very important role. 'Socially connected people,' claims Stevenson (2011, 96), 'who have few friends and connections to the community in which they live are less likely to do well at school and more likely to suffer from psychological problems and low self-esteem.'

Changing this perception can transform schools into enablers of resilience development in many areas of life beyond the academic. A school which is really integrated with its community is

> a school where partnerships between the school and community resources integrate academics, health and social services, youth and community development to improve the quality of academic learning, build stronger families, and develop healthier communities. (Lee et al., 2013, 178)

Gilligan (2004) points out:

> Schools may also serve as a vital local resource in run-down neighbourhoods drained of other facilities and may help to promote and sustain a sense of community in hard-pressed inner cities. (Gilligan, 2004, 96–7)

He goes on to stress that using the resources offered by schools to strengthen 'needy neighbourhoods' can be more effective than focusing 'piecemeal' on families, and that 'there is a very strong case that community development has to be a central part of any comprehensive child welfare and family support strategy in disadvantaged communities' (Gilligan, 2004, 97).

Lee et al. cite the example of a community school in Chicago in which standardised test scores have risen since the school went into partnership with a local community-based organisation. As well as providing students with academic support, the school

> has increased the social-emotional support given to students through mentorship and counseling services. Students identified as 'high risk' were able to make significant personal growth while they improved attendance, behaviour, and levels of self-control. Other students showed dramatic increases in self-esteem, building confidence and creating friendships through enrichment classes. (Lee et al., 2013, 179)

Schools that engage with families are more likely to be able to support students in achieving good educational outcomes, particularly when parents may have had a negative experience of education when they were young and are still anxious about dealing directly with teachers and school management. Conversely, it is perceived that schools that do not actively welcome parents and guardians can contribute to escalating problems when it comes to dealing with problematic behaviours (Lee et al., 2013, 184).

When the school is integrated in the area it serves, the social support that will result makes it easier for the school to 'enhance instructional capacity' and serve its students to the best of its capacity (Newmann, 1998, 94). Brown and Theobald comment that the students who are least happy at school are also the least likely to become involved in organised activities outside of school (Brown and Theobald, 1998, 133).

Schools and community organisations can also come together to increase student participation in extracurricular activities that can help them to build the sort of skills that will contribute to great levels of resilience. Table 8.1 identifies benefits of extracurricular and community engagement activities for children and young people.

Table 8.1 Benefits of extracurricular activities

Researchers	Benefits and gains
Mahoney and Cairns (1997)	Involvement in extracurricular activities is associated with a lower likelihood of dropping out of school.
Cooper et al. (1999)	Involvement in extracurricular activities is associated with better academic outcomes.
Elder et al. (2000)	Involvement in extracurricular activities is associated with lower rates of smoking and alcohol and marijuana consumption.
Mahoney (2000)	Involvement in extracurricular activities is associated with lower rates of delinquency.
Barber et al. (2001)	Involvement in extracurricular activities is associated with lower rates of substance abuse and better psychological adjustment.
Eccles et al. (2003)	Involvement in extracurricular activities helps children to acquire resilience by giving them the opportunity to develop and practise social and cognitive skills, to develop a sense of belonging and of contributing to the community, to develop a positive social network and to learn how to deal with challenge in their lives.
Peck et al. (2008)	Young people who are involved in extracurricular activities are much more likely to display educational resilience. Positive experiences of extracurricular activities give vulnerable young people the chance to experience developmentally appropriate experiences and transferable skills that help with, for example, persistence in education.
Gonzales et al. (2011)	Culture is not only a function of a shared cultural identity (i.e. ethnic group membership) but also is determined by factors such as family socioeconomic status (SES), immigration status and the types of communities in which individuals settle. These multiple influences combine to account for the unique cultural experiences of youth and families in and out of the classroom.

4

Researchers	Benefits and gains
Mason (2012)	The more positive activities young people engage in, the greater their resulting benefit.
Pring (2012)	There is a need for the wider society to flourish, not simply in terms of economic well-being but also in terms of teaching the skills to engage as a citizen.
King and Church (2015)	The choices young people make about the spaces and activities they encounter during their leisure time are considered as crucial for the development of healthy lifestyles in youth and can ultimately further contribute to their future development and guide healthy lifestyles and behaviour choices into adulthood.

Vignette 8.5

Chantelle is a 15-year-old girl attending school in Glasgow. She does her best to work hard, but lately she's been finding it more and more difficult. When she's asked why, she shrugs. 'All the teachers just assume we're only going to leave school early and have babies,' she says. 'So why bother? They won't take me seriously anyway.'

In fact, the area where Chantelle lives is one with high levels of poverty, drug and alcohol misuse, teen pregnancy and a host of other social problems – a fairly large percentage of the kids in Chantelle's school seem likely to drift into less-than-ideal futures. The problem is that this attitude is selling Chantelle and everyone else short. The students feel that nobody cares what happens to them – the teachers show that every day with their lacklustre attitude. Chantelle asked her form teacher for information about getting into university three weeks ago and was upset when Mr Hilton looked astonished. He never got her the information either. Neither of Chantelle's parents finished secondary school, so they don't know anything about it. If Mr Hilton can't help, who can?

'I might as well drop out now,' Chantelle says. 'Nobody around here ever finishes secondary school anyway.'

Discussion

With reference to Chapter 5, explore the cumulative impact of being part of a disadvantaged community on Chantelle's approach to her education and her future goals. Examine how education relationships might be able to support her to aspire and achieve beyond her current social environment.

From a multi-agency perspective, examine how the issues facing the broader community and those facing the school interact with one another, and consider the value of education/community relationships in this context.

Schools and sports groups that fill an integrated role in their communities can, Dyson (2012, 142) claims, be life changing for the students involved and for future generations. In the case of individual families and students, they can build confidence and set young people on a trajectory that will see them completing their education and making a successful entry to the adult world. Dyson also believes that such schools can have a wider 'cultural' influence on the broader community they serve, which he describes as follows:

> Students can begin to feel more positively about themselves, take on leadership roles and experience an enriched range of learning opportunities. The ethos of the school and nature of students' engagement with the school can, accordingly, begin to change. Similarly, there is evidence of actual and potential impacts at community level. Adults facing significant disadvantages can . . . be set on upward trajectories of growing confidence, qualifications and employability. More generally, it seems that the consistent availability of full service and extended provision will, over time, have wider effects across whole communities and will contribute towards making the areas served by schools safer, more cohesive, more attractive to employers and so richer in opportunities. (Dyson, 2012, 143)

Schools also have a role to play in encouraging physical activity by providing sports and recreational facilities to students – even outside of normal school hours (Birnbaum and Linver, 2013, 60).

> Education programs are most efficient in early childhood and pay by their greatest dividends, especially for children from low socio-economic backgrounds or otherwise difficult starting situations. Children who participate in high-quality programs show improved cognitive performance and more motivation in school. They live healthier lives, are more likely to participate in social networks, and have their own families. Furthermore, they have better opportunities for better occupations in life. Infancy researchers must not be surprised by these findings. A supportive environment in early years leads to better adjustment in the children's brain and behavior alike that in turn facilitates knowledge and skill acquisition. Because the prosperity of contemporary culture and economy depend heavily on knowledge, children who receive a good education in early years are more likely to be successful in later life and contribute to civic responsibility. (Pauen, 2012b, 3)

Conclusion

Although there are many things that families can do to promote resilience in growing children, and ways in which to support them in doing so, school remains a very important social as well as educational arena for the growing child and adolescent. Outside of family and immediate social circles, this is where children and adolescents spend most of their time. School and other structured activities offer very reliable opportunities to help students to develop and capitalise on important social and cognitive skills and grow the sort of resilience that will help them to move through life successfully. Clearly, schools need to help students acquire literacy, numeracy and other academic skills, and there is a growing expectation that schools will also facilitate broader personal development opportunities.

Given that schools are where many young people forge close friendships – friendships that will often last a lifetime – and that they are where many form positive relationships with adults outside their own families of origin for the first time, educators and policymakers recognise the important role of schools in helping children to acquire the social and interpersonal skills that are important for that broader promise of resilience as well as educational resilience. To achieve this means acquiring an ability to look beyond 'just' learning academic subjects, to acquire a holistic focus that considers the student as a member of his or her peer group and community, and the school as an integral aspect of the community.

CHAPTER 9

The Promise of Resilience

Introduction

People of every generation face challenges to resilience, and current generations are no exception. No matter how much society changes and evolves, there will always be difficulties to confront, and some people will suffer more setbacks than others. Many societies have already recognised the huge gains to be made from investing in programmes such as social welfare and socialised medicine, and great progress has been made. For the twenty-first century, fostering resilience, for today and for the future, is a specific challenge facing each generation, not least because each individual person has a unique personal narrative with its own opportunities and challenges.

The notion that the resilient adult is vitally important for communities and nations alike has emerged strongly over time, and this means placing social policies, goals and interventions that support resilience as central to policymaking and professional practice. Resilience research (see Chapter 2) has always had a pragmatic mission: to learn better ways of preventing psychopathology and promoting healthy development among children and young people. However, the promise of resilience is not merely about the individual skills and competence that can be gained through a process of personal development. The promise of resilience (Figure 9.1) is positive social and emotional development, culminating in a positive and personal transformation to the benefit of a stable family, community and society. The promise of resilience is held within the positive transformation of each child and young person (at the core of this diagram) through a maze of processes, opportunities and challenges.

The central tenant of this text is that the combined influences of the prevention models and resilience science have over the past two decades strengthened the case for the promise of resilience. Developing policies that promote and enhance resilience have become both politically and socially desirable, and two main drivers can be identified.

Firstly, changing social contexts, including considerable changes to family and community structures, pose significant challenges to support networks and patterns of family social and employment interactions. These changes are occurring at a time when the political appetite for the provision of state welfare across the Western world has been steadily declining. The cultivation of the resilient independent adult is a seen as a mechanism for sustaining this political trajectory without dramatically adding to the nation's social problems.

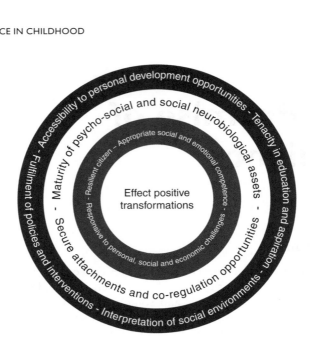

Figure 9.1 The promise of resilience

Secondly, state financial and economic realities suggest that global economic and employment pressures are set to continue well into the twenty-first century and can and will continue to pose numerous social and employment challenges to young people and families. The cultivation of the resilient, socially adaptable and flexible adult is seen as a mechanism for securing future economic security at the levels of the family, the community and the nation state.

By recognising the value of resilience to future lives, there has been a concerted drive by all Western economies to develop policies relating to child care, family support, education and more that are designed to help grow more resilient children, adolescents, families and communities.

The potential gains to society are perceived to be immense – and so of course are the huge gains that can be made in terms of the human rights of the individual people who will benefit from a more targeted investment in their futures. This chapter explores the significance of individual resilience in the twenty-first century and thus examines the important factors driving the perception that building the skills of resilience in childhood promises a strong foundation for future generations and future society and nationhood.

Resilience and policymaking

Frey and Walker argue that 'principles of risk, protection and resilience' can be used to develop social policy in two fundamental ways:

- 'One option requires policymakers to specifically focus efforts on youth who are most likely to experience academic failure and school-related problems. Such a strategy tends to concentrate program and policy efforts on youth

from disadvantaged backgrounds, since socioeconomic status is a key risk factor for social and educational failure.
- 'A second approach uses knowledge of risk, protection and resilience to design promotive social and educational policies that are beneficial for all children irregardless [sic] of risk exposure.' (Frey and Walker, 2006, 83–4)

Figure 1.1 identifies policymaking as one of the key contributory factors is setting and securing the framework of a common understanding of resilience as an emerging and evolving construct (explored in Chapter 1). Much of the research discussed in Chapter 2, which spans a number of decades, has provided the impetus and influence for promoting and recognising the values and benefits to be widely gained from well-adjusted, resilient citizens. Table 9.1 provides an outline of a range of social policies by country that have been used to contribute to developing resilience in individuals, families and communities.

However, despite the fact that state policies can and do have enormous implications for the resilience of individuals and communities, there is often little joined-up thinking around the areas of resilience and social policy. Tully (2002) proposes that this might be because

> resilience has traditionally dealt with human behavior theory related to individuals and their social settings, whereas social policy is often perceived as something that is done, mostly by administrative law-makers, to remedy specifically identified social problems. (Tully, 2002, 321)

Tully proposes that the concept of resliience be revisited in light of our accepted vocabulary around social policy. She suggests:

> In an attempt to link the more animate concept of resilience with the more inanimate construct of social policy, the term resilience means those processes of social policy development and implementation that promote and empower a person affected by that policy (both at the micro- and macro-level). (Tully, 2002, 323)

Tully (2002, 323) believes that every social policy should be considered in terms of whether it enhances or inhibits resilience and in the knowledge that social policies evolve and adapt over time, as society itself goes through changes and as people's requirements change. She adds (2002, 329) that 'whether or not the policy mandate lives up to the requirement of alleviating social ills, there is always a relationship between resilience, human behaviour and social policy'.

Jenson and Fraser (2006, 269–75) propose a number of steps that can be used to create policies that keep resilience centre stage:

- Evaluate risk and protective factors.
- Assign policy responsibility in ways that promote service integration across systems of care.
- Use evidence to create public policy responses.
- Determine the course of specific individual and social interventions.
- Implement, monitor and evaluate policies and interventions.

Table 9.1 Policy drivers by country

Country	Policy priorities	Research
UK	Reducing poverty and increasing employment	Himmelweit and Sigala (2004). Despite successive governments' work in this area, mothers' choices appear to be limited by a range of internal and external factors. Policies can be restrained by various factors, including issues of personal identity. However, positive feedback can be a way to enhance the effects of steps taken, by modifying attitudes and behaviours and by creating policies that increase choice, reduce the cost of being a mother and help to meet long-term goals in this area.
	Reducing obesity and related health problems	Summerbell et al. (2012). In the UK, as elsewhere, obesity and related health problems are a growing challenge for children and families, with huge fiscal repercussions to the state. Various institution-based interventions at school and in early years settings aim to address this issue by encouraging physical activity and healthy eating and creating environments that facilitate the same.
	Fostering positive parenting among low-income families	McDonald et al. (2012). In the UK (and also in the US, Germany and Holland) the FAST (Families and Schools Together) programme provides culturally sensitive parenting interventions to low-income families. The research focuses on the strategies deployed and the associated outcomes. The findings suggest that encouraging parental involvement, fostering positive emotions, increasing social capital and reinforcing attendance are all useful.
USA	Reforming welfare to get more low-income people back to work and out of poverty	Lee et al. (2004). Starting from the late 1990s, welfare reforms were aimed at reducing dependency on welfare and reducing poverty, with positive repercussions for vulnerable young families. However, research carried out in 2004 suggested that sanctions associated with the changes were inversely associated with an increase in earnings and formal employment, and positively associated with informal work and difficulties paying rent.
	Enhancing child nutrition by targeting children from low-income families	Hurley et al. (2008). Low-income mothers partake in a supplemental nutrition programme designed to ensure that they and their children receive adequate nutrition. This research focused on rates and duration of breastfeeding among mothers in this demographic, so as to ascertain how successful the official policy of increasing breastfeeding has been.
	The No Child Left Behind programme	Dee and Jacob (2011). The No Child Left Behind Act of Congress, which was passed in 2011, focuses on school accountability and student assessments, with the intention that children who are educationally vulnerable be identified and helped. The methods and outcomes of the programme have been controversial. Work carried out by Dee and Jacob suggests that the approach resulted in tangible improvements in mathematical ability, but not in reading ability.

Australia	Housing infrastructure projects aimed at improving the health of indigenous Australians	Baillie et al. (2012). Official policy in Australia has been to tackle health and reduce childhood illness in indigenous Australians by improving the poor quality of their housing. However, the authors' research indicates that there has been no obvious improvement in these areas despite clear improvements in matters relating to hygiene. Policies targeting the quality of housing need to be accompanied by broad-based community interventions in a range of areas to see the desired results.
	Reducing bullying across Australian schools	Cross et al. (2011). Australia developed a national, integrated policy to prevent bullying and violence in schools in 2003, becoming one of the first countries to do so. The programme is known as the National Safe Schools Framework (NSSF). However, at the time of writing, practical issues such as school implementation of the programme and a lack of teacher training appear to be hampering the programme's effectiveness in terms of helping students at risk of suffering as a result from these behaviours, or at risk of engaging in them.
	National Framework for Protecting Australia's Children 2009–2020	Winkworth and White (2010). Resulting from the adoption of the policy and set of procedures laid out in this Framework, Australia has invested heavily in child protection and support. However, different areas of service provision fail to work together cooperatively and seamlessly, and some children fall through the gaps. There is a great need for more work across sectors and higher levels of cooperation, for example between child support systems and state child protection.
Canada	Family policies in Quebec which give great emphasis to the role of civil law	Beaujot et al. (2013). Quebec has a markedly different approach to family law to the rest of Canada. With respect to families, its civil law has provided alternative forms of marriage for many years, resulting in different family structures and attitudes to child rearing, and leading to a child care policy that focuses on improving child welfare.
	Reducing problem behaviours	Augimeri et al. (2011). In 1985, Canada passed a law making children under 12 not criminally liable. In parallel, it developed the Stop Now and Plan (SNAP) programme. The programme has been demonstrated over the years to be effective in reducing problem behaviours among young people at risk for becoming involved in criminal activities.
	Working towards full engagement of aboriginal youth with the education system	Nguyen (2011). For complex historical and cultural reasons, aboriginal youth in Canada are more at risk of dropping out of school and are less likely to attend university, among other things. The government-funded Aboriginal Head Start programme is helping young Aboriginals to engage with the education system. It is most effective when it is culturally sensitive.

Country	Policy priorities	Research
Ireland	Improving rates of breast-feeding	Mulcahy et al. (2012). Breastfeeding has been proven to enhance children's health, but Ireland has a particularly low rate. Official policy is to counteract this with support, including from Public Health Nurses, who visit new mothers and provide guidance and support. However, although such nurses are well educated on breast-feeding, resources are not always used as fully as they might be.
	Including children with special educational needs in the mainstream educational system	Meegan and MacPhail (2006). Ireland adopted a policy of inclusive education for children with special educational needs relatively late, in the early 1990s. Various official bodies have supported the transition to a more inclusive form of education, but the education system still does not provide an optimal service in terms of supporting children with an educational vulnerability.
	Providing equity of care to children who have been separated from their families	Mullally (2011). Ireland has a long history of failing to care adequately for children who have been separated from their families. In 2009, the state committed to providing equitably for children in these circumstances, but gaps and inconsistencies remain.
Denmark, Finland and Norway	Providing vulnerable children with care in the home	Pösö et al. (2014). Government policy is to provide children in need with services, including protection services, in the home as far as is possible. In practice, quite high numbers of children in the child protection system are cared for away from home, and overall the child protection system is not resulting in very good outcomes, partly because official policy stresses the universal nature of care and doesn't look closely enough at the specific needs of the individual. A more child-centred approach is needed.
Sweden	Redesigning family law to protect children in vulnerable situations re custody, domestic violence, etc.	Eriksson (2010). From 2006, Swedish family law changed to adopt a more safety-focused approach for dealing with children at risk in family law, particular with respect to domestic violence; children who witness domestic violence are now considered victims rather than witnesses, with far-reaching implications.
	Mandatory reporting suspicions of child maltreatment	Cocozza et al. (2007). Despite the fact that reporting is mandatory for anyone who suspects that a child is being mistreated, some children fall through the cracks of the system. In a given area, 1 per cent of all the children were reported, but 22 per cent of those reports were never investigated.

Bacon et al. (2010, 41) identify a number of areas where, they claim, government policy has been shown to have considerable effect:

- In health, a greater well-being focus would shift the emphasis to positive health and meeting the needs of people with lower-level mental health issues, a group who often make considerable demands on primary health care services.
- In children's services, a well-being focus would tend towards a bigger emphasis on promoting self-expression and identity, and services that underpin self-esteem and resilience in adulthood.
- In community empowerment, a well-being focus would imply spending more on creating social networks and people's sense of belonging and less on formalised consultation processes.
- In arts and culture, well-being could be boosted by spending more on participation and less on enabling people to spectate big events.

In terms of social policy, those who are implementing it need to understand the sort of behaviours that the policy will elicit and what the implications will be for the resilience of the people in question, not just in the short term, but throughout the course of their lives. However, given that public funds are finite, we need to know how they can be best used to make a real and lasting difference.

Vignette 9.1

Sally is a teenage mother living in Manchester. The father of her child is in prison, and in any case he's not very interested in their baby, so Sally is on her own. Her parents have told her they don't want anything to do with her and her son, Thomas. Fortunately for Sally, the UK has various social welfare policies that help. She is entitled to a single mother's allowance, and when Thomas is a little older, there's a place for him in a heavily subsidised crèche, where he will get his first exposure to education. Sally lives in social housing that is far from luxurious, but still quite acceptable – she has a small, clean, safe apartment in a housing complex. Because she is not quite 18, Sally is still a minor, so she receives regular visits from a social worker and the public health nurse to give her advice on how to take care of Thomas.

Although Sally is being helped in many ways by a social welfare policy designed to support people in her situation, both she and Thomas still face multiple hazards to resilience. Life is often lonely, and Sally is very young to live alone. She has a small budget to work on and little experience of managing money. She dropped out of school to have Thomas and doesn't see a way to finish her education without neglecting her child.

Although there are many supports for Sally, services are struggling to integrate all of those supports into a system that could help Sally to fend off challenges to resilience while also growing her strengths.

Discussion

If the promise of resilience is to be reflected in Sally's life experience, from a multi-agency perspective, explore the balance of factors (inhibitors, challenges and opportunities) that are at play in this case study, and examine use of a range of strategies (see Chapters 6 and 8) that could help to improve that balance.

Behaviours on the part of one generation can have profound consequences for the levels of resilience experienced by the next and subsequent generations. Tully (2002, 331) says that policymakers

> need to be aware both of policies that encourage positive behaviours and, in turn, resilience as well as those policy initiatives that may inhibit resilience. For example, welfare policies that limit benefits without providing adequate job training may hinder a single mother's ability to be resilient, whereas policies that provide early prenatal intervention for teens may enhance an adolescent's ability to adapt.

Welfare policies

In the modern period, many countries around the world (certainly the majority of developed countries) have developed welfare programmes that are designed to support citizens, particularly during periods of their lives when they are experiencing difficulty (illness, unemployment, old age). The first state-sponsored social security scheme was introduced in 1889 by Otto von Bismarck and provided for people after retirement at the age of 65. However, it is worth noting that average life expectancy at the time was just 45 (Gilbert, 2013, 83)!

Welfare programmes have made very substantial contributions to citizens' welfare and can be said to have had many positive benefits in terms of enhancing resilience among vulnerable populations. However, there are also a number of potential hazards to resilience, such as when so-called 'welfare traps' fail to provide an effective balance between welfare receipts and opportunities for independence.

> The idea that generous welfare benefits might inhibit one's inclination to work was once viewed as heresy by welfare state advocates – in the United States they charged it was 'blaming the victim'. Yet after years of rising welfare and disability rolls, by the late 1990s the same idea, that welfare benefits produce 'poverty traps' or 'enforced dependency' . . . was widely accepted in OECD countries. (Gilbert, 2013, 84)

According to Gilbert (2013, 85), the shifts that need to take place are ones that redefine 'the role of the state from providing benefits that compensate for risks to one that enables beneficiaries to actively exercise responsibility in coping with risks'. Given that work has many benefits for those who engage in it and in order for a welfare system to be seen as promoting resilience, it is generally accepted that 'welfare policies heretofore providing 'passive' income supports to unemployed people should be replaced by measures designed to promote employment' (Gilbert, 2013, 86).

[T]here has been a normative swing from an emphasis on welfare provisions being given as the social rights of citizenship to the social responsibilities of recipients to behave well, contribute to society . . . and become independent as quickly as possible. (Gilbert, 2013, 88)

Gilbert refers to the changes that take place as representing the shift from a 'welfare' to an 'enabling' state (Gilbert, 2013, 90). Increasingly, the right to obtain welfare is seen by both populations in general and governments as the right to work and receive a living wage in exchange. He sums up these changes as follows:

[A] new contract is being forged about the right to welfare benefits, which seeks to change the balance between entitlements and conditionality. Politically, this contract is driven by two agendas. The responsibility agenda emphasises the obligation to work and emphasises the assurance of work training, employment opportunities, and a living wage. (Gilbert, 2013, 93)

Linking the resilient and independent adult with decreasing levels of welfare has been a common approach across new global economic and financial priorities. Green (1998) addresses some of the 'hazards' to resilience as a dysfunctional welfare system, saying:

[I]f too many people look to the government for the means of life, then this dependency has harmful effects which accumulate over time. The initial harm results from people organising their affairs so that they qualify for benefit. Having crossed the boundary between independent self-support and reliance on the work of others, individuals are inclined to neglect friendships or relationships with people who could provide a helping hand in a spirit of mutual respect. Because their self-respect diminishes, they often become more shameless in their determination to live at the expense of others. They also fail to join organisations like churches or voluntary associations, where they would meet people who would gladly provide temporary, restorative help. As a further consequence, they acquire fewer skills of co-operating with others, and face fewer challenges. In turn, they have fewer opportunities to strengthen their characters by overcoming adversity. (Green, 1998, vii)

Economic and labour policies

The resilient citizen is an enormously important resource at the heart of current social and economic policy. Crucially, for policymakers, the evidence indicates that resilience and well-being can impact positively on both employment and the economy (issues that are typically central to government decision-making). Resilience and well-being indicate substantial and long-term contribution of important skills and competences that include the 'the ability to work as a team, accept criticism, commitment, or management, leadership and oral communication skills' (Bacon et al., 2010, 50).

People who are resilient tend to be better workers and employees. For example, they display enhanced teamwork and communication skills (Bacon et al., 2010, 54). Thus, possessing the qualities of resilience is a very important contributor towards finding and keeping work. Moreover, research shows that employment is beneficial to workers in a range of ways that go far beyond the financial. Bacon et al. (2010) cite a report from the UK's Department of Work and Pensions that concluded that

> work was, overall, good for both physical and mental health and wellbeing. The beneficial effects of work were shown to outweigh the potential harmful effects of long-term worklessness or prolonged sickness absence. Work has a wider function in people's lives, providing us not only income but also with extra meaning. (Bacon et al., 2010, 55)

By investing in resilience, the state can ensure that people will be more resourceful, more entrepreneurial, more independent and better able to engage with their communities and society in a healthy, productive way (Table 9.2).

Table 9.2 Economic value of the resilient citizen

Researchers	Key factor
Frey and Stutzer (2002)	Resilient people are happier, and happier people work better. Happier people do better at work, find work more easily and are more likely to do well at work. They will be net contributors to their economy.
Pecora (2002)	Resilient families are more likely to have healthy relationships, and children are less likely to suffer abuse or neglect. Foster care, institutional care, etc., all have profound ramifications for the individual affected and carry substantial costs to the state in both the short and the long term.
Campanella (2006)	Communities formed of resilient citizens rebound from difficult situations more quickly and at lower cost. The resilience of an urban area springs from the levels of resilience and resourcefulness displayed by its citizens. 'Social fabric' and networks of community, with strong citizen involvement, lead to healthy communities that can withstand challenges.
Rychen et al. (2006)	Today's citizens are expected to be flexible, adaptable and mobile. Nowadays, adults are expected to fill many different roles and deal with multiple challenges in a very complex social and economic situation, including possessing the ability to act alone, to deal with groups of very diverse people and to use a range of tools competently. These abilities are crucial to their successful functioning as individuals and to the well-being of the global economy as a whole.
Moretti and Obsuth (2009)	Resilient people are less likely to become involved in crime. The economic costs of crime are substantial in any society, and they are getting higher. More resilient people result in far lower economic costs in any given society.

Bacon et al. (2010)	Resilient people are better at finding and keeping work. A resilient workforce is a more productive one, as workers are happier, healthier and more engaged with what they are doing. They are less likely to lose jobs frequently and to need support in the form of unemployment and sickness benefits.
Skodol (2010)	Resilient people are better at planning for the future and better at forming good working relationships with others. Individuals who can plan for the future, even when that means putting up with risk or uncertainty or other issues 'today', are better placed to perform well in the workplace and in their social and familial contexts, all of which provides economic benefits to the state.
Aldrich and Meyers (2015)	The first and most common form of social networking available to individuals is bonding social capital. Family ties are central to resilience because kin commonly serve as the first providers of assistance, and higher levels of bonding social capital can translate into greater levels of trust and more widely shared norms among communities. Feelings of mutual trust and dependence in young people can increase awareness of volunteer opportunities and community responsibilities, supporting participation and inclusion.
Hardy (2015)	Resilient communities are less likely to harbour terrorism. Terrorism bears a huge economic as well as social cost, with greater need for policing, for dealing with the aftermath of terrorist activities, insurance, etc.

Resilient people are future oriented, which makes it easier for them to plan ahead, to deal with issues in the short term, and to make sacrifices today that will result in greater gains tomorrow.

> They are motivated to achieve and to be successful in diverse aspects of life. They are goal-directed, industrious and productive. They show determination and persistence in the pursuit of personal goals, while maintaining a sense of balance in their lives and the ability to sustain effort over time. Although generally optimistic about the outcomes of their efforts, they are also flexible in their ability to adapt to challenges, limitations, and changing life circumstances, and can accept setbacks with equanimity. (Skodol, 2010, 115)

However, in addition, aggression, violence and antisocial behaviour in adolescents are pressing concerns in many developed countries. The social and economic costs of violence and antisocial behaviour are substantial and rising. A recent report estimated that the average cost for a career criminal beginning as a juvenile and continuing through adulthood was approximately $2.0 million US dollars (Moretti and Obsuth, 2009, 1347).

There is a persistent assumption that social problems, especially those relating to children and young people, can be eased with greater public financial investment. Although this can be true, it is only part of the story. Programmes that invest wisely in policies that enhance resilience and well-being can make an enormous difference. However, from 2008 onwards the now well-established global recession has meant reduced consumption, investment, employment, production of goods and services, and business profits, along with inflation in most economies. According to Planas et al:

> This situation has ultimately had a significant effect on young people and how youth policies are dealt with and considered. In most cases we can say that the situation has led to a lack of prominence being awarded these policies within social policy as a whole because, while young people have become one of the groups to suffer the effects of the current situation most intensely, public youth policies have been reduced and resources and programmes cut. Estimates by the International Institute for Labour Studies (IILS, 2012) suggest that youth unemployment stood at 12.6% in 2012 and will reach 12.9% by 2017. Today, in developed economies, 35% of young people have not worked for at least six months, and the short-term prospects are no more positive. (Planas et al., 2013, 22)

At a time when resources are scarce, especially for local governments, it may therefore be necessary to prioritise investment of efforts and resources dedicated to youth policy and intervention practice. The alternative is to blur youth policies and distort their orientation, thus setting future generations back decades. This would be at the risk of huge political and social cost given the hopeless outlook for many young people as a consequence of this prolonged economic crisis. Budget constraints should not be an excuse for ignoring an entire generation.

Vignette 9.2

Joshua's home life could hardly have been worse; his mother was a habitual meth user, and his father, a violent criminal, had been shot dead over a drug debt. Joshua was always neglected and frequently abused. Eventually he was taken into public care – Joshua was 10. He was illiterate, displayed seriously oppositional behaviour and wet his bed. By the time he was 14, he had drifted into petty crime like vandalism and shoplifting. The care worker in the home said that he had moments of kindness with the younger children, but most of the time he was just a pain in the neck.

Then Joshua got a new care worker, Tim, who was determined not to take him at face value. He was enormously patient with Joshua and ensured that the teenager got the help he needed at school to learn how to read and write. Because it was often hard for Joshua to concentrate on his homework, he was allowed to do it in Tim's office, where it was quiet. Sometimes Joshua went to sit in the kitchen in the evenings because he said that the other kids were 'doing his head in'. That was where he found out that he was really interested in cooking. Eileen, the home's cook, started off teaching him how to make biscuits and cakes, and it turned out that he had quite a flair for it. Joshua had found something he liked to do. As a result, he became happier and more confident. His schoolwork improved a lot and so did his difficult behaviour.

Then Joshua received some news: he was moving to a different home. Tim tried to get the decision reversed, but to no avail. Joshua was so angry he went into the kitchen and smashed all the windows. He lashed out at Eileen and ended up breaking her arm. Instead of going to another home, he was moved into a juvenile detention centre.

Discussion

The promise of resilience can be illusive for many teenagers and in particular for looked-after children. From a multi-agency perspective, explore how a combined understanding of how (i) stability, (ii) attachment, (iii) self-confidence and (iv) adolescent neurobiological development can be used to develop strategies to help Joshua to develop the social and emotional skills as well as the literacy skills that would help him into positive employment.

Education policies

Education policy has been used across the Western world to promote effective investment in children and young people (see Chapters 7 and 8). The notion that students can learn about citizenship in a formal educational environment is not a new one. In fact, Plato wrote:

> By maintaining a sound system of education you produce citizens of good character, and citizens of sound character, with the advantage of a good education, produce in turn children better than themselves. (cited in Greer, 2012, 106)

Dewey proposed schools as an appropriate environment for developing citizenship (Hansen et al., 2013, 141), and school programmes in many countries do include a 'civics' class which is supposed to introduce students to the adult world of engaging with government, policy and community.

Rowe (2012, 56) points out that when citizenship studies were first introduced to schools, the emphasis tended to be on the taught aspect of the subject, 'ignoring the potential of the school community to offer practical experience of citizenship activities, whilst others argued that the ethos, values and structures of the school were the true site of citizenship learning, neglecting the crucial importance of the taught curriculum and viewing the introduction of a new subject as an unwelcome burden'. A third group of schools, however, 'recognised that citizenship has both a cognitive and an experiential component . . . and that these elements should all be seen as part of a coherent citizenship package or offer'.

Peacock stresses:

> An important aspect of citizenship education is learning to make informed choices. If school presents as a place where compliance and uniformity is the dominant culture, our children, parents and staff are given little room to exercise choice. (Peacock, 2012, 127)

If schools teach citizenship as one subject among many, without actually living the principles that they espouse, the message that students receive is a contradictory one. Instead, by ensuring that schools consistently operate in a manner that is true to the values promoted by citizenship, students are in a position to learn in a much more effective way (Rowe, 2012, 57). They can learn by observing citizenship skills, such as democracy, respect and dialogue, in practice, rather than simply reading about them in a book or listening to a lecture on the topic.

In a major study carried out in secondary schools in England, the authors found that though many schools are increasingly becoming involved in citizenship programmes for students, progress is not uniform (Keating et al., 2009, ii). There are many challenges to developing effective citizenship programmes in today's school. One is the rapid pace of social and political change. Whereas citizenship is commonly associated with the national state, and many didactic programmes around citizenship are predicated on this model, the increasing fluidity of economic and other systems means that we are much more global citizens than previously. This means that any attempt to teach the information and skills necessary to proactive citizenship now encompasses a wide range of issues, including 'religion, gender, antiracism, sustainable development and history; characterisations and forms – including community, multicultural, peace, human rights and global education; and, finally, a section on pedagogy – including curriculum, school and community settings and active citizenship' (Kerr, 2012, 18).

Today, many countries and especially urban areas have become intensely multicultural, a situation that embodies both opportunities and challenges, some of which have been mentioned above. The school environment offers unparalleled opportunities both to teach about and to model citizenship skills that are crucial to succeeding in a globalised, multicultural world (Malik, 2012, 68). Schools provide

> a real opportunity to address local and societal cohesion challenges in a meaningful way through learning about difference within the school and its local community. In each community, the school can become (and indeed in many areas already is) the heart, providing a safe place for children, families and others to interact and break down prejudices, and teach everyone, not just the pupils, the confidence to become good neighbours and active citizens. (Malik, 2012, 70)

The way in which educators behave with respect to citizenship matters as much as what they say. Research has shown that when students experienced classes as open, as places where controversial topics could be safely discussed, they 'reported higher levels of political interest, political efficacy, political trust and a sense of civic duty than did comparable samples who experienced a less open climate' (Hahn, 2012, 53).

Research carried out in the United States concluded that students whose backgrounds pose a hazard to resilience – minority ethnic students from low-income backgrounds – found such a teaching environment particularly helpful in terms of developing an interest in political matters, becoming committed to civic participation and developing the expectation that they would take part in the voting process as adults (Hahn, 2012, 53).

Positive engagement with citizenship is especially important in the case of children and adolescents from more deprived areas, as they are likely to be engaged in fewer 'positive' activities in their communities. One study

> found that around three-quarters of young people participated in some form of positive activity but far fewer young people from lower-income families or from rural areas participated in these activities. (Mason, 2012, 81)

Although there is certainly a place for studying citizenship during a dedicated session set aside for the topic, schools and educators can look at how to integrate elements that will foster civic participation and skills among their students in many other topics too. Subjects such as history have tended to be taught from ethnocentric perspectives that do not lend themselves to the sort of constructive questioning and debate that helps to form resilient citizens (Verma, 2012, 79).

Growing the resilient citizen

Citizens are officially recognised as 'belonging', and they have the right to participate in social and legal processes present in the particular place where they live. There are a number of definitions, including those identified in Box 9.1.

Box 9.1 Definitions of citizenship

1. Citizenship is the state of being a member of a particular country and having rights because of it; the state of living in a particular area or town and behaving in the manner that is expected (Cambridge Dictionaries Online).

2. Citizenship is a social contract with both rights and responsibilities that include the right to vote and participate in the community, and obligations to do certain things (Leary, 2000).

3. Citizenship stems from the extent to which an individual can control his or her own destiny within his or her community in terms of being in a position to influence its government (Taylor et al., 1990).

4. Active citizenship is the idea that members of communities or countries have particular roles and responsibilities, even if they are not in government. For example, volunteering in one's community is often associated with being an active citizen.

Lockyer points out that the concept of 'citizen' is one that has evolved considerably over the years, and that increasingly children are also seen as

> 'citizens now', rather than potential citizens whose active citizenship is to be delayed until they can exercise the same rights as adults. (Lockyer, 2012, 178)

The notion of children as citizens is not entirely a new one. Inspired by the Enlightenment, George Washington was keenly aware of the role of children as 'citizens in waiting' and felt strongly about the importance of educating them in the science of government (Cook and Klay, 2014, 45). Both he and Benjamin Franklin believed that educating young people was essential in order for them to become effective citizens of their nation, and for overall economic prosperity (Cook and Klay, 2014, 46). Washington's views on education are summed up in his words: 'The best means of forming a healthy, virtuous, and happy people, will be found in the right education of youth' (Cook and Klay, 2014, 48).

Over the last decade, most major countries in the world have signed up to the United Nations Convention on the Rights of the Child, prompting much thought on the extent to which children and young people can be actively involved in their communities and nations and in determining their own future. It has been argued that the best way to prepare children to become citizens is through their direct participation in the structures that form their society, such as democracy (Hart, 1997, 3).

In most countries today, children's relationship with the notion of citizenship is ambiguous: they are granted some rights and opportunities to participate, but they are denied others. However, if citizenship is envisioned as a set of behaviours rather than rights and responsibilities, children can be understood as 'citizens now' as well as 'citizens in the making' (Larkins, 2014, 7). One of the problems with viewing children as future citizens is that 'focusing on the future status and well-being of the young too often leads to their current entitlements, needs and qualities being overlooked' (Lockyer, 2012, 178).

Although, in varying forms, training in citizenship, as it exists in the education systems of diverse countries and cultures, represents a tacit understanding of the child as a citizen-in-progress, the role of the child as a citizen now as well as a citizen in the future is increasingly accepted, and scholars and educators seek new ways in which to engage children with the state and process of citizenship. For example, researchers in Iran explored ways of using multimedia software as a way of increasing eight-year-old children's awareness of their own role as citizens in their home country (Ghapanchi and Shahtalebi, 2014, 342–8).

Malik (2012, 71) points out that in many cases today's school students will live and work in a very different world to that of their parents'. Acquiring the social and other skills necessary to being a productive, positively engaged citizen in a world full of 'difference' is more important than ever.

Cultural citizenship

Importantly, citizenship is not just about our formal rights and duties, or how children and adolescents see themselves and their families in relation to the state. It is also about *cultural* citizenship, which implies the 'ability in a shared cosmopolitan context to participate in the polity while being respected and not reduced to an Other' (Stevenson, 2011, 19).

Cultural citizenship, asserts Stevenson (2011),

> is the struggle for a democratic society that enables a diversity of citizens to lead relatively meaningful lives, that respects the formation of complex hybrid identities, offers them the protection of the state and grants them a critical education which seeks to explore the possibility of living in a future that is free from domination and oppression. To be a cultural citizen means to engage in deliberative argument about

what it is ethical to become, and to consider how we might live virtuous and just lives in specific cultural locations and contexts. (Stevenson, 2011, 34)

Hansen et al. (2013, 140) consider the process of civic engagement to consist of three concepts, which they define as: 'civil literacy', referring to a knowledge and understanding of politics and government structure and functions; 'civic competence', referring to skills such as social and leadership skills that can be used in applying civic literacy; and 'civic development', referring to the process by which young people 'learn and become engaged citizens'.

In this era of extensive migration and global employment, resilient children and adolescents are much better equipped to be useful, productive, participatory citizens in challenging communities and cosmopolitan countries. As Skodol (2010, 113–14) says, 'Resilient personalities are characterised by traits that reflect a strong, well-differentiated and integrated sense of self and traits that promote strong, reciprocal interpersonal relationships with others.' Diverse relationships promote self-transformations and a reliance on one's ability to contribute positively and constructively. These abilities form the bedrock of a productive existence as a citizen in changing cultural contexts.

Sustaining resilient communities

Communities have their own characteristics that are formed by the people who live in them, and counterinfluence their inhabitants. Like the family, the community is a dynamic body. Community norms and standards can foster or inhibit the development of resilience; communities themselves can also be described as resilient.

Hall and Zautra (2010) define a resilient community as

one in which all organisations, large and small, formal and informal, work together successfully to enhance the quality of life of all its members . . . From [a] resilience perspective, *health* refers not simply to attending to levels of illness, pain and psychological disturbance but also to taking a social account of balance of opportunities for enrichment in work, family and civic life, the qualities that sustain well-being for individuals and build vibrant communities that can sustain healthy lifestyles for generations. (Hall and Zautra, 2010, 352)

Hall and Zautra also assert:

A resilient community is one that examines the long-term changes within the society, warding off ill outcomes before they arrive and enhancing quality of life over that of previous generations. (Hall and Zautra, 2010, 354)

Sanchez-Jankowski writes:

Neighborhood institutions . . . are social organizations composed of people whose patterns of local morals and values are acted out in a consistent and ordered fashion within their local social arena and have over time evolved into a set of norms governing the interactive behaviour of the neighbourhood's residents. All neighbourhood institutions embody, teach and differentially reinforce local value orientations and social identities, their concomitant activity scripts, and social engagement etiquette. (Sanchez-Jankowski, 2008, 18)

The growing complexity of the societies in which most of us live, and the tendency towards ever-increasing globalisation, means that, it has become imperative now, more than before, for democratic countries to improve the capacity of citizens to engage intelligently in political life, because of changes in scale due to increased internationalism, the growth in the complexity of public affairs, and the increase in the amount of information available through a range of different media of communication (American Political Science Association (2012) Democratic Imperatives: Innovations in Rights, Participation and Economic Citizenship. American Political Science Association. Washington DC).

Researchers have proposed that an 'open classroom' environment 'encourages discussion of controversial or contemporary issues, leading to increased interest or engagement,' that 'open classroom environments were significantly related to civic knowledge, appreciation of conflict, and voting expectations (Hansen et al., 2013, 142)'.

There is growing concern that a large number of the electorate in countries such as the UK have little engagement with their society and community on a civic level. Many are not members of any local or voluntary organisations. They are not politically involved, and they do not engage a great deal with the public institutions in their area.

Active citizenship however, includes active participation in one's community into what has been referred to as 'civic engagement' and defined as:

> a collection of behaviours by either individuals or groups which contribute to the 'common good', often through promoting or delivering positive change. Specific behaviours that potentially fit under this umbrella include form political participation, volunteering, fundraising and participation in decision-making. (Mason, 2012, 81)

Moreover, those who are involved in public decision-making are happier – this prompts Frey and Stutzer to state that

> increased possibilities of directly participating in public decision-making and a decentralized state directly contribute to happiness. This effect is not only due to public policies more closely linked to what the citizens desire but also to the right to participate as such – that is to the utility gained by the possibility of taking an active role in the political process. (Frey and Stutzer, 2002, 174–5)

Daniel and Meyers (2015, 262) suggest that 'one proven way to increase levels of social capital in communities has come from the practices of time banking and community currency'. For young people, both of these systems can provide incentives or rewards for those who volunteer; in exchange for contributions in a communal garden or at a school, for example, participants can receive rewards linked with school status and access to opportunities leading to even greater participation. Drawing out local young people who may otherwise not have volunteered and then connecting them with increased opportunities creates what Daniel and Meyers call a 'virtuous cycle' of social capital.

We can safely assert that people and communities that display higher levels of resilience are also happier – and when people are happy, there are profound consequences for their behaviour that impact on them and society in a variety of very important ways. For example, Frey and Stutzer (2002, 13) isolate the following impacts of greater levels of happiness:

- Happier people are more successful in the labour market. They find a job more easily than unhappy persons, and they tend to progress more quickly in their careers.
- Happier persons more easily find a partner and are thus less exposed to loneliness.
- Happier people are more cooperative; they are more inclined to help others and to incur a risk in doing so.

The contemporary focus is on creating the sort of social environment that will bring out the best in an area's residents and create a 'virtuous circle' in which both individual and community resilience can be fostered. Recently, governments, local and national, have been able to formulate and instigate policies that look at infrastructure not just in terms of roads, houses, schools and so forth, but of structures and systems that facilitate community building. What factors can 'promote greater connectivity, less isolation, and effective communication channels?' (Hall and Zautra, 2010, 363)

Hall and Zautra identify the following community characteristics as what they refer to as 'social infrastructure' – qualities that enhance the building of social capital:

- Places, public and private, for exchange, communication, and dialogue about community issues.
- Sources of community news.
- The full range and number of organizations that connect people at various levels of community (block watches, neighborhood associations, community centers, planning groups, etc.).
- 'Trust index' rates that attempt to measure levels of trust within neighborhoods and communities. (Hall and Zautra, 2010, 364)

A functioning social infrastructure makes it easier for individuals to become engaged with their community and work together (Table 9.3) to create a place to live that is more resilient per se and that facilitates the acquisition and development of resilience in all of its inhabitants.

Kretzmann (2010, 487) identifies the 'asset-focused steps' that resilient communities tend to take. They start by identifying their existing assets; then they start to 'connect them for productive purposes'; and finally they harness their assets to a vision for the future. 'These three steps,' says Kretzmann, 'are not sequential, but continuous.'

Resilient communities, Innes and Jones suggest, embody factors that enable them to withstand threats, real or perceived, and repair themselves. They argue that:

the primary source of resilience to crime and disorder is the presence of collective efficacy in a community whereby a group of people come together around a shared goal, such as improving feelings of safety and security. (Innes and Jones, 2006, 50)

Table 9.3 Social capital in resilient communities

Researchers	Key factors
Knack and Keefer (1997)	Resilient communities are more likely to have more social capital, which has economic pay-off.
	Social capital makes a measurable, positive economic difference. Countries with higher, more equal incomes are more likely to display higher levels of social capital in the form of trust and more prosocial norms, and tend to have higher levels of education.
Frey and Stutzer (2002)	Resilient people are happier, which makes it easier for them to acquire social capital.
	Happy people are more likely to benefit from finding a life partner and enjoying the psychological and physical health benefits of companionship; they are better at cooperating with others, even when doing so entails taking a risk.
Knack (2002)	Higher levels of social capital are associated with better governance.
	Societies with higher levels of social capital, particularly in terms of social trust and volunteering, display better governance.
Moretti and Obsuth (2009)	Resilient people are less likely to become involved in crime.
	Aside from any economic costs associated with crime, there are also social repercussions. Individuals involved in crime, and societies in which crime rates are high, enjoy less social capital, fewer relationships of trust, less cooperation, etc.
Bacon et al. (2010)	Resilient people are better at finding and keeping work.
	Work creates economic value, but that's not all; the sense of meaning and purpose that comes from working in a productive and useful way leads to higher levels of happiness, and lower levels of poor health.
Hall and Zautra (2010)	Resilient communities lead to environments that sustain well-being.
	A resilient community can create a healthy environment in which future generations can grow up, leading to a virtuous circle in which positivity pervades and young people's likelihood of growing up to be resilient is enhanced.
Skodol (2010)	Resilient personalities form strong interrelationships within the community.
	The nature of strong, productive relationships between individuals with strong qualities of resilience can form a significant degree of social capital with which a highly functioning society can be created.
Hardy (2015)	Resilient communities are less likely to harbour terrorism.
	When communities feel or are at risk of terrorism, social capital diminishes as people feel less comfortable engaging with each other, and more fearful of social interactions. More resilient communities are less likely to be at risk in this area.

Neighbourhood factors that aid resilience include

more community order and organisation, greater institutional resources . . . and a general, positive attitude among its residents. (Creasey and Jarvis, 2013a, 7)

Given that the above are typically characteristics of more affluent neighbourhoods, communities that are not resilient and that are not fostering resilience among their young residents can be aided by programmes that are expressly designed to foster community building, including ensuring adequate law enforcement and creating public amenities such as parks (Creasey and Jarvis, 2013b, 7).

None of this is to suggest that the physical nature of the community environment is not important – quite the contrary! For example, the form that housing takes can have a very significant impact on resilience. Higher-quality housing is less likely to lead to a high incidence of asthma, for example. Housing planning that reduces sprawl can result in lower levels of air pollution (Allison et al., 2013, 31). Ensuring adequate green spaces for play and leisure has a wide range of health benefits.

Conclusion

Resilience is often thought of as something that impacts on the individual, or maybe on a family or community. It is certainly true that the word is full of individuals' unique stories of resilience or the lack thereof. However, the importance of resilience goes way beyond these stories because, by creating a society in which everyone is facilitated in being as resilient as they can, the promise is that we are investing in a better future for everyone.

Building the skills of resilience in budding citizens – through childhood and adolescence, and throughout the rest of their life course – may well provide a valid underpinning for future generations. From the human rights viewpoint, it is easy to argue that helping people to develop resilience is fundamental. Resilient people are demonstrably healthier, happier and more successful. They have a better chance of a good family life and satisfying career and are more likely to grow up to become well-adjusted adults and parents.

Yet, as important as human rights are, resilience is perceived to also make an enormous difference in many social, political and economic areas of modern life. As demonstrated throughout this text, stakeholders such as researchers, academics, politicians and practitioners all currently subscribe to a common notion that investing in the development of human resilience can have meaningful and positive ramifications for society in general. The political view that developing resilience from childhood can improve life chances, improve physical and mental health, improve family dynamics, reduce welfare dependency, and generally make our society a happier, safer, better place for everyone, has strengthened over the last decade. As a consequence, the promise of resilience is likely to remain a driving force and continue at the forefront of twenty-first century policymaking.

Bibliography

Agnoli, S, Mancini, G, Pozzoli, T, Baldaro, B, Russo, PM, and Surcinelli, P. (2012) The Interaction between Emotional Intelligence and Cognitive Ability in Predicting Scholastic Performance in School-aged Children. *Personality and Individual Differences.* 53: 660–65

Aldrich, D, and Meyers, M. (2015) Social Capital and Community Resilience. *American Behavioural Scientist.* 59/2: 254–69.

Allison, KW, Broce, RS, and Houston, AJ. (2013) The Importance of Housing, Neighbourhood and Community Contexts. In Creasey, GL, and Jarvis, PA. (Editors) *Adolescent Development and School Achievement in Urban Communities: Resilience in the Neighborhood.* Routledge, NY. 27–37.

Allison, S, Stacey, K, Dadds, V, Roeger, L, Wood, A, and Martin, G. (August 2003) What the Family Brings: Gathering Evidence for Strengths-based Work. *Journal of Family Therapy.* 25/3: 263–84.

Alva, SA. (1991) Academic Invulnerability among Mexican-American Students: The Importance of Protective Resources and Appraisals. *Hispanic Journal of Behavioral Sciences.* 13: 18–34.

Anand, KJS, and Scalzo, FM. (2000) Can Adverse Neonatal Experiences Alter Brain Development and Subsequent Behavior? *Biology of the Neonate.* 77: 69–82.

Anda, RF, Felitti, VJ, Bremner, JD, Walker, JD, Whitfield, C, Perry, BD, Dube, SR, and Giles, WH. (April 2006) The Enduring Effects of Abuse and Related Adverse Experiences in Childhood. *European Archives of Psychiatry and Clinical Neuroscience.* 256/3: 174–86.

Andersen, SL. (January–March 2003) Trajectories of Brain Development: Point of Vulnerability or Window of Opportunity? Brain Development, Sex Differences and Stress: Implications for Psychopathology. *Neuroscience and Biobehavioral Reviews.* 27/1–2: 3–18.

Andersen, SL, Tomada, A, Vicow, E, Valente, E, Polcari, A, and Teicher, M. (2008) Preliminary Evidence for Sensitive Periods in the Effect of Childhood Sexual Abuse on Regional Brain Development. *The Journal of Neuropsychiatry and Clinical Neurosciences.* 20: 292–301.

Appleyard, K, Egeland, B, van Dulmen, M, and Sroufe, L. (2005) When More Is Not Better: The Role of Cumulative Risk in Child Behavior Outcomes. *Journal of Child Psychology and Psychiatry.* 46/3: 235–45.

Armstrong, MI, Birnie-Lefcovitch, S, and Ungar, MT. (June 2005) Pathways Between Social Support, Family Well Being, Quality of Parenting, and Child Resilience: What We Know. *Journal of Child and Family Studies.* 14/2: 269–81.

Arnett, JJ. (1999) Adolescent Storm and Stress, Reconsidered. *American Psychologist.* 54/5: 317–26.

Arnon, S, Shamai, S, and Illatov, Z. (June 2008) Socialization Agents and Activities of Young Adolescents. *Adolescence.* 43/170: 373–97.

Arthur, J, and Cremin, H. (Editors) (2012) *Debates in Citizenship Education.* Routledge.

Atwool, N. (October 2006) Attachment and Resilience: Implications for Children in Care. *Child Care in Practice*. 12/4: 315–30.

Augimeri, LA, Walsh, M, and Slater, N. (2011) Rolling Out Snap; An Evidence Based Intervention: A Summary of Implementation, Evaluation and Research. *International Journal of Child, Youth and Family Studies*. 2/21: 330–52.

Bacon, N, Brophy, M, Mguni, N, Mulgan, G, and Shandro, A. (2010) *The State of Happiness: Can Public Policy Shape People's Wellbeing and Resilience?* The Young Foundation. http://youngfoundation.org/wp-content/uploads/2012/10/The-State-of-Happiness.pdf. Accessed 17 October 2013.

Bagdi, A, and Vacca, J. (December 2005) Supporting Early Childhood Social-emotional Well Being: The Building Blocks for Early Learning and School Success. *Early Childhood Education Journal*. 33/3: 179–90.

Baillie, RS, Stevens, M, and McDonald, E. (2012) The Impact of Housing Improvement and Socio-environmental Factors on Common Childhood Illnesses: A Cohort Study in Indigenous Australian Communities. *Journal Epidemiological Community Health*. 66: 821–31.

Bandura, A. (1995) Exercise of Personal and Collective Efficacy in Changing Societies. In Bandura, A. (Editor) *Self-efficacy in Changing Societies*. Cambridge University Press. 1–45.

Bandura, A. (1997) Self-efficacy and Health Behaviour. In Baum, A, Newman, S, Wienman, J, West, R, and McManus, C. (Editors) *Cambridge Handbook of Psychology, Health and Medicine*. Cambridge University Press. 160–2.

Barber, BL, Eccles, JS, and Stone, MR. (2001) Whatever Happened to the Jock, the Brain, and the Princess? Young Adult Pathways Linked to Adolescent Activity Involvement and Social Identity. *Journal of Adolescent Research*. 16: 429–55.

Barboza, GE, Schiamburg, LB, Oehmke, J, Korzeniewski, P, Lori, A, and Heraux, CG. (January 2009) Individual Characteristics and the Multiple Contexts of Adolescent Bullying: An Ecological Perspective. *Journal of Youth and Adolescence*. 38/1: 101–21.

Barnard, P, and Morland, I. (1999) When Children Are Involved in Disasters. In Barnard, P, Morland, I, and Nagy, J. (Editors) *Children, Bereavement and Trauma: Nurturing Resilience*. Jessica Kingsley Publishers. 21–30.

Barnard, P, Morland, I, and Nagy, J. (Editors) (1999) *Children, Bereavement and Trauma; Nurturing Resilience*. Jessica Kingsley Publishers.

Barnett, DW, Bauer, AM, Ehrhardt, KE, Lentz, FE, and Stollar, SA. (1996) Keystone Targets for Change: Planning for Widespread Positive Consequences. *School Psychology Quarterly*. 11/2: 95–117.

Bauer-Wu, S. (2010) Integrative Oncology: Mindfulness Meditation. *Oncology* (Supplement, Nurse Edition). 10: 36–40.

Bava, S, and Tapert, SF. (2010) Adolescent Brain Development and the Risk for Alcohol and Other Drug Problems. *Neuropsychology Review*. 20/4: 398–413.

Beardslee, WR, Gladstone, TRG, Wright, EJ, and Cooper, AB. (2003) A Family-based Approach to the Prevention of Depressive Symptoms in Children at Risk: Evidence of Parental and Child Change. *Pediatrics*. 112/2: 119–31.

Beaujot, R, Jianggin Du, C, and Ravanera, Z. (June 2013) Family Policies in Quebec and the Rest of Canada: Implications for Fertility, Child-care, Women's Paid Work, and Child Development Indicators. *Canadian Public Policy*. 39/2: 221–40.

Benard, B. (1991) *Fostering Resiliency in Kids: Protective Factors in the Family, School and Community*. Portland, Oregon: Western Center for Drug-free Schools and Communities. http://friendsofthechildrenboston.org/mentors/articles/Benard%20-%20%20Fostering%20Resiliency.pdf. Accessed 26 July 2013.

Benard, B. (1993) Fostering Resiliency in Kids. *Educational Leadership*. 51/3: 44–8.

Benard, B. (2001) *Competence and Resilience Research: Lessons for Prevention*. National Resilience Resource Center. http://www.nationalresilienceresource.com/CAPT_Competence_and_Resilience_F_2012.pdf. Accessed 26 July 2013.

Benard, B. (2009) Using Strengths-based Practice to Tap the Resilience of Families. In Saleebey, D. (Editor) *The Strengths Perspective in Social Work Practice*. Pearson. 197–220.

Benard, B, and Truebridge, SL. (2009) A Shift in Thinking: Influencing Social Workers' Beliefs About Individual and Family Resilience in an Effort to Enhance Well-being and Success for All. In Saleeby, D. (Editor) *The Strengths Perspective in Social Work Practice*. Pearson. 201–19.

Biddle, BJ. (Editor) (2001) *Social Class, Poverty and Education: Policy and Practice*. Routledge Falmer.

Birnbaum, AS, and Linver, MR. (2013) Adolescent Physical Development and Health. In Creasey, GL, and Jarvis, PA. (Editors) *Adolescent Development and School Achievement in Urban Communities: Resilience in the Neighbourhood*. Routledge. 53–64.

Biro, F, Greenspan, L, and Gatvaz, M. (2012) Puberty in Girls of the 21st Century. *Journal of Pediatric and Adolescent Gynaecology*. 25/5: 289–94.

Bleuler, M. (1978) *The Schizophrenic Disorders: Long Term Patient and Family Studies*. Yale University Press.

Blinn Pike, L. (1999) Why Abstinent Adolescents Report They Have Not Had Sex: Understanding Sexually Resilient Youth. *Orig. Family Relations*. 48: 3. http://extension.missouri.edu/hdfs/journal.htm. Accessed 25 July 2013.

Block, J, and Kremen, AM. (1996) IQ and Ego-resiliency: Conceptual and Empirical Connections and Separateness. *Journal of Personality and Social Psychology*. 70/2: 349–61.

Bloom Lewkowicz, A. (2007) *Teaching Emotional Intelligence; Strategies and Activities for Helping Students Make Effective Choices*. Corwin Press.

Blundo, R. (2001) Learning Strengths-based Practice: Challenging Our Personal and Professional Frames. *Families in Society: The Journal of Contemporary Social Services*. 82/3: 296–304.

Bodrova, E, and Leong, DG. (March 2008) Developing Self-regulation in Kindergarten; Can We Keep All the Crickets in the Basket? Beyond the Journal. *Young Children on the Web*. https://www.naeyc.org/files/yc/file/200803/BTJ_Primary_Interest.pdf. Accessed 23 July 2014.

Bogin, B. (1999) Evolutionary Perspective on Human Growth. *Annual Review of Anthropology*. 28: 10–54.

Borman, K, and Schneider, B. (1998) *The Adolescent Years: Social Influences and Educational Challenges*. Ninety-seventh Yearbook of the National Society for the Study of Education.

Bostock, L. (2004) *Social Care Institute for Excellence: Promoting Resilience in Fostered Children and Young People*. The Policy Press.

Bowlby, J. (1953) *Child Care and the Growth of Love*. Penguin Books.

Bowlby, J. (1957) An Ethological Approach to Research in Child Development. *British Journal of Medical Psychology*. 30: 230–40.

Bowlby, J. (1958) The Nature of the Child's Tie to His Mother. *International Journal of Psychoanalysis*. 37/5: 350–73.

Bowlby, J. (1959) Separation Anxiety. *International Journal of Psycho-analysts*. XLI: 1–25.

Bowlby, J. [1969] (1999) Attachment, 2nd edn. *Attachment and Loss* (vol. 1). Basic Books.

Bowlby, J. (1989) *A Secure Base: Parent-child Attachment and Healthy Human Development*. Basic Books.

Bowlby, J. (2005, orig. 1957) *The Making and Breaking of Affectional Bonds*. Routledge Classics.

Bowlby, J. (2005) *A Secure Base; Clinical Applications of Attachment Theory*. Routledge Classics.

Bowlby, J, Ainsworth, M, Boston, M, and Rosenbluth, D. (1956) The Effects of Mother-child Separation: A Follow-up Study. *British Journal of Medical Psychology*. 29: 211–47.

Brackenreed, D. (2010) Resilience and Risk. *International Education Studies*. 3: 111–21.

Bradley, RH, Whiteside, L, Mundrom, DJ, Casey, PH, Kelleher, KJ, and Pope, SK. (1994) Contribution of Early Intervention and Early Caregiving Experiences to Resilience in Low-birthweight, Premature Children Living in Poverty. *Journal of Clinical Child Psychology*. 23/4: 425–34.

Bratburg, GH. (July 2007) Pubertal Timing – Antecedent to Risk or Resilience? Doctoral thesis. Epidemiological Studies on Growth, Maturation and Health Risk Behaviours; The Young HUNT study, Nord-Trøndelag, Norway. http://www.diva-portal.org/smash/get/diva2:122846/FULLTEXT01.pdf. Accessed 25 July 2013.

Bronfenbrenner, U. (1972) *Two Worlds of Childhood: US and USSR*. George Allen and Unwin Ltd.

Bronfenbrenner, U. (Editor) (1972) *Influences on Human Development*. The Dryden Press Inc.

Bronfenbrenner, U. (1979) *The Ecology of Human Development: Experiments by Nature and Design*. Harvard University Press.

Bronfenbrenner, U. (1986) Ecology of the Family as a Context for Human Development: Research Perspectives. *Developmental Psychology*. 22: 723–42.

Bronfenbrenner, U. (1989) Ecological Systems Theory. *Annals of Child Development*. 6: 187–249.

Brooks, R, and Goldstein, S. (2002) *Raising Resilient Children: Fostering Strength, Hope and Optimism in Your Child*. McGraw-Hill.

Brown, BB, and Theobald, W. (1998) Learning Contexts Beyond the Classroom: Extracurricular Activities, Community Organizations, and Peer Groups. In Borman, K, and Schneider, B. (Editors) *The Adolescent Years: Social Influences and Educational Challenges*. Ninety-seventh Yearbook of the National Society for the Study of Education. 109–41.

Brown, J, Ross, H, and Munn, P. (2012) *Democratic Citizenship in Schools: Teaching Controversial Issues, Traditions and Accountability*. Dunedin.

Brown, JH. (2004) Resilience: From Program to Process. *The California School Psychologist*. 9: 83–92.

Brown, JH, D'Emidio-Caston, M, and Benard, B. (Editors) (2001) *Resilience Education*. Corwin Press.

Brun, C, and Rapp, RD. (2001) Strengths-based Case Management: Individuals' Perspectives on Strengths and the Case Manager Relationship. *Social Work*. 46/3: 278–88.

Burchinal, MR. (May 1999) Child Care Experiences and Developmental Outcomes. *The Annals of the American Academy of Political and Social Science*. 563/1: 73–97.

Burkam, DT, and Lee, VF. (2002) *Inequality at the Starting Gate: Social Background Differences in Achievement as Children Begin School*. Executive Summary. http://www.epi.org/publication/books_starting_gate/. Accessed 23 July 2014.

Burns, GW. (2010) Can You Be Happy in Pain? Applying Positive Psychology, Mindfulness and Hypnosis to Chronic Pain Management. In Burns, GW. (Editor)

Happiness, Healing, Enhancement; Your Casebook Collection for Applying Positive Psychology in Therapy. John Wiley & Sons. 202–14.

Calkins, SD, Blandon, AY, Williford, AP, and Keane, SP. (2007) Biological, Behavioral, and Relational Levels of Resilience in the Context of Risk for Early Childhood Behavior Problems. *Development and Psychopathology.* 19: 675–700.

Calkins, S, and Keane, S. (2009) Developmental Origins of Early Anti-social Behaviour. *Development and Psychopathology.* 21/4. 1095–109.

Cambridge Dictionaries Online, http://dictionary.cambridge.org/dictionary/british/.

Campanella, T. (2006) Urban Resilience and the Recovery of New Orleans. *Journal of the American Planning Association.* 72/2: 141–6.

Carey, N. (2012) *The Epigenetics Revolution: How Modern Biology Is Rewriting Our Understanding of Genetics, Disease and Inheritance.* Icon Books Ltd.

Carnegie Council on Adolescent Development. (1995) *Turning Points: Preparing American Youth for 21st Century: Report of Task Force on Education of Young Adolescents.* Carnegie Foundation.

Casey, BJ, Gledd, J, and Thomas, K. (October 2000) Structural and Functional Brain Development and its Relation to Cognitive Development. *Biological Psychology.* 54/1–3: 241–57.

Casey, BJ, Jones, R, and Hare, TA. (March 2008) The Adolescent Brain. *The Year in Cognitive Neuroscience.* 1124: 111–26.

Centre for Excellence and Outcomes in Children's and Young People's Services. (2010) *Risk and Resilience in the Early Years, Proven Practice.* http://www.communitycare.co.uk/2010/06/18/proven-practice-the-benefits-of-early-intervention/. Accessed 26 July 2013.

Chassin, L, Carle, AC, Nissim-Sabat, D, and Kumpher, KL. (2004) Fostering Resilience in Children of Alcoholic Parents. In Maton, KI, Schellenbach, CJ, Leadbeater, BJ, and Solarz, AL. (Editors) *Investing in Children, Youth, Families, and Communities: Strengths-based Research and Policy.* American Psychological Association.

Cherlin, AJ, Furstenberg, FF, Chase-Lansdale, PL, Keiran, KE, Robins, PK, Morrison, DR, and Tritler, JO. (1991) Longitudinal Studies of the Effects of Divorce on Children in Great Britain and the United States. *Science.* 252: 1386–9.

Cicchetti, D, and Rogosch, FA. (1997) The Role of Self-organization in the Promotion of Resilience in Maltreated Children. *Development and Psychopathology.* 9: 797–816.

Cicchetti, D, and Rogosch, F. (2001) The Impact of Child Maltreatment and Psychopathology on Neuroendocrine Functioning. *Development and Psychopathology.* 13: 783–804.

Cocozza, M, Gustafsson, PA, and Sydsjö, G. (2007) Who Suspects and Reports Child Maltreatment to Social Services in Sweden? Is There a Reliable Mandatory Reporting Process? *European Journal of Social Work.* 10/2: 209–23.

Conrad, C. (Editor) (2011a) *The Handbook of Stress; Neurological Effects on the Brain.* Wiley-Blackwell.

Conrad, C. (2011b) Chronic Stress and Hippocampus Vulnerability to Functional Changes and Health in the Adult. In Conrad, C. (Editor) *The Handbook of Stress: Neurological Effects on the Brain.* Wiley-Blackwell. 324–48.

Cook, M. (2012) *Levels of Personality.* Cambridge University Press.

Cook, SA, and Klay, WE. (2014) George Washington and Enlightenment Ideas on Educating Future Citizens and Public Servants. *Journal of Public Affairs Education.* 20/1: 45–55.

Cooper, H, Valentine, JC, Nye, B, and Lindsay, JJ. (1999) Relationships between Five After-school Activities and Academic Achievement. *Journal of Educational Psychology.* 91: 369–78.

Cox, K. (June 2006) Investigating the Impact of Strength-based Assessment on Youth with Emotional or Behavioral Disorders. *Journal of Child and Family Studies.* 15/3: 278–92.

Creasey, GL, and Jarvis, PA. (Editors) (2013a) *Adolescent Development and School Achievement in Urban Communities: Resilience in the Neighbourhood.* Routledge.

Creasey, GL, and Jarvis, PA. (2013b) Urban and Underserviced Communities. In Creasey, GL, and Jarvis, PA. (Editors) *Adolescent Development and School Achievement in Urban Communities: Resilience in the Neighbourhood.* Routledge. 1–11.

Cross, D, Epstein, M, Hearn, L, Slee, P, Shaw, T, and Monks, H. (September 2011) National Safe Schools Framework: Policy and Practice to Reduce Bullying in Australian Schools. *International Journal of Behavioral Development.* 35/5: 398–404.

Crossley, N. (2013) Habit and Habitus. *Body and Society.* 19/2–3: 136–61.

Csikszentmihalyi, M. (1993) Context of Optimal Growth in Childhood. *Daedalus.* 122/1: 33–55.

Curtis, WJ, and Cicchetti, D. (2003) Moving Research on Resilience into the 21st Century: Theoretical and Methodological Considerations in Examining the Biological Contributors to Resilience. *Development and Psychopathology.* 15: 773–810.

Curtis, WJ, and Nelson, CA. (2003) Towards Building a Better Brain: Neurobehavioural Outcomes, Mechanisms, and Processes of Environmental Enrichment. In Luthar, SS. (Editor) *Resilience and Vulnerability: Adaptation in the Context of Childhood Adversities.* Cambridge University Press. 243–66.

Daniel, B. (2010) Concepts of Adversity, Risk, Vulnerability and Resilience: A Discussion in the Context of the Child Protection System. *Social Policy and Society.* 9/2: 231–41.

Daniel, B, Taylor, J, Scott, J, Derbyshire, D, and Neilson, D. (2011) *Recognizing and Helping the Neglected Child.* Kingsley.

Daniel, B, and Wassell, S. (2002a) *The Early Years: Assessing and Promoting Resilience in Vulnerable Children.* Jessica Kingsley Publishers.

Daniel, B, and Wassell, S. (2002b) *The School Years: Assessing and Promoting Resilience in Vulnerable Children.* Jessica Kingsley Publishers.

Daniel, B, Wassell, S, and Gilligan, R. (2011) *Child Development for Child Care and Protection Workers,* 2nd edn. Kingsley.

Davies, M. (2002) A Few Thoughts about the Mind, the Brain and a Child with Early Deprivation. *Journal of Analytical Psychology.* 47: 421–35.

Davis, BM. (2006) *How to Teach Students Who Don't Look Like You: Culturally Relevant Teaching Strategies.* Corwin Press.

Daunic, A, Corbett, N, Smith, S, Barnes, T, Santiago-Poventud, L, Chalfant, P, Pitts, D, and Gleaton, J. (November 2013) Brief Report: Integrating Social-emotional Learning with Literacy Instruction: An Intervention for Children at Risk for Emotional and Behavioural Disorders. *Behavioral Disorders.* 39/1: 43–51.

Dearden, J. (2004) Resilience: A Study of Risk and Protective Factors from the Perspective of Young People with Experience of Local Authority Care. *Support for Learning.* 19/4: 187–93.

Dee, TS, and Jacob, B. (2011) The Impact of No Child Left Behind on Student Achievement. *Journal of Policy Analysis and. Management.* 30: 418–46.

Deming, D. (2009) Early Childhood Intervention and Life-cycle Skill Development: Evidence from Head Start. *American Economic Journal.* 1/3: 111–34.

Denham, SA, Bassett, H, Mincic, M, Kalb, S, Way, E, Wyatt, T, and Segal, Y. (2012) Social-emotional Learning Profiles of Preschoolers' Early School Success: A Person-centered Approach. *Learning and Individual Differences.* 22: 178–89.

Department for Education. (2014) *Statutory Framework for the Early Years Foundation Stage.* Department for Education: London.

Dowling, M. (2010) *Young Children's Personal, Social and Emotional Development.* Sage.

Doyle, D. (April 2012) *Breaking the Cycle of Deprivation: An Experimental Evaluation of an Early Childhood Intervention.* UCD Centre for Economic Research. Working Paper Series.

DuBois, DL. (2001) Family Disadvantage, the Self and Academic Achievement. In Biddle, BJ. (Editor) *Social Class, Poverty and Education: Policy and Practice.* Routledge Falmer. 133–73.

Dulmus, C, Sowers, K, Thyer, B. (2012) *Human Behaviour in Social Work Practice: Theories for Social Work Practice.* John Wiley and Sons.

Dyson, A. (2012) Teachers Working with the Community and Other Professionals: Full Service and Extended Schools. In Hill, M, Head, G, Lockyer, A, Reid, B, and Taylor, R. (Editors) *Children's Services: Working Together.* Pearson. 140–50.

Early, TJ, and Glenmaye, F. (2000) Valuing Families: Social Work Practice with Families from a Strengths Perspective. *Social Work.* 45/2: 118–30.

Ebata, AT, Petersen, C, and Conger, J. (1990) The Development of Psychopathology in Adolescence. In Rolf, J, Masten, A, Nuechterlein, K, and Weintraub, S. (Editors) *Risk and Protective Factors in the Development of Psychopathology.* Cambridge University Press. 308–33.

Eccles, JS, Barber, BL, Stone, M, and Hunt, J. (2003) Extracurricular Activities and Adolescent Development. *Journal of Social Issues.* 59: 865–89.

Elder, C, Leaver-Dunn, D, Wang, MQ, Nagy, S, and Green, L. (2000) Organized Group Activity as a Protective Factor Against Adolescent Substance Use. *American Journal of Health Behavior.* 24: 108–13.

Eriksson, M. (2010) Children Who 'Witness' Violence as Crime Victims and Changing Family Law in Sweden. *Journal of Child Custody.* 7/2: 93–116.

Evers, A, and Guillemard, AM. (Editors) (2013) *Social Policy and Citizenship: The Changing Landscape.* Oxford University Press.

Farah, MJ, Shera, DM, Savage, JH, Betancourt, L, Gianetta, JM, Brodsky, NL, Malmud, EK, and Hurt, H. (September 2006) Childhood Poverty: Specific Associations with Neurocognitive Development. *Brain Research.* 1110/1: 166–74.

Feder, A, Nestler, EJ, Westphal, M, and Charney, DS. (2010) Psychobiological Mechanisms of Resilience to Stress. In Reich, JW, Zautra, AJ, and Stuart Hall, J. (Editors) *Handbook of Adult Resilience.* The Guilford Press. 35–54.

Fergus, S, and Zimmerman, MA. (2005) Adolescent Resilience: A Framework for Understanding Healthy Development in the Face of Risk. *Annual Review of Public Health.* 26: 399–419.

Figueroa-Sanchez, M. (2008) Building Emotional Literacy; Groundwork to Early Learning. Annual Theme. *Childhood Education.* 84/5: 301–4.

Fleming, J, and Ledogar, RJ. (Summer 2008) Resilience, an Evolving Concept: A Review of Literature Relevant to Aboriginal Research. *Pimatisiwin.* 6/2: 7–23.

Flouri, E, Midouhas, E, Joshi, H, and Tzavidis, N. (2015). Emotional and Behavioural Resilience to Multiple Risk Exposure in Early Life: The Role of Parenting. *European Child and Adolescent Psychiatry.* 24/7: 745–55.

Fogel, A, and Garvey, A. (2007) Alive Communication. *Infant Behavior and Development.* 30: 251–7.

Fox, E. (2008) *Emotion Science.* Palgrave Macmillan.

Fox, J. (2012) *Resilience: A Framework of Positive Practice.* http://www.scotland.gov.uk/Publications/2005/05/18120009/00124. Accessed 18 March 2014.

Frey, AJ, and Walker, M. (2006) Education Policy for Children, Youth and Families. In Jenson, J, and Fraser, MW. (Editors) *Social Policy for Children and Families: A Risk and Resilience Perspective.* Sage Publications. 67–92.

Frey, BS, and Stutzer, A. (2002) *Happiness and Economics: How the Economy and Institutions Affect Human Well-being.* Princeton University Press.

Fröhlich-Gildhoff, K, and Rönnau-Böse, M. (2012) Prevention of Exclusion: The Promotion of Resilience in Early Childhood Institutions in Disadvantaged Areas. *Journal of Public Health.* 20: 131–9.

Garbarino, J, Dubrow, N, Kostelny, K, and Pardo, C. (1992) *Children in Danger: Coping with the Consequences of Community Violence.* Jossey-Bass.

Garmezy, N. (1974) The Study of Competence in Children at Risk from Severe Psychology. In Anthony, EJ, and Koupernik, C. (Editors) *The Child in His Family: Children at Psychiatric Risk.* Wiley. 3: 77–97.

Garmezy, N. (1983) *Stress, Coping and Development in Children.* McGraw-Hill.

Garmezy, N. (1990) A Closing Note: Reflections on the Future. In Rolf, J, Masten, RA, Cicchetti, D, Nuechterlein, K, and Weintraub, S. (Editors) *Risk and Protective Factors in the Development of Psychopathology.* Cambridge University Press. 527–34.

Garmezy, N. (1991) Resiliency and Vulnerability to Adverse Developmental Outcomes Associated with Poverty. *The American Behavioural Scientist.* Mar/Apr: 416–31.

Garmezy, N, Masten, AS, and Tellegen, A. (1984) The Study of Stress and Competence in Children: A Building Block for Developmental Psychopathology. *Child Development.* 55/1: 97–111.

Gendron, B. (2004) Why Emotional Capital Matters in Education and in Labour? Toward an Optimal Exploitation of Human Capital and Knowledge Management. In *Les Cahiers de la Maison des Sciences Economiques.* Série Rouge. No. 113. Paris. http://halshs.archives-ouvertes.fr/hal-00201223/. Accessed 29 April 2014.

Ghapanchi, A, and Shahtalebi, B. (2014) Investigating Effectiveness of Multimedia Software-based Citizenship Education on Increasing Citizenship Awareness of 8 Year-old Children. *Journal of Applied Environmental Biological Science.* 4/2: 342–8.

Gilbert, N. (2013) Citizenship in the Enabling State: The Changing Balance of Rights and Obligations. In Evers, A, and Guillemard, A-M. (Editors) *Social Policy and Citizenship; The Changing Landscape.* Oxford University Press. 80–96.

Gilbert, PS, Allan, S, Trent D, et al. (1991) A Social Comparison Scale: Psychometric Properties and Relationship to Psychopathology. *Personality and Individual Differences.* 19/3: 293–9.

Gilbert, R, Spatz Widom, C, Browne, K, Fergusson, D, Webb, E, and Janson, S. (January 2009) Burden and Consequences of Child Maltreatment in High-income Countries. *The Lancet.* 373/9657: 68–81.

Gilligan, R. (1997) Beyond Permanence? The Importance of Resilience in Child Placement Practice and Planning. *Adoption and Fostering.* 21/1: 12–20.

Gilligan, R. (1999) Enhancing the Resilience of Children and Young People in Public Care by Mentoring Their Talents and Interests. *Child and Family Social Work.* 4: 187–96.

Gilligan, R. (2000) Adversity, Resilience and Young People: The Protective Value of Positive School and Spare Time Experiences. *Children and Society.* 14/1: 37–47.

Gilligan, R. (2004) Promoting Resilience in Child and Family Social Work: Issues for Social Work Practice, Education and Policy. *Social Work Education: The International Journal.* 23/1: 93–104.

Gilligan, R. (2007) Adversity, Resilience and the Educational Progress of Young People in Public Care. *Emotional and Behavioural Difficulties.* 12/2: 135–45.

Gilligan, R. (2009) *Promoting Resilience; Supporting Children and Young People Who Are in Care, Adopted or in Need,* 2nd edn. London: British Association for Adoption and Fostering.

Gokiert, RJ, Georgis, R, Tremblay, M, Krishnan, V, Vandenberghe, C, and Lee, C. (2014) Evaluating the Adequacy of Social-emotional Measures in Early Childhood. *Journal of Psychoeducational Assessment.* 32: 441.

Goldstein, S, and Brooks, RB. (2006) Why Study Resilience? In Goldstein, S, and Brooks, RB. (Editors) *Handbook of Resilience in Children.* Springer. 3–14.

Goleman, D. (1996) *Emotional Intelligence: Why It Can Matter More Than IQ.* Bantam Books.

Goleman, D. (1998) What Makes a Leader? *Harvard Business Review.* http://hbr.org/2004/01/what-makes-a-leader/ar/1. Accessed 26 July 2013.

Gonzales N, Coxe, S, Roosa, M, White, R, Knight, G, Zeiders, K, and Saenz, D. (2011) Economic Hardship, Neighborhood Context, and Parenting: Prospective Effects on Mexican–American Adolescent's Mental Health. *American Journal of Community Psychology.* 47/1–2: 98–113.

Gordon, EW, and Song, LD. (1994) Variations in the Experience of Resilience. In Wang, MC, and Gordon, EW. (Editors) *Educational Resilience in Inner-city America: Challenges and Prospects.* Routledge. 27–43.

Gormley, WT, Phillips, DA, Newmark, K, Wetli, K, and Adelstein, S. (November–December 2011) Social-emotional Effects of Early Childhood Education Programs in Tulsa. *Child Development.* 82/6: 2095–109.

Green, DG. (1998) Benefit Dependency: How Welfare Undermines Independence. *Choice in Welfare No. 41.* The Institute of Economic Affairs.

Greenberg, MT. (December 2006) Promoting Resilience in Children and Youth: Preventive Interventions and Their Interface with Neuroscience. *Annals of the New York Academy of Sciences.* 1094: 139–50.

Greer, K. (2012) Getting the Society We Deserve: Accountability for Citizenship Education. In Brown, J, Ross, H, and Munn, P. (Editors) *Democratic Citizenship in Schools: Teaching Controversial Issues, Traditions and Accountability.* Dunedin. 106–119.

Greybeal, C. (2001) Strengths-based Social Work Assessment: Transforming the Dominant Paradigm. *Families in Society: The Journal of Contemporary Social Services.* 82/3: 233–42.

Grossmann, T, and Johnson, MH. (2007) The Development of the Social Brain in Human Infancy. *European Journal of Neuroscience.* 25: 909–19.

Gu, J, and Kanai, R. (April 2014) What Contributes to Individual Differences in Brain Structure? *Frontiers in Human Neuroscience.* http://journal.frontiersin.org/Journal/88305/abstract. Accessed 28 April 2014.

Hahn, C. (2012) The Citizenship Teacher and Teaching Controversial Issues: A Comparative Perspective. In Brown, J, Ross, H, and Munn, P. (Editors) *Democratic Citizenship in Schools: Teaching Controversial Issues, Traditions and Accountability.* Dunedin. 48–59.

Hall, JS, and Zautra, AJ. (2010) Indicators of Community Resilience: What Are They, Why Bother? In Reich, JW, Zautra, AJ, and Stuart Hall, J. (Editors) *Handbook of Adult Resilience.* The Guilford Press. 350–71.

Hammond, W. (2010) Principles of Strengths-based Practice. *Resiliency Initiatives.* http://www.ayscbc.org/Principles%20of%20Strength-2.pdf. Accessed 12 May 2014.

Hansen, DM, Jessop, NJ, and Crawford, MJ. (2013) Civic Engagement: Volunteerism, Community Involvement and Political Action. In Creasey, GL, and Jarvis, PA (Editors) *Adolescent Development and School Achievement in Urban Communities: Resilience in the Neighbourhood.* Routledge. 140–50.

Hansenne, M, and Legrand, J. (2012) Creativity, Emotional Intelligence, and School Performance in Children. *International Journal of Educational Research.* 53: 264–68.

Hardy, K. (2015) Resilience in UK Counter-terrorism: Theoretical Criminology. 19/1: 77–94.

Harris T, Brown, GW, and Bilfulco, A. (1986) Loss of Parent in Childhood and Adult Psychiatric Disorder: The Role of Lack of Adequate Parental Care. *Psychological Medicine*. 16: 641–59.

Hart, RA. (1997) *Children's Participation: The Theory and Practice of Involving Young Citizens in Community Development and Environmental Care.* Routledge.

Hassed, C. (2010) Doing Nothing, Changing Profoundly: The Paradox of Mindfulness in a Case of Anxiety. In Burns, GW. (Editor) *Happiness, Healing, Enhancement: Your Casebook Collection for Applying Positive Psychology in Therapy.* John Wiley and Sons. 164–75.

Hauser, ST, Allen, JP, and Schultz, MS. (2012) Exceptional Outcomes: Using Narratives and Family Observations to Understand Resilience. In Kerig, P, Schultz, M, and Hauser, ST. (Editors) *Adolescence and Beyond: Family Processes and Development.* Oxford University Press. 231–49.

Herba, C, and Phillips, M. (2004) Annotation: Development of Facial Expression Recognition from Childhood to Adolescence: Behavioural and Neurological Perspectives. *Journal of Child Psychology and Psychiatry*. 45/7: 1185–98.

Herrman, H, Stewart, DE, Diaz-Granados, N, Berger, EL, Jackson, B, and Yuen, T. (May 2011) What Is Resilience? *The Canadian Journal of Psychiatry*. 56/5: 2258–65.

Hill, M, Head, G, Lockyer, A, Reid, B, and Taylor, R. (Editors) (2012) *Children's Services: Working Together*. Pearson.

Himmelweit, S, and Sigala, M. (July 2004) Choice and the Relationship between Identities and Behaviour for Mothers with Pre-school Children: Some Implications for Policy from a UK Study. *Journal of Social Policy*. 33/3: 455–78.

Howard, S, and Johnson, B. (2000) Young Adolescents Displaying Resilient and Non-resilient Behaviour: Insights from a Qualitative Study – Can Schools Make a Difference? Australian Association for Research in Education. http://aare.edu.au. Accessed 24 July 2013.

Howell, KH, Graham-Bermann, SA, Czyz, E, and Lilly, M. (2010) Assessing Resilience in Children Exposed to Intimate Partner Violence and Victims. *Violence and Victims.* 25/2: 150–64.

Hudley, C, and Duran, R. (2013) Urban Schools and Adolescent Development. In Creasey, GL, and Jarvis, PA. (Editors) *Adolescent Development and School Achievement in Urban Communities: Resilience in the Neighbourhood.* Routledge. 115–26.

Hurley, KM, Black, MM, Papas, MA, and Quigg, AM. (2008) Variation in Breastfeeding Behaviours, Perceptions, and Experiences by Race/Ethnicity among a Low-income Statewide Sample of Special Supplemental Nutrition Program for Women, Infants, and Children (WIC) Participants in the United States. *Maternal and Child Nutrition Journal*. 4/2: 95–105.

Hutchings, J, Bywater, T, Daley, D, Gardner, F, Whitaker, C, Jones, K, Eames, C, et al. (2007) Parenting Intervention in Sure Start Services for Children at Risk of Developing Conduct Disorder: Pragmatic Randomised Controlled Trial. *British Medical Journal*. 334/7595: 678.

Iacoboni, M, Horan, W, Cross, K, Korb, A, Lee, J, Nori, P, Quintana, J, Wynn, J, Green, M. (2014) Self-Reported Empathy and Neural Activity during Action Imitation and Observation in Schizophrenia. *NeuroImage: Clinical*. 5: 100–8.

Innes, M, and Jones, V. (2006) *Neighbourhood Security and Urban Change: Risk, Resiliency and Recovery.* Joseph Rowntree Foundation.

Jacobson, L. (2 October 2002) Kindergarten Study Links Learning Deficits to Poverty. *Education Week. Across the Nation.* 22/5: 10.

Jaffee, SR. (2007) Sensitive, Stimulating Caregiving Predicts Cognitive and Behavioral Resilience in Neurodevelopmentally At-risk Infants. *Development and Psychopathology.* 19: 631–47.

Jennings, WG, and Reingle, JM. (2012) On the Number and Shape of Developmental/ Lifecourse Violence, Aggression, and Delinquency Trajectories: A State-of-the-Art Review. *Journal of Criminal Justice.* 40/6: 472–89.

Jenson, J, and Fraser, MW. (2006) Toward the Integration of Child, Youth and Family Policy: Applying Principles of Risk, Resilience and Ecological Theory. In Jenson, J, and Frazer, MW. (Editors) *Social Policy for Children and Families: A Risk and Resilience Perspective.* Sage Publications. 265–79.

Johnson, B. (November 2008) Teacher-student Relationships Which Promote Resilience at School: A Micro-level Analysis of Students' Views. *British Journal of Guidance and Counselling.* 36/4: 385–98.

Johnson, M. (July 2001) Functional Brain Development in Humans. *Nature Reviews Neuroscience.* 2: 475–83.

Johnson, M, Crosnoe, R, and Elder, G. (2011) Insights on Adolescence from a Life Course Perspective. *Journal of Research on Adolescence.* 21/1: 273–80.

Kabat-Zinn, J, and Davidson, R. (Editors) (2011) *The Mind's Own Physician: A Scientific Dialogue with the Dalai Lama on the Healing Power of Meditation.* Mind and Life Institute. New Harbinger Publications.

Karatsoreos, IN, and McEwen, BS. (1 May 2012) Resilience and Vulnerability: A Neurobiological Perspective. F1000 Reports. Faculty of 1000 Ltd. http://f1000. com/prime/reports/b/5/13/pdf. Accessed 4 June 2013.

Kärkkäinen, R, Raty, H, and Kasanen, K. (2009) Parents' Perceptions of Their Child's Resilience and Competencies. *European Journal of Psychology of Education.* 24/3: 405–19.

Karoly, LA, Kilburn, M, and Cannon, J. (2005) *Early Childhood Interventions; Proven Results, Future Promise.* Prepared for The PNC Financial Services Group.

Keating, A, Kerr, D, Lopes, J, Featherstone, G, and Benton, T. (2009) *Embedding Citizenship Education in Secondary Schools in England (2002–8): Citizen Educational Longitudinal Study Seventh Annual Report.* National Foundation for Educational Research. Department for Children, Schools and Families.

Kerr, D. (2012) Comparative and International Perspectives on Citizenship Education. In Arthur, J, and Cremin, H. (Editors) *Debates in Citizenship Education.* Routledge. 17–31.

King, E, and Sheikh, S. (January 2011) *Resilience and Integration: A Way Forward. Public Service Briefing.* Office for Public Management.

King, K, and Church, A. (2015) Questioning Policy, Youth Participation and Lifestyle Sports. *Leisure Studies.* 34/3: 282–302.

Kliewer, W, Goodman, K, and Reid-Quiñones, K. (2013) The Urban Family. In Creasey, GL, and Jarvis, PA (Editors) *Adolescent Development and School Achievement in Urban Communities: Resilience in the Neighbourhood.* Routledge. 91–102.

Knack, S. (October 2002) Social Capital and the Quality of Government: Evidence from the States. *American Journal of Political Science.* 46/4: 772–85.

Knack, S, and Keefer, P. (1997) Does Social Capital Have an Economic Payoff? A Cross-country Investigation. *The Quarterly Journal of Economics.* 112/4: 1251–88.

Knitzer, J. (2000) *Promoting Resilience, Helping Young Children and Parents Affected by Substance Abuse, Domestic Violence and Depression in the Context of Welfare Reform.* National Centre for Children in Poverty. Issue Brief 8.

Knowland, V, and Thomas, M. (2014) Educating the Adult Brain: How the Neuroscience of Learning Can Inform Educational Policy. *International Review of Education.* 60/1. 99–122.

Kretzmann, JP. (2010) Asset-based Strategies for Building Resilient Communities. In Reich, JW, Zautra, AJ, and Stuart Hall, J. (Editors) *Handbook of Adult Resilience*. The Guilford Press. 484–95.

Laboni, M. (2009) Neurobiology of Imitation. *Current Opinion in Neurobiology*. 19: 661–5.

Landry, SH, Smith, KE, and Swank, PR. (2006) Responsive Parenting: Establishing Early Foundations for Social, Communication, and Independent Problem-solving Skills. *Developmental Psychology*. 42/4: 627–42.

Lareau, A. (2001) Linking Bourdieu's Concept of Capital to the Broader Field: The Case of Family-school Relationships. In Biddle, BJ. (Editor) *Social Class, Poverty and Education: Policy and Practice*. Routledge Falmer. 77–100.

Larkins, C. (February 2014) Enacting Children's Citizenship: Developing Understandings of How Children Enact Themselves as Citizens through Actions and Acts of Citizenship. *Childhood*. 21/1: 7–21.

Leary, V. (2000) Citizenship. Human Rights and Diversity. In Cairns, AC, Courtney, JC, MacKinnon, P, Michellmann, HJ, and Smith, DE. (Editors) *Citizenship, Diversity, and Pluralism: Canadian and Comparative Perspectives*. McGill-Queen's Press. 247–64.

Lee, BJ, Slack, KS, and Lewis, DA. (September 2004) Are Welfare Sanctions Working as Intended? Welfare Receipt, Work Activity, and Material Hardship among TANF-Recipient Families. *Social Service Review*. 78/3: 370–403.

Lee, JH, Nam, SK, Kim, AR, Kim, B, Young Lee, M, and Lee, SM. (July 2013) Resilience: A Meta-analytic Approach. *Journal of Counseling & Development*. 91/3: 269–79.

Lee, RE, Pacione-Zayas, C, Bosch, S, Blackwell, K, and Pawlicki, D. (2013) Partnerships Between Schools, Teachers, Children, Families and Communities. In Creasey, GL, and Jarvis, PA. (Editors) *Adolescent Development and School Achievement in Urban Communities: Resilience in the Neighbourhood*. Routledge. 177–89.

Lee, VE, Brooks-Gunn, J, Schnur, E, and Liaw, FR. (1990) Are Head Start Effects Sustained? A Longitudinal Follow-up Comparison of Disadvantaged Children Attending Head Start, No Preschool, and Other Preschool Programs. *Child Development*. 61: 495–507.

Lesch, KP. (2001) When the Serotonin Transporter Gene Meets Adversity: The Contribution of Animal Models to Understanding Epigenetic Mechanisms in Affective Disorders and Resilience. *Current Topics in Behavioral Neuroscience*. 7: 251–80.

Lester, P, Stein, J, Saltzman, W, Woodward, K, MacDermind, SW, Milburn, N, Mogil, C, and Beardslee, W. (August 2013) Psychological Health of Military Children: Longitudinal Evaluation of a Family-centered Prevention Program to Enhance Family Resilience. *Military Medicine*. 178/8: 838–45.

Lipina, SJ, and Colombo, JA. (2009) *Poverty and Brain Development during Childhood: An Approach from Cognitive Psychology and Neuroscience*. Human Brain Development Series. American Psychological Association.

Lockyer, A. (2012) Taking Children's Citizenship Seriously. In Hill, M, Head, G, Lockyer, A, Reid, B, and Taylor, R. (Editors) *Children's Services: Working Together*. Pearson. 175–90.

Luecken, LJ, and Gress, JL. (2010) Early Adversity and Resilience in Emerging Adulthood. In Reich, JW, Zautra, AJ, and Stuart Hall, J. (Editors) *Handbook of Adult Resilience*. The Guilford Press. 238–57.

Luecken, LJ, Roubinov, D, and Purdom, C. (2011) Clinical Implications of Childhood Stress. In Conrad, C. (Editor) *The Handbook of Stress: Neurological Effects on the Brain*. Wiley-Blackwell. 304–24.

Lundberg, U, and Cooper, CL. (2011) *The Science of Occupational Health: Stress, Psychobiology and the New World of Work*. Wiley-Blackwell.

Luthar, Suniya (1991) Vulnerability and Resilience: A Study of High-Risk Adolescence. *Child Development*. 62/3: 600–66.

Luthar, SS. (Editor) (2003) *Resilience and Vulnerability: Adaptation in the Context of Childhood Adversities*. Cambridge University Press.

Luthar, SS, and Cicchetti, D. (2000) The Construct of Resilience: Implications for Interventions and Social Policies. *Developmental Psychopathology*. 12/4: 857–85.

Luthar, SS, and Zigler, E. (1991) Vulnerability and Competence: A Review of Research on Resilience in Childhood. *American Journal of Orthopsychiatry*. 61/1: 6–22.

Mahoney, JL. (2000) School Extracurricular Activity Participation as a Moderator in the Development of Antisocial Patterns. *Child Development*. 71: 502–16.

Mahoney, JL, and Cairns, RB. (1997) Do Extracurricular Activities Protect against Early School Dropout? *Developmental Psychology*. 33/2: 241–53.

Maguire, EA, Gadian, DG, Johnsrude, IS, Good, CD, Ashburner, J, Frackowiak, RSJ, and Frith, CD. (2000) Navigation-related Structural Change in the Hippocampi of Taxi Drivers. *Proceedings of the National Academy of Sciences of the United States of America*. 97/8: 4398–403.

Malik, A. (2012) Citizenship Education, Race and Community Cohesion. In Arthur, J, and Cremin, H. (Editors) *Debates in Citizenship Education*. Routledge. 67–79.

Marshal, K. (2004) Resilience Research and Practice: Bridging the Gap. In Waxman, HC, Padron, YN, and Gray, J. (Editors) *Educational Resiliency: Student, Teacher and School Perspectives*. Information Age Publishing.

Martin, A, and Marsh, H. (2008) Academic Buoyancy: Towards an Understanding of Students' Everyday Academic Resilience. *Journal of School Psychology*. 46: 53–83.

Martin, A, and Marsh, H. (2009) Academic Resilience and Academic Buoyancy: Multidimensional and Hierarchical Conceptual Framing of Causes, Correlates and Cognate Constructs. *Oxford Review of Education*. 35/3: 353–70.

Mason, C. (2012) The Civic Engagement of Young People Living in Areas of Socio-economic Disadvantage. In Arthur, J, and Cremin, H. (Editors) *Debates in Citizenship Education*. Routledge. 80–91.

Masten, A. (2007) Resilience in Developing Systems: Progress and Promise as the Fourth Wave Rises. *Development and Psychopathology*. 19: 912–30.

Masten, A. (2011) Resilience in Children Threatened by Extreme Adversity: Frameworks for Research, Practice and Translational Synergy. *Development and Psychopathology*. 23/2: 493–506.

Masten, A. (2014) Global Perspectives on Resilience in Children and Youth. *Child Development*. 85/1. 6–20.

Masten, A., Best, K, and Garmezy, N. (1990) Resilience and Development: Contributions from the Study of Children Who Overcame Adversity. *Development and Psychopathology*. 2/4: 425–44.

Mayer, S. (2010) The Relationships between Income Inequality and Inequality in Schooling. *Theory and Research in Education*. 8/1: 5–20.

McDonald, L, Fitzroy, S, Fuchs, I, Fooken, I, and Klasen, H. (2012) Evidence-based Parent Education Programmes to Promote Positive Parenting. Strategies for High Retention Rates of Low-income families in FAST (Families and Schools Together): An Evidence-based Parenting Programme in the USA, UK, Holland and Germany. *European Journal of Developmental Psychology*. 9/1: 75–88.

McGrath, D, and van Buskirk, W. (1999) Cultures of Support for At-risk Students. In Shaw, KM, Valadex, JR, and Rhoads, RA. (Editors) *Community Colleges as Cultural*

Texts: Qualitative Explorations of Organizational and Student Culture. SUNY Press. 15–37.

Meegan, S, and MacPhail, A. (2006) Inclusive Education: Ireland's Education Provision for Children with Special Educational Needs. *Irish Educational Studies.* 25/1: 53–62.

Meyers, A, and Hickey, AM. (2014) Multilevel Prospective Dynamics in School-based Social and Emotional Learning Programs. *Journal of Cognitive Education and Psychology.* 13/2: 218–31.

Miller-Lewis, L, Searle, AK, Sawyer, MG, Baghurst, PA, and Hedley, D. (2013) Resource Factors for Mental Health Resilience in Early Childhood: An Analysis with Multiple Methodologies. *Child and Adolescent Psychiatry and Mental Health.* 7/6: 1–23.

Mindess, M, Chen, MH, and Brenner, R. (November 2008) Social-emotional Learning in the Primary Curriculum. *Beyond the Journal. Young Children on the Web.* http://journal.naeyc.org/btj/200811/pdf/btjsocialemotional.pdf. Accessed 25 August 2013.

Montt, G. (2011) Cross-national Differences in Educational Achievement Inequality. *Sociology of Education.* 84/1: 49–68.

Mooney-Somers, J, and Maher, L. (2009) The Indigenous Resiliency Project: A Worked Example of Community-based Participatory Research. *New South Wales Public Health Bulletin.* 20/8: 112–8.

Morales, E. (2010) Linking Strengths: Identifying and Exploring Protective Factor Clusters in Academically Resilient Low-socio-economic Urban Students of Color. *Roeper Review.* 32: 164–75.

Moretti, M, and Obsuth, I. (2009) Effectiveness of an Attachment-focused Manualized Intervention for Parents of Teens at Risk for Aggressive Behaviour. *Journal of Adolescence.* 32/6: 1347–57.

Morey, LC. (2007) *Personality Assessment Inventory Professional Manual, 2nd edn.* Psychological Assessment Resources.

Morrison, G, Brown, M, D'Incau, B, Larson O'Farrell, S, and Furlong, M. (2006) Understanding Resilience in Educational Trajectories: Implications for Protective Possibilities. *Psychology in the Schools.* 43/1: 19–31.

Morse, R, Rojahn, J, and Smith, A. (2014) Effects of Behaviour Problems, Family Functioning and Family Coping on Parent Stress in Families with a Child with Smith-Magenis Syndrome. *Journal of Developmental and Physical Disabilities.* 26/4: 391–401.

Mulcahy, H, Phelan, A, Corcoran, P, and Leahy-Warren, P. (April 2012) Examining the Breastfeeding Support Resources of the Public Health Nursing Services in Ireland. *Journal of Clinical Nursing.* 21/7–8: 1097–108.

Mullally, S. (2011) Separated Children in Ireland: Responding to 'Terrible Wrongs'. *International Journal of Refugee Law.* 23/4: 632–55.

Nagy, E. (2011) The Newborn Infant: A Missing Stage in Infant Psychology. *Infant and Child Development.* 20: 3–19.

Nelson, CA, Fox, NA, and Zeanah, CH. (2012) *Romania's Abandoned Children: Deprivation, Brain Development and the Struggle for Recovery.* Harvard University Press.

Nelson, CA, Fox, NA, and Zeanah, CH. (2013) Early Hazards to Brain Development: The Effects of Early Institutionalization on Brain and Behavioral Development. In Pauen, S. (Editor) *Early Childhood Development and Later Outcome. The Jacobs Foundation Series on Adolescence.* Cambridge University Press. 148–67.

Nesheiwat, KM, and Brandwein, D. (2011) Factors Related to Resilience in Preschool and Kindergarten Students. *Child Welfare.* 90/1: 7–24.

Newman, T. (2002) Promoting Resilience: A Review of Effective Strategies for Child Care Services. Prepared for the Centre for Evidence-based Social Services, University of Exeter. http://www.barnardos.org.uk/resources/researchpublications/documents/RESILSUM.PDF. Accessed 29 July 2013.

Newmann, F. (1998) How Secondary Schools Contribute to Academic Success. In Borman, K, and Schneider, B. (Editors) *The Adolescent Years: Social Influences and Educational Challenges.* Ninety-seventh Yearbook of the National Society for the Study of Education. 88–108.

Nguyen, M. (2011) Closing the Education Gap: A Case for Aboriginal Early Childhood Education in Canada, a Look at the Aboriginal Headstart Program. *Canadian Journal of Education.* 35/3: 229–48.

Niesel, R, and Griebel, W. (2005) Transition Competence and Resiliency in Educational Institutions. *International Journal of Transitions in Childhood.* 1: 4–11.

Obradovic, J. (2012) How Can the Study of Physiological Reactivity Contribute to Our Understanding of Adversity and Resilience Processes in Development? *Development and Psychopathology.* 24: 371–87.

Olsson, CA, Bond, L, Burns, JM, and Vella-Brodrick, DA. (February 2003) Adolescent Resilience; A Concept Analysis. *Journal of Adolescence.* 26/1: 1–11.

Ong, AC, Bergeman, CS, and Boker, SM. (December 2009) Resilience Comes of Age: Defining Features in Later Adulthood. *Journal of Personality.* 77/6: 1777–804.

Onwuegbuzie, A., Collins, K, and Frels, R. (2013) Using Bronfenbrenner's Ecological Systems Theory to Frame Quantitative, Qualitative and Mixed Research. *International Journal of Multiple Research Approaches.* 7/6: 2–8.

Parto, M, and Besharat, MA. (2011) Mindfulness, Psychological Well-being and Psychological Distress in Adolescents: Assessing the Mediating Variables and Mechanisms of Autonomy and Self-regulation. *Procedia – Social and Behavioral Sciences.* 30: 578–82.

Pauen, S. (Editor) (2012a) *Early Childhood Development and Later Outcome.* The Jacobs Series on Adolescence. Cambridge University Press.

Pauen, S. (2012b) Looking Back and Looking Forward: Milestones in Research on Early Childhood Development. In Pauen, S. (Editor) *Early Childhood Development and Later Outcome.* The Jacobs Series on Adolescence. Cambridge University Press. 1–8.

Payler, J, and Georgeson, J. (2013) Multiagency Working in the Early Years: Confidence, Competence and Context. *Early Years.* 33/4: 380–97.

Peacock, A. (2012) Developing Outward-facing Schools Where Citizenship Is a Lived Experience. In Brown, J, Ross, H, and Munn, P. (Editors) *Democratic Citizenship in Schools: Teaching Controversial Issues, Traditions and Accountability.* Dunedin. 120–32.

Pecora, P. (2012) Maximizing Educational Achievement of Youth in Foster Care and Alumni: Factors Associated with Success. *Children and Youth Services,* 34/6. 1121–29.

Peale, NV. (1996, orig. 1952) *The Power of Positive Thinking.* Ballantine Books.

Peck, SC, Roeser, RW, Zarrett, N, and Eccles, JS. (2008) Exploring the Roles of Extracurricular Activity Quantity and Quality in the Educational Resilience of Vulnerable Adolescents: Variable- and Pattern-centered Approaches. *Journal of Social Issues.* 64/1: 135–56.

Pecora, J. (2006) Child Welfare Policies and Programs. In Jenson, J, and Fraser, MW. (Editors) *Social Policy for Children and Families: A Risk and Resilience Perspective.* Sage Publications. 19–66.

Pedro-Carroll, JL. (2005) Fostering Resilience in the Aftermath of Divorce: The Role of Evidence-based Programs for Children. *Family Court Review.* 43: 52–64.

Pence, A. (1996) *Canadian National Child Care Study: Shared Diversity: An International Report on Childcare in Canada.* Statistics Canada.

Perry, BD, Pollard, RA, Blaicley, TL, Baker, WL, and Vigilante, D. (1995) Childhood Trauma, the Neurobiology of Adaptation, and 'Use-dependent' Development of the Brain: How 'States' Become 'Traits'. *Infant Mental Health Journal.* 16/4: 271–91.

Petrides, KD, Frederickson, N, and Furnham, A. (2004) The Role of Trait Emotional Intelligence in Academic Performance and Deviant Behaviour at School. *Personality and Individual Differences.* 26: 277–93.

Piaget, J. (1962) *Play, Dreams and Imitation in Childhood.* Norton.

Pitman, E, and Matthey, S. (2004) The SMILES Program: A Group Program for Children with Mentally Ill Parents or Siblings. *American Journal of Orthopsychiatry.* 74: 383–8.

Planas, A, Soler, P, and Montserrat, V. (2014) Assessing Youth Policies. A System of Indicators for Local Government. *Evaluation and Program Planning.* 45: 22–28.

Pösö, T, Skivenes, M, and Hestbæk, AD. (2014) Child Protection Systems within the Danish, Finnish and Norwegian Welfare States – Time for a Child Centric Approach? *European Journal of Social Work.* 17/4: 475–90.

Pring, R. (2012) Accountability, Assessment and Education for Citizenship. In Brown, J, Ross, H, and Munn, P. (Editors) *Democratic Citizenship in Schools: Teaching Controversial Issues, Traditions and Accountability.* Dunedin. 92–105.

Prinz, RJ, Sanders, MR, Shapiro, CJ, Whitaker, DJ, and Lutzker, JR. (2009) Population-based Prevention of Child Maltreatment: The U.S. Triple P System Population Trial. *Prevention Science.* 10: 1–12.

Radke-Yarrow, M, and Sherman, T. (1990) Hard Growing: Children Who Survive. In Rolf, J, Masten, AS, Cicchetti, D, Nüchterlein, KH, and Weintraub, S. (Editors) *Risk and Protective Factors in the Development of Psychopathology.* Cambridge University Press. 120–40.

Rapp, CA, Saleebey, D, and Sullivan, W. (Spring 2005) The Future of Strengths-based Social Work. *Advances in Social Work.* 6/1: 79–90.

Reebye, P. (February 2005) Aggression During Early Years – Infancy and Preschool. *Canadian Child and Adolescent Psychiatry Review.* 14/1: 16–20.

Reebye, P, Nq, T, and Misri, S. (2012) Affect Expression and Self-regulation Capabilities of Infants Exposed in Utero to Psychotropics. *Frontiers in Psychiatry.* 3: 11–22.

Reich, JW, Zautra, AJ, and Stuart Hall, J. (2010) *Handbook of Adult Resilience.* The Guilford Press.

Reid, A, and Reynolds, L. (Editors) (2013) *Equity and Education: Exploring New Directions for Equity in Australian Education.* Australian College of Educators. 1–104.

Resnick, M. (February 2000) Protective Factors, Resiliency and Healthy Youth Development. *Adolescent Medicine: State of the Art Reviews.* 11/1: 157–64.

Richardson, GE. (2002) The Metatheory of Resilience and Resiliency. *Journal of Clinical Psychology.* 58/3: 307–21.

Roberts, H. (2000) What Is Sure Start? *Archives of Disease in Childhood.* 82: 435–7.

Robinson, M. (2008) *Child Development 0–8: A Journey through the Early Years.* Open University Press.

Rolf, J, Masten, AS, Cicchetti, D, Nüchterlein, KH, and Weintraub, S. (Editors) (1990) *Risk and Protective Factors in the Development of Psychopathology.* Cambridge University Press.

Romeo, RD, and Karatsoreos, IN. (2011) Adolescence and Stress; From Hypothalamic-pituitary-adrenal Function to Brain Development. In Conrad, C. (Editor) *The Handbook of Stress; Neurological Effects on the Brain.* Wiley-Blackwell. 269–85.

Romeo, RD, and McEwen, BS. (2006) Stress and the Adolescent Brain. *Annals of the New York Academy of Sciences.* 1094: 202–14.

Ross, A, Dooly, M, and Hartsmar, N. (2012) *Equalities and Education in Europe: Explanations and Excuses for Inequality.* Cambridge Scholars Publishing.

Rowe, D. (2012) Schools and Their Communities. In Arthur, J, and Cremin, H. (Editors) *Debates in Citizenship Education.* Routledge. 56–66.

Rutter, M. (1971) Parent-child Separation: Psychological Effects on the Child. *Journal of Child Psychology and Psychiatry.* 12: 233–60.

Rutter, M. (1984) Resilient Children. *Psychology Today.* 3: 57–65.

Rutter, M. (1987) Psychosocial Resilience and Protective Mechanisms. *American Journal of Orthopsychiatry.* 57: 316–31.

Rutter, M. (1990) Psychosocial Resilience and Protective Mechanisms. In Rolf, J, Masten, AS, Cicchetti, D, Nüchterlein, KH, and Weintraub, S. (Editors) *Risk and Protective Factors in the Development of Psychopathology.* Cambridge University Press. 181–214.

Rutter, M. (1999a) Social Context: Meanings, Measures and Mechanisms. *European Review.* 7: 139–49.

Rutter, M. (1999b) Resilience Concepts and Findings: Implications for Family Therapy. *Journal of Family Therapy.* 21: 119–44.

Rutter, M. (2000) Resilience Reconsidered: Conceptual Considerations, Empirical Findings and Policy Implications. In Meisels, S, and Shonkoff, J. (Editors) *Handbook of Early Childhood Intervention.* Cambridge University Press. 651–83.

Rutter, M. (2005) Environmentally Mediated Risks for Psychopathology: Research Strategies and Findings. *Journal of the American Academy of Child and Adolescent Psychiatry.* 44/1: 3–18.

Rutter, M. (2012) Resilience: Causal Pathways and Social Ecology. In Ungar, M. (Editor) *The Social Ecology of Resilience: A Handbook of Theory and Practice.* Springer. 33–42.

Rychen, DS, and Salganik, LH. (Editors) (2003) *Key Competencies for a Successful Life and a Well-functioning Society.* Hogrefe and Huber.

Rychlak, J. (1968) *A Philosophy of Science for Personality Theory.* Houghton Mifflin.

Ryle, G. (2009, orig. 1949) *The Concept of Mind.* Routledge.

Sameroff, AJ, Bartko, WT, Baldwin, A, Baldwin, C, and Seifer, R. (1998) Family and Social Influences on the Development of Child Competence. In Lewis, M, and Feiring, C. (Editors) *Families, Risk, and Competence.* Erlbaum. 161–85.

Sameroff, AJ, and Seifer, R. (1990) Early Contributors to Developmental Risk. In Rolf, J, Masten, AS, Cicchetti, D, Nüchterlein, KH, and Weintraub, S. (Editors) *Risk and Protective Factors in the Development of Psychopathology.* Cambridge University Press. 52–66.

Sanchez-Jankowski, M. (2008) *Cracks in the Pavement: Social Change and Resilience in Poor Neighbourhoods.* University of California Press.

Saracho, ON, and Spodek, B. (1998) *Multiple Perspectives of Play in Early Childhood Education.* State University of New York Press

Schoggen, P. (1978) Ecological Psychology and Mental Retardation. In Sackett, G. (Editor) *Observing Behaviour.* University Park Press. 33–62.

Schoggen, P, and Schoggen, M. (1989) Student Voluntary Participation and High School Size. *The Journal of Educational Research.* 81/5. 288–93.

Schoon, I. (2006) *Risk and Resilience; Adaptations in Changing Times.* Cambridge University Press.

Schore, AN. (1997) Early Organization of the Nonlinear Right Brain and Development of a Predisposition to Psychiatric Disorders. *Development and Psychopathology.* 9: 595–631.

Schultz, D, Jayox, LH, Hickman, LK, Setodki, C, Kofner, A, Harris, R, and Barnes, D. (2013) The Relationship Between Protective Factors and Outcomes for Children Exposed to Violence. *Violence and Victims.* 28/4: 697–714.

Schwartz, RM. (1986) The Internal Dialogue: On the Asymmetry between Positive and Negative Coping Thoughts. *Cognitive Therapy and Research*. 10/6: 591–605.

Seale, A, Miller-Lewis, L, Sawyer, M, and Baghurst, P. (2013) Predictors of Children's Kindergarden Classroom Engagement: Preschool Adult-Child Relationships, Self-concept and Hyperactivity/Inattention. *Early Education and Development*. 24/8: 1112–36.

Seccombe, K. (May 2002) Beating the Odds Versus Changing the Odds. *Journal of Marriage and Family*. 64: 384–94.

Segal, Z. (2011) Mindfulness-based Cognitive Therapy and the Prevention of Relapse in Recurrent Depression. In Kabat-Zinn, J, and Davidson, R. (Editors) *The Mind's Own Physician: A Scientific Dialogue with the Dalai Lama on the Healing Power of Meditation*. Mind and Life Institute. New Harbinger Publications. 102–10.

Shapiro, S, Carlson, L, Astin, J, and Freedman, B. (2006) Mechanisms of Mindfulness. *Journal of Clinical Psychology*. 62/3: 373–86.

Sheard, M, Ross, S, and Cheung, A. (2012) Educational Effectiveness of an Intervention Programme for Social-emotional Learning. *International Journal of Multiple Research Approaches*. 6/3: 264–84.

Shim, JM. (2012) Pierre Bourdieu and Intercultural Education: It Is Not Just about Lack of Knowledge about Others. *Intercultural Education*. 23/3: 209–20.

Shonkoff, JP, and Phillips, DA. (2000) *From Neurons to Neighborhoods: The Science of Early Childhood Development*. National Academy Press.

Siegel, D. (2001) Toward an Interpersonal Neurobiology of the Developing Mind: Attachment Relationships, 'Mindsight,' and Neural Integration. *Infant Mental Health Journal*. 22/1–2: 67–94.

Siegel, D. (2014) *Brainstorm: The Power and Purpose of the Teenage Brain*. Harper.

Silberg, JL, and Eaves, LJ. (2012) Unravelling the Effect of Genes and Environment in the Transmission of Parental Anti-social behavior to Children's Conduct Disturbance, Depression and Hyperactivity. *Journal of Child Psychology and Psychiatry*. 53: 668–77.

Sisk, C, and Zehr, J. (October–December 2005) Pubertal Hormones Organize the Adolescent Brain and Behavior. *Frontiers in Neuroendocrinology*. 26/3–4: 163–74.

Skodol, AE. (2010) The Resilient Personality. In Reich, JW, Zautra, AJ, and Stuart Hall, J. (Editors) *Handbook of Adult Resilience*. The Guilford Press. 112–25.

Sletten, MA. (2010) Social Costs of Poverty: Leisure Time Socializing and the Subjective Experience of Social Isolation among 13–16 Year Old Norwegians. *Journal of Youth Studies*. 13/3: 308.

Spratt, E, Friedenberg, S, LaRosa, A, De Belliss, MD, Macias, MM, Summer, AP, Hulsey, TC, Runyan, DK, and Brady, KT. (2012) The Effects of Early Neglect on Cognitive, Language, and Behavioral Functioning. *Childhood Psychology*. 3/2: 175–82.

Squeglia, LM, Jacobus, J, and Tapert, SF. (January 2009) The Influence of Substance Use on Adolescent Brain Development. *Clinical EEG and Neuroscience*. 40/1: 31–8.

Standards and Testing Agency. (2012) *Early Years Foundation Stage Profile Handbook*. Standards and Testing Agency, Department for Education: London.

Stanton-Salazar, RD. (2001) Defensive Network Orientation as Internalized Oppression: How Schools Mediate the Influence of Social Class on Adolescent Development. In Biddle, BJ. (Editor) *Social Class, Poverty and Education: Policy and Practice*. Routledge Falmer. 101–31.

Stawicki, JA, and Hirsch, BJ. (2013) Adolescent Development in Underserved Communities: A Conceptual Framework. In Creasey, GL, and Jarvis, PA (Editors) *Adolescent Development and School Achievement in Urban Communities: Resilience in the Neighbourhood*. Routledge. 15–26.

Steinberg, L. (March 2008) A Social Neuroscience Perspective on Adolescent Risk-taking. *Developmental Review*. 28/1: 78–106.

Steinberg, L. (April 2011) The Middle/High Years/Demystifying the Adolescent Brain. *Educational Leadership*. 68/7: 42–6.

Steinmetz, G. (2011) Bourdieu, Historicity, and Historical Sociology. *Cultural Sociology*. 5: 45–56.

Stevenson, N. (2011) *Education and Cultural Citizenship*. Sage.

Strathearn, L. (2007) Exploring the Neurobiology of Attachment. In Peter Fonagy, Mayes, L, and Target, M. (Editors) *Developmental Science and Psychoanalysis: Integration and Innovation*. Karnac Books. 117–31.

Stuckler, D, and Sanjay, B. (2011) Evaluating the Health Burden of Chronic Diseases. In Stuckler, D and Siegel, K. (Editors) *Sick Societies: Responding to the Global Challenge of Chronic Disease*. Oxford University Press. 1–26.

Summerbell, CD, Moore, HJ, Vögele, C, Kreichauf, S, Wildgruber, A, Manios, Y, Douthwaite, W, Nixon, CA, Gibson, EL, and ToyBox-study Group. (2012) Evidence-based Recommendations for the Development of Obesity Prevention Programs Targeted at Children. *Obesity Reviews*. 13: 129–32.

Sun, RCF, and Shek, DTL. (2013) Longitudinal Influences of Positive Youth Development and Life Satisfaction on Problem Behaviour among Adolescents in Hong Kong. *Social Indicators Research*. 114: 1171–97.

Synder, R, Shapiro, S, and Treleaven, D. (2012) Attachment Theory and Mindfulness. *Journal of Child and Family Studies*. 21/5: 709–19.

Taylor, D, Turner, B, and Hamilton, P. (Editors) (1990) *Citizenship: Critical Concepts*. Routledge.

Tein, JY, Sandler, IN, Ayers, TS, and Wolchik, TA. (June 2006) Mediation of the Effects of the Family Bereavement Program on Mental Health Problems of Bereaved Children and Adolescents. *Prevention Science*. 7/2: 179–95.

Theron, LC, and Engelbrecht, P. (2012) Caring Teachers: Teacher-youth Transactions to Promote Resilience. In Ungar, M. (Editor) *The Social Ecology of Resilience: A Handbook of Theory and Practice*. Springer. 265–80.

Thomas, MSC, and Knowland, V. (2009) Sensitive Periods in Brain Development – Implications for Education Policy. *European Psychiatric Review*. 2/1: 17–20.

Thompson, RA. (2014) Stress and Child Development. *The Future of Children*. 24/1: 41–59.

Trickett, PK, Negriff, S, Juye, J, and Peckins, M. (2011) Child Maltreatment and Adolescent Development. *Journal of Research on Adolescence*. 21/1: 3–20.

Ttofi, MM, and Farrington, DP. (2011) Effectiveness of School-based Programs to Reduce Bullying: A Systematic and Meta-analytic Review. *Journal of Experimental Criminology*. 7: 27–56.

Tully, T. (2002) Social Work Policy. In Green, Roberta C. (Editor) *Resiliency: An Integrated Approach to Practice, Policy and Research*. NASW Press. 321–35.

Tzoumakis, S, Lussier, P, and Corrado, R. (2014) The Persistence of Early Childhood Physical Aggression: Examining Maternal Delinquency and Offending, Mental Health, and Cultural Differences. *Journal of Criminal Justice*. 42/5: 408–20.

Ungar, M. (2005) Introduction: Resilience across Cultures and Contexts. In Ungar, M. (Editor) *Handbook for Working with Children and Youth: Pathways to Resilience Across Cultures and Contexts*. Sage Publications. xv–xxxix.

Ungar, M. (May 2006) Nurturing Hidden Resilience in At-risk Youth in Different Cultures. *Journal of the Canadian Academy of Child and Adolescent Psychiatry*. 15/2: 53–8.

Ungar, M. (2008) Resilience across Cultures. *British Journal of Social Work*. 38: 218–35.

Ungar, M. (Editor) (2012) *The Social Ecology of Resilience; A Handbook of Theory and Practice*. Springer.

Verma, R. (2012) Between Spaces of 'Otherness' and Belonging: Lessons on Global Citizenship and Controversy in the Classroom. In Brown, J, Ross, H, and Munn, P. (Editors) *Democratic Citizenship in Schools: Teaching Controversial Issues, Traditions and Accountability*. Dunedin. 74–87.

Vidal Rodeiro, CL, Emery, JL, and Bell, JF. (2012) Emotional Intelligence and Academic Attainment of British Secondary School Children: A Cross-sectional Survey. *Educational Studies*. 38/5: 521–39.

Vygotsky, LS. (1978) *Mind in Society*. Harvard University Press.

Walsh, F. (1996) The Concept of Family Resilience: Crisis and Challenge. *Family Process*. 35/3: 261–81.

Wang, MC, Haertel, GD, and Walberg, HJ. (1994) Educational Resilience in Inner Cities. In Wang, MC, and Gordon, EW. *Educational Resilience in Inner-City America: Challenges and Prospects*. Laurence Eribaum. 45–72.

Ward, F, and Thurston, M. (2006) *Understanding Risk and Protective Factors: Findings from a Sample of Vulnerable Children and Young People in Crewe*. Centre for Public Health Research, University of Chester.

Waugh, C, Frederickson, BL, and Taylor, F. (2008) Adapting to Life's Slings and Arrows: Individual Differences in Resilience When Recovering from an Anticipated Threat. *Journal of Research in Personality*. 42/4: 1031–46.

Waxman, SR, and Goswami, U. (2012) Learning about Language: Acquiring the Spoken and Written Word. In Pauen, S. (Editor) *Early Childhood Development and Later Outcome*. The Jacobs Series on Adolescence. Cambridge University Press. 89–117.

Webster-Stratton, C, and Reid, JM. (2004) Strengthening Social and Emotional Competence in Young Children – The Foundation for Early School Readiness and Success; Incredible Years Classroom Social Skills and Problem-solving Curriculum. *Infants and Young Children*. 17: 96–113.

Weist, MD. (1997) Expanded School Mental Health Services: A National Movement in Progress. In Ollendick, T, and Priar, RJ. (Editors) *Advances in Clinical Child Psychology*. 19: 319–52.

Wentzel, KR. (1991) Social Competence at School: Relations between Social Responsibility and Between Social Responsibility and Academic Achievement. *Review of Educational Research*. 61: 1–24.

Werner, E. (1989) High Risk Children in Young Adulthood: A Longitudinal Study from Birth to 32 Years. *American Journal of Orthopsychiatry*. 59: 72–81.

Werner, E. (1993) Risk, Resilience and Recovery: Perspectives from the Kauai Longitudinal Study. *Development and Psychopathology*. 5/4: 503–15.

Werner, E. (1998) Protective Factors and Individual Resilience. In Meisels, S, and Shonkoff, J. (Editors) *Handbook of Early Childhood Intervention*. Cambridge University Press. 115–32.

Werner, E. (2012) Risk, Resilience and Recovery. *Reclaiming Children and Youth*. 21/1. 18–22.

Werner, E, and Smith, RS. (1982) *Vulnerable but Invincible; A Longitudinal Study of Resilient Children and Youth*. McGraw-Hill.

West, D, and Farrington, D. (1973) *Who Becomes Delinquent?* Second Report of the Cambridge Study in Delinquent Development. London: Heinemann.

Whiteford, C, Walker, S, and Berthelsen, D. (2013) Australian Children with Special Health Care Needs: Social-emotional and Learning Competencies in the Early Years. *International Journal of Early Childhood*. 45: 35–50.

Windingstad, S, McCallum, RS, Bell, SM, and Dunn, P. (2011) Measures of Emotional Intelligence and Social Acceptability in Children: A Concurrent Validity Study. *Canadian Journal of School Psychology*. 26/2: 107–26.

Winfield, L. (1991) Resilience, Schooling and Development in African-American Youth: A Conceptual Framework. *Education and Urban Society*. 24/1: 5–14.

Winkworth, G, and White, M. (May 2010) May Do, Should Do, Can Do: Collaboration between Commonwealth and State Service Systems for Vulnerable Children. Communities. *Children and Families Australia*. 5/1: 5–20.

Wolin, SJ, and Wolin, S. (1993) *The Resilient Self*. Villard Books.

Wolin, S, and Wolin, SJ. (1995) Resilience among Youth Growing Up in Substance Abusing Families. *Pediatric Clinics of North America* 42/2: 415–29.

Woods, PA. (2011) *Transforming Education Policy; Shaping a Democratic Future*. Policy Press.

Wright, T. (2010) Learning to Laugh, a Portrait of Risk and Resilience in Early Childhood. *Harvard Educational Review*. 80/4: 444–63.

Yates, TM, Egeland, B, and Sroufe, LA. (2003) Rethinking Resilience; A Developmental Process Perspective. In Luthar, SS. (Editor) *Resilience and Vulnerability: Adaptation in the Context of Childhood Adversities*. Cambridge University Press. 243–66.

Yates, TM, and Masten, AS. (2004) Fostering the Future: Resilience Theory and the Practice of Positive Psychology. In Linley, P and Joseph, S. (Editors) *Positive Psychology in Practice*. John Wiley and Sons. 521–39.

Zembylas, M. (December 2007) Emotional Capital and Education: Theoretical Insights from Bourdieu. *British Journal of Educational Studies*. 55/4: 443–63.

Zimmerman, MA, Bingenheimer, JB, and Notoro, PC. (April 2002) Natural Mentors and Adolescent Resilience: A Study with Urban Youth. *American Journal of Community Psychology*. 30/2: 221–43.

Zimmerman, MA, and Brenner, AB. (2010) Resilience in Adolescence: Overcoming Neighborhood Disadvantage. In Reich, JW, Zautra, AJ, and Stuart Hall, J. (Editors) *Handbook of Adult Resilience*. The Guilford Press. 284–308.

Zolkoski, SM, and Bullock, LM. (2012) Resilience in Children and Youth: A Review. *Children and Youth Services Review*. 34: 229.

Index